Date Due

BIBLIOGRAPHY

OF

EUROPEAN

LITERATURE

BIBLIOGRAPHY OF

European Literature

COMPANION TO
ESSENTIALS OF EUROPEAN LITERATURE

BY

VINCENT F. HOPPER

PROFESSOR OF GENERAL LITERATURE
NEW YORK UNIVERSITY

AND

BERNARD D. N. GREBANIER

PROFESSOR OF ENGLISH
BROOKLYN COLLEGE

BARRON'S EDUCATIONAL SERIES, INC.
Great Neck, New York

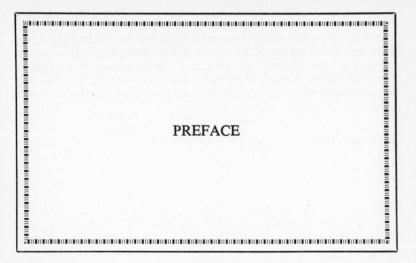

PREFACE

THE ORIGINAL plan for this bibliography was to print it as an appendix, half in each of the two volumes of the authors' *Essentials of European Literature*. But two reasons made it clear that it would be wiser to issue the bibliography as a separate volume: it began to take on such bulk as would have rendered the appendix disproportionate to the volumes proper; also, the complete dearth of bibliographical materials for the study in English of European literature made the publication of such a bibliography by itself seem a possible contribution to the work of advanced scholar and undergraduate alike. Once the authors had decided on issuing this as a unit, they expanded the original and brought it up to its date of publication.

The authors have limited themselves to *books* in English on the subjects discussed in *Essentials of European Literature:* the leading writers and their works, the crucial periods of literary production, the minor writers of such periods, the national literatures generally. The authors, understandably perhaps, desiring to live to see their bibliography published, exclude the innumerable magazine articles on these subjects. Anthologies (even though one is fathered by a co-author of this volume) are also omitted because they are of so many different sorts and usually include partial reprints of works available elsewhere in complete form.

This bibliography, pioneering as it does, can lay claim only to such completeness as it achieves. It is hoped that the contents will be welcomed as supplying a pressing need, and will encourage a vaster work on the subject.

Among the uses which the authors suggest for this bibliography is the discovery, which a study of these pages should make clear, of the astonishing gaps in translations, biographies, and critical writings in the field of European letters. A series of profitable and needed works, we hope, will be inaugurated when the many comparatively virgin territories are noted.

B. D. N. G.
V. F. H.

December, 1953.

TABLE OF CONTENTS

Chapter One: THE EARLY MIDDLE AGES

Chapter Two: THE HEIGHT OF THE MIDDLE AGES

Chapter Three: THE RENAISSANCE

Chapter Four: NEOCLASSICISM

Chapter Five: THE ROMANTIC MOVEMENT IN
FRANCE AND ITALY

Chapter Six: THE GOLDEN AGE OF GERMAN LITERATURE

Chapter Seven: THE RISE OF REALISM

Chapter Eight: THE RISE OF RUSSIAN LITERATURE

Chapter Nine: OTHER NINETEENTH-CENTURY DEVELOPMENTS

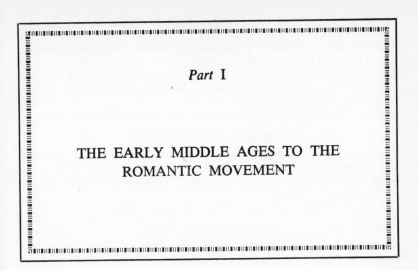

Part I

THE EARLY MIDDLE AGES TO THE
ROMANTIC MOVEMENT

GENERAL

Barnes, H. E., *An Intellectual and Cultural History of the Western World* (Random House, 1937)

Drinkwater, J., *The Outline of Literature* (G. P. Putnam's Sons, 1931)

Guérard, A., *Preface to World Literature* (H. Holt & Co., 1940)

Gunn, S., *The Story of Literature* (J. H. Sears & Co., 1940)

Horton, R. W. and Hopper, V. F., *Backgrounds of European Literature* (Horton & Hopper, Rowayton, Conn., 1948)

Knowlton, E. C., *An Outline of World Literature* (Ronald Press Co., 1929)

Laird, C. (ed.), *The World through Literature* (Appleton-Century-Crofts, Inc., 1951)

Macy, J., *The Story of the World's Literature* (Boni & Liveright, 1925)

Magnus, L., *Dictionary of European Literature* (E. P. Dutton & Co., 1927), *A History of European Literature* (Nicholson, 1934)

Moulton, R. G., *World Literature and Its Place in General Culture* (The Macmillan Co., 1911)

Nicoll, A., *World Drama: From Aeschylus to Anouilh* (Harcourt, Brace & Co., 1950)

Powys, J. C., *The Enjoyment of Literature* (Simon & Schuster, 1938)

Rascoe, B., *Titans of Literature* (G. P. Putnam's Sons, 1932)

Sismondi, J. C. L. S. de, *Historical View of the Literature of the South of Europe* (G. Bell & Sons, 1872-77)

1

Smith, H. (ed.), *Columbia Dictionary of Modern European Literature* (Columbia University Press, 1947)

Townsend, A. H., *Good Reading* (Mentor Books, New American Library, 1947-48), *A Guide to Good Reading* (Hendricks House, Farrar Straus, 1935-48)

Wordsworth, J. C., *Adventures in Literature* (Heath Cranton, 1929)

DUTCH LITERATURE

Bowring, J., *Batavian Anthology* (Taylor & Hessey, 1824), *Sketch of the Language and Literature of Holland* (Diederichs Bros., 1829)

Gosse, Sir E. W., *Studies in the Literature of Northern Europe* (C. K. Paul & Co., 1879)

Greshoff, J., *Harvest of the Lowlands* (Querido, 1945)

FRENCH LITERATURE

Aldington, R., *Literary Studies and Reviews* (Allen, 1924)

Babbitt, I., *French Literature* (American Library Assn., 1928)

Besant, W., *The French Humorists* (Roberts & Bros., 1874)

Brèmond, H., *A Literary History of Religious Thought in France* (The Macmillan Co., 1928)

Brogan, D. W., *French Personalities and Problems* (H. Hamilton, 1946)

Brunetière, F., *Essays in French Literature* (C. Scribner's Sons, 1898)

Butler, K. T., *A History of French Literature* (E. P. Dutton & Co., 1923)

Cohn, A., *French Literature* (Columbia University Press, 1911)

Demogeot, J. C., *History of French Literature* (Rivingtons, 1874)

Des Granges, C. M., *An Illustrated History of French Literature* (Hatier, 1921)

Dowden, E., *A History of French Literature* (D. Appleton & Co., 1897)

Duhamel, G., *In Defense of Letters* (E. F. Bozman, tr.) (Greystone Press, 1939)

Faguet, E., *A Literary History of France* (T. F. Unwin, 1907)

Guyer, F. E., *The Main Stream of French Literature* (D. C. Heath & Co., 1932)

Hatzfeld, H., *Literature through Art* (Oxford University Press, 1952)

Jensen, E. M., *The Influence of French Literature on Europe* (R. G. Badger, 1919)

Konta, Mrs. A., *The History of French Literature* (D. Appleton & Co., 1910)

Mauriac, F., *Men I Hold Great* (E. Pell, tr.) (Philosophical Library, 1951)

Nitze, W. A. and Dargan, E. P., *A History of French Literature* (H. Holt & Co., 1927)

Ritchie, R. L. G., *France: A Companion to French Studies* (Methuen & Co., Ltd., 1937)

Saintsbury, G., *French Literature and Its Masters* (A. A. Knopf, 1946), *A Short History of French Literature* (Clarendon Press, 1901)
Schiefley, W. H., *Essays on French Literature* (Wetzel Publishing Co., Inc., 1930)
Smith, M. S., *The Spirit of French Letters* (The Macmillan Co., 1912)
Smith, M. A., *Short History of French Literature* (H. Holt & Co., 1924)
Strachey, L., *Landmarks in French Literature* (H. Holt & Co., 1912)
Van Laun, H., *History of French Literature* (Chatto & Windus, 1883)
Waite, V., *An Approach to French Literature* (G. G. Harrap, 1947)
Wright, C. H. C., *A History of French Literature* (Oxford University Press, 1912)

ITALIAN LITERATURE

Baretti, G., *The Italian Library: An Account of the Lives and Works of the Most Valuable Authors of Italy* (London, 1757)
De Sanctis, F., *History of Italian Literature* (Harcourt, Brace & Co., 1931)
Flamini, F. A., *A History of Italian Literature* (E. M. O'Connor, tr.) (The National Alumni, 1906)
Foligno, C., *Epochs of Italian Literature* (Clarendon Press, 1920)
Foster, M. A., *Italian Literature* (W. & R. Chambers, 1853)
Gardner, E. G., *The Arthurian Legend in Italian Literature* (J. M. Dent & Sons, Ltd., 1930), *A History of Italian Literature* (D. Appleton & Co., 1898), *Italy, a Companion to Italian Studies* (Methuen & Co., Ltd., 1934), *The Story of Italian Literature* (Harper & Brothers, 1927)
Herbert, C., *Italy and Italian Literature* (Gilbert & Piper, 1835)
Kennard, J. S., *A Literary History of the Italian People* (The Macmillan Co., 1941)
Marshall, R., *Italy in English Literature* (Columbia University Press, 1934)
Sanctis, F. de, *History of Italian Literature* (J. Redfern, tr.) (Harcourt, Brace & Co., 1931)
Trail, F., *A History of Italian Literature* (V. Ciocia, 1903-04), *The Scholar's Italy* (Williams & Wilkins Co., 1923)

GERMAN LITERATURE

Bithell, J., *Germany* (Methuen & Co., 1947)
Francke, K., *A History of German Literature as Determined by Social Forces* (H. Holt & Co., 1901)
Gostwick, J., *German Literature* (Lippincott, Grambo & Co., 1854)
Gostwick, J. and Harrison, R., *Outlines of German Literature* (Schönhof & Möller, 1873)
Hosmer, J. K., *A Short History of German Literature* (C. Scribner's Sons, 1899)

Menzel, W., *German Literature* (D. A. Talboys, 1840)

Metcalfe, F., *History of German Literature* (Longman, Brown, Green, Longmans, & Roberts, 1858)

Moore, R. W., *History of German Literature* (Bay View Reading Club, 1903)

Moschyisker, F. A., *A Guide to German Literature* (London, 1850)

Priest, G. M., *A Brief History of German Literature* (C. Scribner's Sons, 1909)

Robertson, J. G., *A History of German Literature* (W. Blackwood & Sons, 1902), *The Literature of Germany* (Home University Library of Modern Knowledge, H. Holt & Co., 1913), *Outlines of the History of German Literature* (G. P. Putnam's Sons, 1911)

Rose, W., *Men, Myths, and Movements in German Literature* (G. Allen & Unwin, Ltd., 1931)

Scherer, W., *History of German Literature* (C. Scribner's Sons, 1886)

Staël-Holstein, A. L. G., *Germany* (Houghton, Mifflin & Co., 1882)

Taylor, B., *Studies in German Literature* (G. P. Putnam's Sons, 1879)

Thomas, C., *A History of German Literature* (Appleton Dollar Library, D. Appleton & Co., 1928)

Waterhouse, G., *A Short History of German Literature* (Methuen & Co., 1942)

Zeydel, E. H., *The Holy Roman Empire in German Literature* (Columbia University Press, 1918)

PORTUGUESE LITERATURE

Bell, A. F. G., *Portuguese Literature* (Oxford University Press, 1922)

Prestage, E., *Portuguese Literature to the End of the 18th Century* (Sherratt & Hughes, 1909)

Young, G. (ed.), *Portugal, an Anthology* (Clarendon Press, 1916)

SCANDINAVIAN LITERATURE

Blankner, F., *The History of the Scandinavian Literatures* (Dial Press, 1938)

Horn, F. W., *History of the Literature of the Scandinavian North* (S. C. Griggs & Co., 1884)

Jorgenson, T., *History of Norwegian Literature* (The Macmillan Co., 1933)

Larsen, H. A., *Scandinavian Literature* (American Library Association, 1930)

SPANISH LITERATURE

Adams, N. B., *The Heritage of Spain* (H. Holt & Co., 1949)

Bell, A. F. G., *Castilian Literature* (Clarendon Press, 1938)

Bouterwek, F., *History of Spanish and Portuguese Literature* (London, 1823)

Brenan, G., *The Literature of the Spanish People from Roman Times to the Present Day* (Cambridge University Press, 1951)

Clarke, H. B., *Spanish Literature* (G. Allen & Unwin, Ltd., 1921)

Fitzmaurice-Kelly, J., *Chapters on Spanish Literature* (A. Constable & Co., 1908), *A History of Spanish Literature* (D. Appleton & Co., 1920), *A New History of Spanish Literature* (H. Milford, 1926), *Some Masters of Spanish Verse* (Oxford University Press, 1924)

Ford, J. D. M., *Main Currents of Spanish Literature* (H. Holt & Co., 1919)

Foster, A. F., *Hand-book of Spanish Literature* (W. & R. Chambers, 1851)

Laborde, E. D., *A History of Spanish Literature* (W. Heinemann, Ltd., 1931)

Madariaga, S. de, *The Genius of Spain* (Clarendon Press, 1933)

Mérimée, E., and Morley, S. G., *A History of Spanish Literature* (H. Holt & Co., 1930)

Northrup, G. T., *An Introduction to Spanish Literature* (The University of Chicago Press, 1936)

Peers, E. A. (ed.), *Spain; a Companion to Spanish Studies* (Dodd, Mead & Co., 1929)

Perrier, J. L., *A Short History of Spanish Literature* (J. L. Perrier, 1925)

Sedgwick, H. D., *Spain* (Little, Brown & Co., 1937)

Ticknor, G., *History of Spanish Literature* (Harper & Brothers, 1849)

CHAPTER ONE

THE EARLY MIDDLE AGES

GENERAL

Artz, F. B., *The Mind of the Middle Ages* (A. A. Knopf, 1953)

Betterson, H. (ed.), *Documents of the Christian Church* (World's Classics, Oxford University Press, 1947)

Bulfinch's Mythology (The Modern Library, Random House, 1943)

Coulton, G. G., *Life in the Middle Ages* (Cambridge University Press, 1930)

Curtius, E. R., *European Literature and the Latin Middle Ages* (Pantheon, 1953)

Duckett, E. S., *Gateway to the Middle Ages* (Macmillan Co., 1938)

Duncan, E., *The Story of Minstrelsy* (C. Scribner's Sons, 1907)

Hamilton, E., *Mythology* (Little, Brown & Co., 1942)

Hopper, V. F., *Medieval Number Symbolism* (Columbia University Press, 1938)

Ker, W. P., *The Dark Ages* (C. Scribner's Sons, 1904), *Epic and Romance* (The Macmillan Co., 1922)

Krüger, G., *History of Early Christian Literature* (The Macmillan Co., 1897)

Labriolle, P. de, *History and Literature of Christianity* (A. A. Knopf, 1925)

Laistner, M. L. W., *Thought and Letters in Western Europe A. D. 500-900* (Dial Press, 1931)

Newell, W. W., *King Arthur and the Table Round* (Houghton Mifflin & Co., 1897)

Nutt, A., *Celtic and Medieval Romance* (D. Nutt, 1904)

Palfrey, T. R., *Medieval French Literature* (Appleton-Century Co., 1934)

Rand, E. K., *Founders of the Middle Ages* (Harvard University Press, 1928)

Ritson, J., *A Dissertation on Romance and Minstrelsy* (E. G. Goldsmid, 1891)

Roberts, A. and Donaldson, J. (eds.), *Ante-Nicene Christian Library: Translations of the Fathers down to 325 A. D.* (T. & T. Clark, 1867-72)

Schaff, P. (ed.), *A Select Library of the Nicene and Post-Nicene Fathers of the Christian Church* (The Christian Literature Co., 1886-90)

Taylor, H. O., *The Classical Heritage of the Middle Ages* (Macmillan Co., 1944)

Wendell, B., *The Traditions of European Literature from Homer to Dante* (C. Scribner's Sons, 1920)

Weston, J. L., *The Romance Cycle of Charlemagne and His Peers* (D. Nutt, 1901), *From Ritual to Romance* (Peter Smith, 1941), *The Quest of the Holy Grail* (G. Bell & Sons, Ltd., 1913)

AUGUSTINE

Translations: Dods, M. (ed.), *Works* (T. & T. Clark, 1871-1874); Healey, J., *The City of God* (J. Grant, 1909; The Temple Classics, J. M. Dent & Sons, 1934; The Hafner Library of Classics, Hafner Publishing Co., 1948); Pilkington, J. G., *The Confessions* (Boni & Liveright, 1927); Pusey, E. B., *Confessions* (The New American Edition of Everyman's Library, E. P. Dutton & Co., 1950), *Confessions of Saint Augustine* (Pocket Books, Inc., 1952), *The Confessions of St. Augustine* (Peter Pauper Press, 1945); Sheed, F. J., *The Confessions* (Sheed & Ward, 1943); Watts, W., *The Confessions* (Loeb Classical Library, W. Heinemann, 1912)

Abercrombie, N., *Saint Augustine and French Classical Thought* (Clarendon Press, 1938)

Baynes, N. H., *The Political Ideas of St. Augustine's De Civitate Dei* (G. Bell & Sons, 1936)

Bourke, V. J., *Augustine's Quest of Wisdom* (Bruce Publishing Co., 1945)

Cutts, E. L., *St. Augustine* (Society for Promoting Christian Knowledge, 1914)

D'Arcy, M. C., *A Monument to St. Augustine* (Sheed & Ward, 1930)

Figgis, J. N., *The Political Aspects of S. Augustine's 'City of God'* (Longmans, Green, & Co., 1921)

McCabe, J., *St. Augustine and His Age* (Duckworth, 1902)

McDougall, E., *St. Augustine, a Study in His Personal Religion* (R. R. Smith, 1930)

Osmun, G. W., *Augustine, the Thinker* (The Abingdon Press, 1924)

Papini, G., *Saint Augustine* (Harcourt, Brace & Co., 1930)

Ryan, A. H., *Perennial Philosophers* (Clonmore & Reynolds, 1946)

Simpson, W. J. S., *St Augustine's Conversion* (The Macmillan Co., 1930), *St. Augustine's Episcopate* (The Macmillan Co., 1944)

West, R., *St. Augustine* (D. Appleton & Co., 1933)

BOETHIUS

Translations: Cardale, J. S., *King Alfred's Anglo-Saxon Version of Boethius De Consolatione Philosophiae* (W. Pickering, 1829); Colville, G., *Boethius' Consolation of Philosophy* (Tudor Library, D. Nutt, 1897); Cooper, W. V., *The Consolation of Philosophy* (The Temple Classics, J. M. Dent & Co., 1902; The Modern Library, Random House, 1941); Fox, S., *King Alfred's Anglo-Saxon Version of Boethius De Consolatione Philosophiae* (Bohn's Antiquarian Library, H. G. Bohn, 1864, G. Bell, 1901; Clarendon Press, 1900); Furnivall, F. J. (ed.), *Chaucer's 'Boece'* (Chaucer Society, N. Trübner & Co., 1886); Morris, R. (ed.), *Chaucer's Translation of Boethius' "De Consolatione Philosophiae"* (Early English Text Society, N. Trübner & Co., 1868); Pemberton, C. (ed.), *Queen Elizabeth's Englishings of Boethius, De Consolatione Philosophie* (Early English Text Society, K. Paul Trench, Trübner & Co., 1899); Sedgefield, W. J., *King Alfred's Version of the Consolations of Boethius* (Clarendon Press, 1900); Stewart, H. F. and Rand, E. K., *The Theological Tractates* and "I. T.," *The Consolation of Philosophy* (Loeb Classical Library, G. P. Putnam's Sons, 1926); Walton, J., *Boethius: De Consolatione Philosophiae* (Early English Text Society, Oxford University Press, 1927)

Barrett, H. M., *Boethius* (Cambridge University Press, 1940)

Jefferson, B. L., *Chaucer and the Consolation of Philosophy of Boethius* (Princeton University Press, 1917)

Patch, H. R., *The Tradition of Boethius* (Oxford University Press, 1935)

Ryan, A. H., *Perennial Philosophers* (Clonmore & Reynolds, 1946)

THE CID

Translations: Arnaud, L., *Poem of the Cid* (Barron's Educational Series, Inc., 1953); Huntington, A. M., *Poem of the Cid* (Hispanic Society of America, 1907-08); Ormsby, J., *The Poem of the Cid* (Longmans, Green & Co., 1897); Rose, R. S. and Bacon, L., *The Lay of the Cid* (University of California Press, 1919); Sherwood, M., *The Tale of the Warrior Lord* (Longmans, Green & Co., 1930); Southey, R., *Chronicle of the Cid* (Morley's Universal Library, G. Routledge & Sons, 1885), *The Chronicle of the Cid* (The Chandos Library, F. Warne & Co., 1873)

Huidobro, V., *Portrait of a Paladin* (H. Liveright, Inc., 1932)

Matulka, B., *The Cid as a Courtly Hero* (Columbia Institute of French Studies, 1928)

Pidal, R. M., *The Cid and His Spain* (J. Murray, 1934)

Salinas, P., *Reality and the Poet in Spanish Poetry* (The Johns Hopkins Press, 1940)

DARES AND DICTYS

Griffin, N. E., *Dares and Dictys; an Introduction to the Study of Medieval Versions of the Story of Troy* (J. H. Furst Co., 1907)

THE EDDAS AND SAGAS

Translations: Anderson, R. B., *The Younger Edda* (S. C. Griggs & Co., 1880); Bellows, H. A., *The Poetic Edda* (The American-Scandinavian Foundation, 1923); Beresford, J., *The Song of the Sun* (J. Johnson, 1805); Bray, O., *The Elder or Poetic Edda* (Viking Club, 1908); Brodeur, A. G., *The Prose Edda* (Scandinavian Classics, The American-Scandinavian Foundation, 1916); Coomaraswamy, A. K., *Voluspa* (Essex House Press, 1909); Dasent, G. W., *The Prose or Younger Edda* (W. Pickering, 1842); Hollander, L. M., *The Poetic Edda* (University of Texas, 1928); Larned, A., *Tales from the Norse Grandmother* (Phillips & Hunt, 1881); Mabie, H. W., *Norse Stories Retold from the Eddas* (Roberts Bros., 1896; Dodd, Mead & Co., 1900; Rand, McNally & Co., 1902); Magnussan, E. and Morris, W., *Volsunga Saga* (F. S. Ellis, 1870; The W. Scott Publishing Co., Ltd., 1888; Longmans, Green & Co., 1901; Norroena Society, 1907); Morris, W., *The Story of Sigurd the Volsung* (Ellis & White, 1876; Kelmscote Press, 1898; Longmans, Green, & Co., 1910); Philojuvenis (pseud.) (ed.), *Edda* (J. Nisbet & Co., 1875); Thorp, B., *The Elder Edda of Saemund Sigfusson* and Blackwell, J. A., *The Younger Edda of Snorre Slurteson* (Anglo-Saxon Classics, Norroena Society, 1906); Schlauch, M., *The Saga of the Volsungs* (W. W. Norton & Co., Inc., 1930)

Bugge, S., *The Home of the Eddic Poems* (Grimm Library, D. Nutt, 1899)

Craigie, W. A., *The Icelandic Sagas* (Cambridge University Press, 1913)
Hermannsson, H., *Bibliography of the Eddas* (Cornell University Library, 1920)
Koht, H., *The Old Norse Sagas* (W. W. Norton & Co., 1931)
Liestøl, K., *The Origin of the Icelandic Family Sagas* (H. Aschehoug & Co., 1930)
Phillpotts, B. S., *Edda and Saga* (Home University Library of Modern Knowledge, H. Holt & Co., 1931), *The Elder Edda and Ancient Scandinavian Drama* (Cambridge University Press, 1920)
Schlauch, M., *Romance in Iceland* (Princeton University Press, 1934)
Thorpe, B., *Northern Mythology* (E. Lumley, 1851-52)

ISIDORE OF SEVILLE

Bréhaut, E., *An Encyclopaedist of the Dark Ages, Isidore of Seville* (Columbia University Press, 1912)

JACOPO DA VORAGINE

Translations: Caxton, W., *Jacobus de Varagine: The Golden Legend* (William Caxton, 1484; Holbein Society, 1878; Kelmscott Press, 1892; The Temple Classics, J. M. Dent & Sons, 1900-35); Ryan, G. and Ripperger, H., *The Golden Legend of Jacobus de Voragine* (Longmans, Green & Co., 1941)
Butler, P., *Legenda Aurea* (John Murphy Co., 1899)
Richardson, E. C., *Materials for a Life of Jacopo da Varagine* (The H. W. Wilson Co., 1935)

THE NIBELUNGENLIED

Translations: Armour, M., *The Fall of the Nibelungs* (J. M. Dent & Co., 1897; Everyman's Library, E. P. Dutton & Co., 1908); Birch, J., *Das Nibelungen Lied* (A. Duncker, 1848); Horton, A., *The Lay of the Nibelungs* (G. Bell & Sons, 1901); Lettsom, W. N., *The Fall of the Nibelungers* (Williams & Norgate, 1850); *The Nibelungenlied* (The Colonial Press, 1901); Needler, G. H., *The Nibelungenlied* (H. Holt & Co., 1904); Shumway, D. B., *The Nibelungenlied* (Houghton Mifflin Co., 1909)
Bohning, E. S., *The Concept 'Sage' in Nibelungen Criticism* (Times Publishing Co., 1944)
Carlyle, T., *The Nibelungenlied* (The Platt & Peck Co., 189-?)
Layton, K. A., *The Nibelungen of Wagner* (Urbana University Press, 1909)
Sawyer, W. C., *Teutonic Legends in the Nibelungen Lied and the Nibelungen Ring* (J. B. Lippincott Co., 1904)
Thorp, M., *The Study of the Nibelungenlied* (Clarendon Press, 1940)

THE SAGAS

See The *Eddas* and *Sagas*

THE SONG OF ROLAND

Translations: *The Song of Roland* (Faber & Faber, Ltd., 1937); Bacon, L., *The Song of Roland* (Yale University Press, 1914); Butler, I., *The Song of Roland* (Houghton, Mifflin & Co., 1904); Moncrieff, C. S., *The Song of Roland* (Chapman & Hall, Ltd., 1919; The Limited Editions Club, 1938); O'Hagan, J., *The Song of Roland* (C. K. Paul & Co., 1880; W. Small, 1900); Rabillon, L., *Le Chanson de Roland* (Library of Foreign Poetry, H. Holt & Co., 1885); Sherwood, M., *The Song of Roland* (Longmans, Green & Co., 1938); Way, A. S., *The Song of Roland* (Cambridge University Press, 1913)

THE VOLSUNG SAGA

See The *Eddas* and *Sagas*

CHAPTER TWO

THE HEIGHT OF THE MIDDLE AGES

GENERAL

Adams, H., *Mont St. Michel and Chartres* (Houghton, Mifflin & Co., 1904)

Artz, F. B., *The Mind of the Middle Ages* (A. A. Knopf, 1953)

Betterson, H. (ed.), *Documents of the Christian Church* (World's Classics, Oxford University Press, 1947)

Carlyle, T., *Carlyle's Unfinished History of German Literature* (H. Shine, ed.) (University of Kentucky Press, 1951)

Coulton, G. C., *Medieval Panorama* (Cambridge University Press, 1939)

Crump, C. G. and Jacobs, E. F. (eds.), *The Legacy of the Middle Ages* (Clarendon Press, 1943)

Flick, A. C., *The Decline of the Medieval Church* (A. A. Knopf, 1930)

Gaspary, A., *A History of Early Italian Literature to the Death of Dante* (Bohn's Standard Library, G. Bell & Sons, 1901)

Haskins, C. H., *The Renaissance of the Twelfth Century* (Harvard University Press, 1927)

Hearnshaw, F. J. C. (ed.), *Medieval Contributions to Modern Civilization* (H. Holt & Co., 1922)

Hearnshaw, F. J. C., *The Social and Political Ideas of Some Great Medieval Thinkers* (H. Holt & Co., 1923)

Hopper, V. F., *Medieval Number Symbolism* (Columbia University Press, 1938)

Janssen, J., *History of the German People at the Close of the Middle Ages* (K. Paul, Trench & Trübner, 1906-1928)

Ker, W. P., *Essays on Medieval Literature* (The Macmillan Co., 1905)

Labriolle, P. de, *History and Literature of Christianity* (A. A. Knopf, 1925)

Mott, L. F., *The Provençal Lyric* (W. R. Jenkins, 1901), *The System of Courtly Love* (Ginn & Co , 1896)

Rahman, F., *Avicenna's Philosophy* (Oxford University Press, 1953)

Ross, J. B. and McLaughlin, M. M. (eds.), *Medieval Reader* (The Portable Library, The Viking Press, 1949)

Rutherford, J., *The Troubadours* (London, 1873)

Sandys, J. E., *A History of Classical Scholarship* (Cambridge University Press, 1903-08)

Simpson, L. F., *The Literature of Italy* (R. Bentley, 1851)

Smith, J. H., *The Troubadours at Home* (G. P. Putnam's Sons, 1899)

Taylor, A., *Problems in German Literary History of the Fifteenth and Sixteenth Centuries* (Oxford University Press, 1939)

Taylor, H. O., *Classical Heritage of the Middle Ages* (The Macmillan Co., 1925), *The Medieval Mind* (The Macmillan Co., 1927)

Vossler, K., *Medieval Culture: An Introduction to Dante and His Times* (Harcourt, Brace & Co., 1929)

Waddell, H., *The Wandering Scholars* (Houghton Mifflin Co., 1927)

Wulf, M. de, *History of Medieval Philosophy* (Longmans, Green & Co., 1935-38)

AQUINAS

Translations: The English Dominican Fathers, *The Summa contra Gentiles* (Burns Oates & Washbourne, 1927-35); Fathers of the English Dominican Province, *The "Summa Theologica" of St. Thomas Aquinas* (R. & T. Washbourne, 1911-25); Grabmann, M., *Introduction to the Summa* (B. Herder Book Co., 1930); Herbert, A. G. (ed.), *God and His Works* (The Macmillan Co., 1936); Pegis, A. C., *Basic Writings of Saint Thomas Aquinas* (Random House, 1945), *Introduction to Thomas Aquinas* (The Modern Library, 1948); Shapcote, L., *On Man* (The Great Books Foundation, 1951)

Carré, M. H., *Realists and Nominalists* (Oxford University Press, 1946)

Chesterton, G. K., *St. Thomas Aquinas* (Hodder & Stoughton, Ltd., 1933)

Coffey, R. M., *The Man from Rocca Sicca* (Bruce Publishing Co., 1944)

Diggs, B. J., *Love and Being, An Investigation into the Metaphysics of St. Thomas Aquinas* (S. F. Vanni, 1947)

Easby-Smith, M., *The Scholastic Synthesis according to the Mind of Saint Thomas Aquinas* (The Dolphin Press, 1932)

Farrell, W., *A Companion to the Summa* (Sheed & Ward, 1939-42)

Gerrity, B., *Nature, Knowledge and God* (Bruce Publishing Co., 1947)

Gilson, E. H., *The Philosophy of St. Thomas Aquinas* (W. Heffer & Sons, Ltd., 1929)

Grabmann, M., *The Interior Life of St. Thomas Aquinas* (Bruce Publishing Co., 1951), *Thomas Aquinas* (Longmans, Green & Co., 1928)

Hoenen, P. H. J., *Reality and Judgment According to St. Thomas* (H. Regnery Co., 1952)

Kluberantz, G. P., *The Discursive Power* (Modern Schoolman, 1952)

Maritain, J., *The Angelic Doctor* (J. F. Scanlon, tr.) (The Dial Press, 1931)

O'Donnell, C. M., *The Psychology of St. Bonaventure and St. Thomas Aquinas* (The Catholic University of America, 1937)

Passerin d'Entrèves, *The Medieval Contribution to Political Thought* (Oxford University Press, 1939)

Patterson, R. L., *The Conception of God in the Philosophy of Aquinas* (G. Allen & Unwin, Ltd., 1933)

Reilly, G. C., *The Psychology of Saint Albert the Great Compared with that of Saint Thomas* (The Catholic University of America, 1934)

Ryan, A. H., *Perennial Philosophers* (Clonmore & Reynolds, 1946)

Sertillanges, A., *Foundations of Thomistic Philosophy* (Catholic Library of Religious Knowledge, Sands & Co., 1931)

Vann, G., *Saint Thomas Aquinas* (Benziger Bros., 1940)

Wulf, M. M., *Medieval Philosophy Illustrated from the System of Thomas Aquinas* (Harvard University Press, 1922)

AUCASSIN AND NICOLETTE

Translations: Housman, L., *Of Aucassin and Nicolette* (Chatto & Windus, 1925); Lang, A., *Aucassin and Nicolette* (T. B. Mosher, 1895; The Fleuron Press, 1924; G. E. Stechert & Co., 1928; Holiday House, 1936; Golden Eagle Press, 1946); Mason, E., *Aucassin and Nicolette and Other Medieval Romances and Legends* (Everyman's Library, E. P. Dutton & Co., 1910); Smith, D. L., *Aucassin and Nicolette* (A. Melrose, 1914)

CRESTIEN DE TROYES

Translations: Comfort, W. W., *Eric and Enid* (Everyman's Library, E. P. Dutton & Co., 1914); Gardiner, L. J., *Cligés: A Romance* (New Medieval Library, Chatto & Windus, 1912)

Cross, T. P., *Launcelot and Guenivere; a Study on the Origins of Courtly Love* (University of Chicago Press, 1930)

Griffith, R. H., *Sir Perceval of Galles* (University of Chicago Press, 1911)

Lewis, C. B., *Classical Mythology and Arthurian Romance* (Oxford University Press, 1932)

Newell, W. W., *King Arthur and the Table Round* (Houghton, Mifflin & Co., 1893)

Rachbauer, M. A., *Wolfram von Eschenbach* (The Catholic University of America, 1934)

Ritson, J., *A Dissertation on Romance and Minstrelsy* (E. G. Goldsmid, 1891)

Weston, J. L., *The Legend of Sir Lancelot du Lac* (Grimm Library, D. Nutt, 1901), *The Legend of Sir Perceval* (Grimm Library, D. Nutt, 1906-09)

DANTE

Translations: Anderson, M. B., *The Comedy of Dante Alighieri* (J. H. Nash, 1929), *La Divina Commedia* (World Book Co., 1921), *The Divine Comedy* (The Heritage Press, 1924); Bergin, T. G., *Inferno* (Crofts Classics, Appleton-Century-Crofts, Inc., 1947), *Purgatorio* (Crofts Classics, Appleton-Century-Crofts, Inc., 1953); Bickersteth, G. L., *The Paradiso of Dante Alighieri* (Cambridge University Press, 1932); Binyon, L., *Dante's Inferno* (Macmillan & Co., Ltd., 1933), *Dante's Paradiso* (Macmillan & Co., Ltd. 1943), *Dante's Purgatorio* (Macmillan & Co., Ltd., 1938), *The Divine Comedy* in *The Portable Dante* (Viking Press, 1947); Bodey, R. T., *The Divine Comedy of Dante Alighieri* (H. Cleaver, Ltd., 1938); Boyd, H., *The Divina Commedia of Dante Alighieri* (T. Cadell, Jr. & W. Davies, 1802); Brewer, W., *Dante's Eclogues* (The Cornhill Publishing Co., 1927); Butler, A. J., *The Paradise of Dante Alighieri* (Macmillan & Co., 1885), *The Purgatory of Dante Alighieri* (Macmillan & Co., 1880); Carlyle, J. A., *The Inferno of Dante Alighieri* (Chapman & Hall, 1849; Harper & Brothers, 1849; The Temple Classics, J. M. Dent & Sons, 1900); Carlyle, J. A. and Wicksteed, P. H., *The Divine Comedy of Dante Alighieri* (The Modern Library, 1932; Modern Library College Editions, The Modern Library, Random House, 1950); Cary, H. F., *The Divine Comedy of Dante Alighieri* (The Colonial Press, 1901), *The Vision* (Taylor & Hessey, 1819; J. Taylor, 1831; W. Smith, 1844; H. G. Bohn, 1847; D. Appleton & Co., 1850; Longman, Brown, Green & Longmans, 1855; Cassell, Pelter, & Galpin, 1868; T. Crowell & Co., 1881; J. M. Lovell, 1881; The Co-Operative Publishing Society, 1901); Cary, T., *The Divine Comedy* (Everyman's Library, E. P. Dutton & Co., 1908); Cayley, C. B., *The Purgatory* (Longman, Brown, Green, & Longmans, 1853); Church, R. W., *De Monarchia* in *Dante* (Macmillan & Co., 1879); Dugdale, W. S., *The Purgatorio* (Bohn's Collegiate Series, G. Bell & Sons, 1883); Fletcher, J. B., *The Divine Comedy of Dante Alighieri* (The Macmillan Co., 1931); Henry, A., *The De Monarchia* (Houghton, Mifflin & Co., 1904); How, L., *The Comedy of Dante Alighieri* (The Harbor Press, 1934); Howell, A. G. F. and Wicksteed, P. H., *A Translation of the Latin Works of Dante Alighieri* (The Temple Classics, J. M. Dent & Sons,

Ltd., 1904); Hunt, L., *The Italian Poets Translated into English Prose* (H. W. Derby, 1861); Johnson, H., *La Comedia di Dante Alighieri* (Yale University Press, 1915); Longfellow, H. W., *The Divine Comedy of Dante Alighieri* (Ticknor & Fields, 1867; B. Tauchnitz, 1867; J. R. Osgood & Co., 1876; Houghton, Mifflin & Co., 1881); Lucchi, L. de', *The Minor Poems of Dante* (Oxford University Press, 1926); Mackenzie, D. J., *The Vision* (Longmans, Green & Co., Ltd., 1927); Milano, P. (ed.), *The Portable Dante* (The Viking Press, 1947); Money, A. L., *The Purgatorio of Dante Alighieri* (G. Allen & Sons, 1910); Murray, E. V., *The Inferno of Dante* (The Merrymount Press, 1920); Musgrave, G., *Dante's Inferno* (Oxford University Press, 1933); Norton, C. E., *The Divine Comedy of Dante Alighieri* (Houghton, Mifflin & Co., 1895-97), *The New Life* (Houghton, Mifflin & Co., 1909); Okey, T., *The Purgatorio of Dante Alighieri* (The Temple Classics, J. M. Dent & Sons, Ltd., 1901); Okey, T. and Wicksteed, P. H., *The Vita Nuova and Canzoniere of Dante Alighieri* (The Temple Classics, J. M. Dent & Sons, Ltd., 1906); Parsons, T. W., *The Divine Comedy of Dante Alighieri* (Houghton, Mifflin & Co., 1893); Pyne, J., *An English Dante* (A. & C. Boni, 1914); Rossetti, D. G., *Dante and His Circle* (Ellis & White, 1874), *The New Life* (R. H. Russell, 1901; Ellis & Elvey, 1903; T. Y. Crowell & Co., 1904), *La Vita Nuova* in *The Portable Dante* (The Viking Press, 1947); Sayers, D. L., *The Divine Comedy, I: Hell* (Penguin Books, Inc., 1949), *II: Purgatory* (Penguin Books Inc., 1954?), *III: Paradiso* (Penguin Books, Inc., 1955?); Shadwell, C. L., *The Paradise of Dante* (Macmillan & Co., Ltd., 1915); Sinclair, J. D., *The Divine Comedy of Dante Alighieri* (John Lane, 1939-46; Oxford University Press, 1948); Schneider, H. W., *On World Government* [*De Monarchia*] (The Library of Liberal Arts, The Liberal Arts Press, Inc., 1949); Toynbee, P., *Dantis Aligherii Epistolae; The Letters of Dante* (Clarendon Press, 1920); Vincent, M. R., *The Inferno* (C. Scribner's Sons, 1904); Wheeler, C. E., *The Divine Comedy* (E. P. Dutton & Co., 1911); White, L. G., *The Divine Comedy* (Pantheon Books, 1948); Wicksteed, P. H., *The Convivio of Dante Alighieri* (The Temple Classics, J. M. Dent & Sons, Ltd., 1903), *A Translation of the Latin Works of Dante Alighieri* (with Howell A. G. F.) (The Temple Classics, J. M. Dent & Sons, Ltd., 1904), *The Paradiso of Dante Alighieri* (The Temple Classics, J. M. Dent & Sons, Ltd., 1899), also in *The Divine Comedy of Dante Alighieri* (The Modern Library, 1932; Modern Library College Editions, The Modern Library, Random House, 1950); Wright, S. F., *The Inferno* (F. Wright, Ltd., 1928)

Anderson, M. B., *The Florence of Dante Alighieri* (J. H. Nash, 1929)

Arensberg, W. C., *The Cryptography of Dante* (A. A. Knopf, 1921)

Blow, S. E., *A Study of Dante* (G. P. Putnam's Sons, 1886)

Boccaccio, G., *Life of Dante,* tr. by P. H. Wicksteed (The Riverside Press, 1904)

Botticelli, S., *Drawings for Dante's Inferno* (Lear Publishers, Inc., 1947)

Boynton, H. W., *The World's Leading Poets* (H. Holt & Co., 1912)

Butler, A. J., *Dante, His Times and His Work* (Macmillan & Co., 1902), *The Forerunners of Dante* (Oxford University Press, 1910)

Buxton, C. R., *Prophets of Heaven and Hell* (Cambridge University Press, 1945)

Carpenter, G. R., *A Translation of Giovanni Boccaccio's Life of Dante* (The Grolier Club, 1900)

Carroll, J. S., *Exiles of Eternity* (Hodder & Stoughton, 1903), *Prisoners of Hope* (Hodder & Stoughton, 1906)

Croce, B., *The Poetry of Dante* (H. Holt & Co., 1922)

Dinsmore, C. A., *Aids to the Study of Dante* (Houghton, Mifflin & Co., 1903), *Life of Dante Alighieri* (Houghton Mifflin Co., 1919)

Dole, N. H., *A Teacher of Dante, and Other Studies in Italian Literature* (Moffat, Yard & Co., 1908)

Dunbar, H. F., *Symbolism in Medieval Thought and Its Consummation in the Divine Comedy* (Yale University Press, 1929)

Eliot, T. S., *Dante* (Faber & Faber, 1929), *The Sacred Wood* (Methuen & Co., Ltd., 1920)

Federn, K., *Dante and His Time* (McClure, Phillips & Co., 1902)

Flamini, F., *Introduction to the Study of the Divine Comedy* (Ginn & Co., 1910)

Fletcher, J. B., *Dante* (H. Holt & Co., 1916), *The Religion of Beauty in Women* (The Macmillan Co., 1911), *Symbolism of the Divine Comedy* (Columbia University Press, 1921)

Friedrich, W. P., *Dante's Fame Abroad, 1350-1850* (University of North Carolina Press, 1950)

Gardner, E. G., *Dante* (Oxford University Press, 1921; E. P. Dutton & Co., 1923), *Dante and the Mystics* (E. P. Dutton & Co., 1913), *Dante's Ten Heavens* (A. Constable & Co., 1900)

Gilbert, A. H., *Dante's Conception of Justice* (Duke University Press, 1925)

Gilson, E. H., *Dante the Philosopher* (D. Moore, tr.) (Sheed & Ward, 1949)

Grandgent, C. H., *Dante* (Duffield & Co., 1916), *Discourses on Dante* (Harvard University Press, 1924), *The Ladies of Dante's Lyrics* (Harvard University Press, 1917), *The Power of Dante* (Marshall Jones Co., 1918)

Gurteen, S. H. V., *The Epic of the Fall of Man* (G. P. Putnam's Sons, 1896)

Harrower, R. B., *A New Theory of Dante's Metelda* (Cambridge University Press, 1926)

Hopper, V. F., *Medieval Number Symbolism* (Columbia University Press, 1938)

Howell, A. G. F., *Dante; His Life and Work* (T. C. & E. C. Jack, 1912)

Hunt, L., *Stories from the Italian Poets* (Chapman & Hall, 1846)

Jourdain, E. F., *A Study in the Symbolism of the Divina Commedia* (E. E. Speight, 1902)

Kavanagh, M., *Dante's Mystic Love* (Sands & Co., 1921)

Ker, W: P., *Essays on Medieval Literature* (Macmillan Co., 1905)

Koch, T. W., *Dante in America* (Ginn & Co., 1896)

Kohler, K., *Heaven and Hell in Comparative Religion* (The Macmillan Co., 1923)

Kuhns, L. O., *Dante and the English Poets from Chaucer to Tennyson* (H. Holt & Co., 1904), *The Treatment of Nature in Dante's 'Divina Commedia'* (E. Arnold, 1897)

La Piana, A., *Dante's American Pilgrimage; a Historical Survey of Dante Studies in the United States, 1804-1944* (Yale University Press, 1948)

Leigh, G., *New Light on the Youth of Dante* (Houghton Mifflin Co., 1930), *The Passing of Beatrice* (Faber & Faber, Ltd., 1932)

Lowell, J. R., *Among My Books* (Second Series) (Houghton Mifflin Co., 1876)

Mabie, H. W., *Essays in Literary Interpretation* (Dodd, Mead & Co., 1900)

Mitchell, E. M., *The Paradise of Dante* (Hall & M'Chesney, 1898)

Moore, E., *Studies in Dante* (First—Fourth Series) (Clarendon Press, 1896-1917)

Mott, L. F., *Dante and Beatrice* (W. R. Jenkins, 1892)

O'Neill, A., *Guide to the Student of Dante* (Franklin Printing House, 1937)

Oliphant, M., *The Makers of Florence* (Macmillan & Co., 1892)

Osgood, C. G., *Poetry as a Means of Grace* (Oxford University Press, 1941)

Page, T. N., *Dante and His Influence* (C. Scribner's Sons, 1922)

Papini, G., *Dante Vivo* (L. Dickson, 1934)

Passerin d'Entrèves, A., *Dante as a Political Thinker* (Clarendon Press, 1952)

Pradeau, *A Key to the Time Allusions in the Divine Comedy of Dante Alighieri* (Methuen & Co., 1902)

Reade, W. H. V., *The Moral System of Dante's Inferno* (Clarendon Press, 1909)

Rossetti, M. F., *A Shadow of Dante* (Roberts, 1886)

Rossetti, W. M., *Dante and His Convito* (Elkin Mathews, 1910)

Santayana, G., *Three Philosophical Poets* (Harvard University, 1927)

Schaff, P., *Dante and the Divina Commedia* (C. Scribner's Sons, 1890), *Literature and Poetry* (C. Scribner's Sons, 1890)

Shattuck, H. R., *The Story of Dante's Divine Comedy* (J. B. Alden, 1887)

Silber, G. R., *The Influence of Dante and Petrarch on Certain of Boccaccio's Lyrics* (George Banta Publishing Co., 1940)

Singleton, C. S., *An Essay on the Vita Nuova* (Harvard University Press, 1949)

Snider, J. D., *Dante: The Divine Comedy* (The H. W. Miner Co., Inc., 1921)

Symonds, J. A., *An Introduction to the Study of Dante* (Macmillan & Co., Ltd., 1899)

Toynbee, P., *Concise Dictionary of Proper Names and Notable Matters in the Works of Dante* (Clarendon Press, 1914), *Dante Alighieri, His Life and Work* (The Macmillan Co., 1910), *Dante in English Literature from Chaucer to Cary* (Methuen & Co., 1909), *Dante Studies* (Clarendon Press, 1921)

Tozer, H. F., *An English Commentary on Dante's Divina Commedia* (Clarendon Press, 1901)

Vernon, W. W., *Readings on the Paradiso of Dante* (Methuen & Co., 1909)

Vossler, K., *Medieval Culture: an Introduction to Dante and His Times* (Harcourt, Brace & Co., 1929)

Walsh, G. G., *Dante Alighieri* (Bruce Publishing Co., 1946)

Whitfield, J. H., *Dante and Virgil* (B. Blackwell, 1949)

Whiting, M. B., *Dante and His Poetry* (G. G. Harrap & Co., Ltd., 1932), *Dante, the Man and the Poet* (D. Appleton & Co., 1923)

Wicksteed, P. H., *Dante* (E. Mathews & J. Lane, 1892), *Dante and Aquinas* (E. P. Dutton & Co., 1913), *Dante and Giovanni del Virgilio* (Constable & Co., Ltd., 1902), *From Vita Nuova to Paradiso* (Manchester University Press, 1922), *Life of Dante* (The Riverside Press, 1904)

Wilkins, E. H., *Dante: Poet and Apostle* (University of Chicago Press, 1921)

Williams, C., *The Figure of Beatrice* (Faber & Faber, Ltd., 1943)

Witte, J. H. F., *Essays on Dante* (Houghton, Mifflin & Co., 1898)

Wordsworth, J. C., *Adventures in Literature* (Heath Craton, Ltd., 1929)

Wright, W. J. P., *Dante and the Divine Comedy* (J. Lane, 1902)

OUR LADY'S TUMBLER

Translations: Bellamy, F. Le F., *The Jongleur's Story* (The Woman's Press, 1926); Butler, I., *Our Lady's Tumbler* (Copeland & Day, 1898); France, A., *Our Lady's Juggler* (English Book Shop, 1933; W. E. Rudge's Sons, 1938); Smith, C. R., *The Story of Jean, The*

Jongleur (Privately Printed, New York, 1927); Wicksteed, P. H., *Our Lady's Tumbler* (T. B. Mosher, 1904)

THE ROMANCE OF THE ROSE

Translations: Chaucer, G. (?), *The Romaunt of the Rose* (The Chaucer Society, K. Paul, Trench, Trübner & Co., 1891; Florence Press, 1908); Ellis, F. S., *The Romance of the Rose* (The Temple Classics, J. M. Dent & Co., 1900)

Fansler, D. S., *Chaucer and the Roman de la Rose* (Columbia University Press, 1914)

Tatlock, J. S. P., *A Concordance to the Complete Works of Geoffrey Chaucer and to the Romaunt of the Rose* (Carnegie Institution of Washington, 1927)

VILLON

Translations: *Ballades & Lyrics of François Villon* (The Peter Pauper Press, 1940); *Ballads Done into English from the French of François Villon* (T. B. Mosher, 1904); *The Book of François Villon* (International Pocket Library, *c.* 1931); *The Lyrics of François Villon* (The Limited Editions Club, 1933); Chaney, E. C., *The Poems of François Villon* (B. H. Blackwell, Ltd., 1940); Heyer, G., *The Retrospect of François Villon* (H. Milford, 1924); Lepper, J. H., *The Testaments of François Villon* (The Casanova Society, 1924; Boni & Liveright, 1926); McCaskie, H. B., *The Poems of François Villon* (Cresset Press, 1946); Nicolson, J. U., *The Complete Works of François Villon* (Covici, Friede, 1931); Payne, J., *Poems of François Villon* (J. W. Luce & Co., 1917; Boni & Liveright, 1918), *Sundry Ballades of François Villon* (The Grabhorn Press, 1922); Stabler, J. H., *The Jargon of Master François Villon* (The Riverside Press, 1918); Stacpoole, H. de Vere, *The Poems of François Villon* (John Lane Co., 1914)

Barry, P. B., *Sinners Down the Centuries* (Jarrolds, Pref., 1928)

Belloc, H., *Avril* (Sheed & Ward, 1945)

Carco, F., *The Romance of Villon* (A. A. Knopf, 1927)

Chaney, E. F., *François Villon in His Environment* (B. H. Blackwell, 1946)

Deutsch, B., *Rogue's Legacy* (Coward-McCann, Inc., 1942)

Erskine, J., *The Brief Hour of François Villon* (The Bobbs-Merrill Co., 1937)

French, J. L. (ed.), *The Book of the Rogue* (Boni & Liveright, 1926)

Lewis, D. B. W., *François Villon* (The Literary Guild of America, 1928)

Mackworth, C., *François Villon, a Study* (Westhouse, 1947)

Rice, W. H., *The European Ancestry of Villon's Satirical Testaments* (The Corporate Press, 1941)

Stacpoole, H. de Vere, *François Villon, His Life and Times* (Hutchinson & Co., 1916)

Stevenson, R. L., *Familiar Studies of Men and Books* (C. Scribner's Sons, 1902), *François Villon, Student Poet, and Housebreaker* (T. B. Mosher, 1911), *A Lodging for the Night* (T. B. Mosher, 1916)

CHAPTER THREE

THE RENAISSANCE

GENERAL

Adams, H., *Mont-Saint-Michel and Chartres* (Houghton Mifflin Co., 1904)

Crawford, R. M., *The Renaissance, and Other Essays* (Melbourne University Press, 1947)

Durant, W., *The Renaissance* (Simon & Schuster, 1953)

Ferguson, W. K., *The Renaissance* (H. Holt & Co., 1940)

Flick, A. C., *The Decline of the Medieval Church* (A. A. Knopf, 1930)

Greg, W. W., *Pastoral Poetry and Pastoral Drama* (A. H. Bullen, 1906)

Haydn, H., *The Counter-Renaissance* (C. Scribner's Sons, 1950)

Huizinga, J., *The Waning of the Middle Ages* (E. Arnold & Co., 1937)

Pater, W., *The Renaissance* (Macmillan & Co., 1910)

Roeder, R., *The Man of the Renaissance* (The Viking Press, 1933)

Sichel, E., *The Renaissance* (H. Holt & Co., 1914)

Taylor, H. O., *Thought and Expression in the Sixteenth Century* (The Macmillan Co., 1920)

Whitcomb, M., *Literary Source-Book of the Renaissance* (University of Pennsylvania Press, 1904)

THE RENAISSANCE IN FRANCE

Hannay, D., *The Late Renaissance* (C. Scribner's Sons, 1898)

Keating, L. C., *Studies in the Literary Salon in France, 1550-1615* (Harvard University Press, 1941)

Tilley, A., *The Dawn of the French Renaissance* (Cambridge University Press, 1918), *The Literature of the French Renaissance* (Cambridge University Press, 1904), *Studies in the French Renaissance* (Cambridge University Press, 1922)

THE RENAISSANCE IN ITALY

Andrews, M., *Courts and Camps of the Italian Renaissance* by Christopher Hare (pseud.) (Harper & Brothers, 1908)

Burckhardt, J. C., *The Civilization of the Renaissance in Italy* (Harper & Brothers, 1929)

Cotterill, H. B., *Italy from Dante to Tasso* (Frederick A. Stokes Co., 1919)

Crane, T. F., *Italian Social Customs of the Sixteenth Century* (Yale University Press, 1920)

Fletcher, J. B., *Literature of the Italian Renaissance* (The Macmillan Co., 1934)

Gardner, E. G. (ed.), *Italy; a Companion to Italian Studies* (Methuen & Co., 1934)

Gardner, E. G., *The Story of Florence* (J. M. Dent & Co., 1910)

Hueffer, F., *Italian and Other Studies* (E. Stock, 1883)

Jackson, T. G., *A Holiday in Umbria* (J. Murray, 1917)

Paget, V., *Euphorion* by Vernon Lee (pseud.) (T. F. Unwin, 1884)

Robb, N. A., *Neoplatonism of the Italian Renaissance* (G. Allen & Unwin, Ltd., 1935)

Schevill, F., *The First Century of Italian Humanism* (F. S. Crofts & Co., 1928)

Symonds, J. A., *Renaissance in Italy* (H. Holt & Co., 1888; J. Murray, 1929; The Modern Library, Random House, 1935)

Vaughan, H. M., *Studies in the Italian Renaissance* (Methuen & Co., Ltd., 1930)

Woodward, W. H., *Vittorino da Feltre and Other Humanist Educators* (Cambridge University Press, 1921)

THE RENAISSANCE IN SPAIN

Bell, A. F. G., *Luis de Leon: Á Study of the Spanish Renaissance* (Oxford University Press, 1925)

Deferrari, H. A., *The Sentimental Moor in Spanish Literature before 1600* (Pennsylvania University, 1927)

Entwistle, W. J., *The Arthurian Legend in the Literatures of the Spanish Peninsula* (J. M. Dent & Sons, Ltd., 1925)

Hannay, D., *The Late Renaissance* (C. Scribner's Sons, 1898)

Madariaga, S. de, *The Genius of Spain* (Clarendon Press, 1923)

Salinas, P., *Reality and the Poet in Spanish Poetry* (The Johns Hopkins Press, 1940)

THE AMADIS DE GAULA

Translations: Rose, W. S., *Amadis de Gaul* (T. Cadell, 1803); Southey, R., *Amadis of Gaul* (J. R. Smith, 1872)

ARETINO

Chubb, T. C., *Aretino, Scourge of Princes* (Reynal & Hitchcock, 1940)

Hutton, E., *Pietro Aretino, the Scourge of Princes* (A. Constable & Co., 1922)

Roeder, R., *The Man of the Renaissance* (The Viking Press, 1933)

ARIOSTO

Translations: Harington, J., *Orlando Furioso* (Richard Field, 1591);
Holle, J., *Orlando Furioso* (G. Nicol, 1785; H. Hudson, 1816); Hunt,
L., *The Italian Poets Translated into English Prose* (H. W. Derby,
1861); Rose, W. S., *Orlando Furioso* (J. Murray, 1823-31)

Cameron, A. V., *The Influence of Ariosto's Epic and Lyric Poetry on
Ronsard and His Group* (The Johns Hopkins Press, 1930)

Croce, B., *Ariosto, Shakespeare, and Corneille* (H. Holt & Co., 1920)

Edwards, E. W., *The Orlando Furioso and its Predecessor* (Cambridge
University Press, 1924)

Fragonard, J. H., *Drawings for Ariosto* (Pantheon, 1945)

Gardner, E. G., *The King of Court Poets* (E. P. Dutton & Co., 1906)

Hunt, L., *Stories from the Italian Poets* (Chapman & Hall, 1846)

McMurphy, S. J., *Spenser's Use of Ariosto* (University of Washington
Press, 1924)

Nicholson, J. S., *Life and Genius of Ariosto* (Macmillan & Co., Ltd., 1914)

BAIF

Cameron, A. V., *The Influence of Ariosto's Epic and Lyric Poetry on
Ronsard and His Group* (The Johns Hopkins Press, 1930)

Clements, J. J., *Critical Theory and Practice of the Pléiade* (Harvard
University Press, 1942)

Levengood, S. L., *The Use of Color in the Verse of the Pléiade* (Les
Presses Universitaires de France, 1927)

BELLEAU

Cameron, A. V., *The Influence of Ariosto's Epic and Lyric Poetry on
Ronsard and His Group* (The Johns Hopkins Press, 1930)

Clements, J. J., *Critical Theory and Practice of the Pléiade* (Harvard University Press, 1942)

Levengood, S. L., *The Use of Color in the Verse of the Pléiade* (Les
Presses Universitaires de France, 1927)

BOCCACCIO

Translations: *Decameron Tales* (J. H. Sears & Co., 1925); *The Decameron*
(Stewart & Kidd Co., 1920; The Heritage Club, 1940; The Limited
Editions Club, 1940; The Living Library, The World Publishing
Co.); *The Little Decameron* (E. P. Dutton & Co., 1923); Aldington,
R., *The Decameron of Giovanni Boccaccio* (Covici, Friede, 1930;
Garden City Publishing Co., 1938); Bell, T., *The Most Pleasant and
Delectable Questions of Love* (Illustrated Editions Co., 1931); Car-
penter, G. R., *A Translation of Giovanni Boccaccio's Life of Dante*
(The Grolier Club, 1900); Cummings, H., *Il Filostrato* (Princeton
University Press, 1924); Griffin, N. E. and Myrick, A. B., *The*

Filostrato of Giovanni Boccaccio (University of Pennsylvania Press, 1929); Hutton, E., *Thirteene Most Pleasaunt and Delectable Questions* (from *Il Philocopo*) (Peter Davies, 1927); Kelly, W. W., *The Decameron* (H. G. Bohn, 1885); Orson, S. W., *The Decameron* (Pocket Books, Inc., 1948); Osgood, C. G., *Boccaccio on Poetry* (Princeton University Press, 1930); Payne, J., *The Decameron of Giovanni Boccaccio* (Villon Society, 1886; Boni & Liveright, 1925; Blue Ribbon Books, 1931; The Modern Library, Random House, 1931); Rigg, J. M., *The Decameron of Giovanni Boccaccio* (Everyman's Library, E. P. Dutton & Co., 1930); Wicksteed, P. H., *Life of Dante* (The Riverside Press, 1904); Winwar, F., *The Decameron* (Limited Editions Club, 1930); Yong, B., *Amorous Fiametta* (Rarity Press, 1931)

Carswell, C. R., *The Tranquil Heart, a Portrait of Giovanni Boccaccio* (Harcourt Brace & Co., 1937)

Chubb, C., *The Life of Giovanni Boccaccio* (A. & C. Boni, Inc., 1930)

Cummings, H. M., *The Indebtedness of Chaucer's Works to the Italian Works of Boccaccio* (Banta Publishing Co., 1916)

Dole, N. H., *A Teacher of Dante, and Other Studies in Italian Literature* (Moffat, Yard & Co., 1908)

Hutton, E., *Giovanni Boccaccio* (J. Lane, 1910)

Ker, W. P., *Essays on Medieval Literature* (The Macmillan Co., 1905)

Krutch, J. W., *Five Masters* (J. Cape & H. Smith, 1930)

McManus, F., *Boccaccio* (Sheed & Ward, 1947)

Silber, G. R., *The Influence of Dante and Petrarch on Certain of Boccaccio's Lyrics* (George Banta Publishing Co., 1940)

Symonds, J. A., *Giovanni Boccaccio as Man and Author* (J. C. Nimmo, 1895)

BOIARDO

Translations: Hunt, L., *The Italian Poets Translated into English Prose* (H. W. Derby, 1861); Rose, W. S., *Orlando Innamorato* (W. Blackwood, 1823)

Edwards, E. W., *The Orlando Furioso and its Predecessor* (Cambridge University Press, 1924)

Grillo, G., *Two Aspects of Chivalry, Pulci and Boiardo* (The Excelsior Press, Inc., 1942)

Hunt, L., *Stories from the Italian Poets* (Chapman & Hall, 1846)

Paget, V., *Euphorion* by Vernon Lee (pseud.) (T. F. Unwin, 1899)

Wordsworth, J. C., *Adventures in Literature* (Heath Cranton, Ltd., 1929)

CALDERON

Translations: Fitzgerald, E., *Six Dramas of Calderon* (W. Pickering, 1853), *Eight Dramas of Calderon* (The Macmillan Co., 1921), *Six*

Plays (Everyman's Library, E. P. Dutton & Co., 1928), *Works of Edward Fitzgerald,* Vol. II (Houghton Mifflin Co., 1887); Mac-Carty, D. F., *Calderon's Dramas* (H. S. King & Co., 1873), *Love, the Greatest Enchantment, The Sorceries of Sin, The Devotion of the Cross* (Longman Green, Longman & Roberts, 1861), *Mysteries of Corpus Christi* (J. Duffy, 1867); Shelley, P. B., *The Wonder-working Magician* in Shelley's *Works* (Any Edition)

Madariaga, S., *Shelley and Calderon* (Constable & Co., 1920)

Owen, J., *The Five Great Skeptical Dramas of History* (G. P. Putnam's Sons, 1896)

Trench, R. C., *Calderon: His Life and Genius* (Redfield, 1856), *An Essay on the Life and Genius of Calderon* (Macmillan & Co., Ltd., 1880)

CALVIN

Translations: Allen, J., *Institutes of the Christian Religion* (P. H. Nicklin, 1816); Allen, J. and Warfield, B. B., *God and Political Duty* (The Library of Liberal Arts, The Liberal Arts Press, Inc., 1950); Beveridge, H., *Institutes of the Christian Religion* (T. T. Clark, 1869)

Harkness, G. E., *John Calvin, The Man and His Ethics* (H. Holt & Co., 1931)

Palm, F. C., *Calvinism and the Religious Wars* (H. Holt & Co., 1932)

CAMOENS

Translations: Atkinson, W. C., *Lusiads* (Penguin Books, Inc., 1952); Aubertin, J. J., *The Lusiads* (C. K. Paul & Co., 1879); Bacon, L., *The Lusiads of Luis de Camoes* (Hispanic Society of America, 1950); Fanshawe, R., *The Lusiad* (Harvard University Press, 1940); Mickle, W. J., *The Lusiad* (G. Bell & Sons, 1877)

Adamson, J., *Memoirs of the Life and Writings of Luis de Camoens* (Longman, Hurst, Rees, Orne, & Brown, 1820)

Bowra, C. M., *From Virgil to Milton* (Macmillan & Co., Ltd., 1945)

Burton, Sir R. F., *Camoens* (B. Quaritch, 1881)

Goldberg, I., *Camoens* (Little Blue Books, Haldeman-Julius, 1924)

CASTIGLIONE

Translations: Hoby, T., *The Book of the Courtier* (Everyman's Library, E. P. Dutton & Co., 1928); Opdycke, L. E., *The Book of the Courtier* (C. Scribner's Sons, 1903)

Ady, J. C., *Baldassare Castiglione* (J. Murray, 1908)

Andrews, M., *Courts and Camps of the Italian Renaissance,* by Cristopher Hare (pseud.) (Harper & Brothers, 1908)

Roeder, R., *The Man of the Renaissance* (The Viking Press, 1933)

CELLINI

Translations: Cust, R. H., *The Memoirs of Benvenuto Cellini* (Duffield, Green & Co., 1932); Macdonell, A., *Memoirs of Benvenuto Cellini* (Everyman's Library, E. P. Dutton & Co., 1910); Nugent, T., *The Life of Benvenuto Cellini* (Hunt & Clarke, 1828); Rascoe, T., *Memoirs of Benvenuto Cellini* (H. G. Bohn, 1847), *Memoirs Written by Himself* (World's Classics, Oxford University Press, 1927); Symonds, J. A., *Autobiography of Benvenuto Cellini* (Brentano's, 1906; The Macmillan Co., 1924; The Modern Library, 1927; The Black & Gold Library, H. Liveright, 1932)

Dark, S., *Twelve Bad Men*, (Thomas Y. Crowell Co., 1929)

Spinatelli, C. J., *The Florentine* (Prentice-Hall, 1953)

Thaddeus, V., *Benvenuto Cellini and His Florentine Dagger* (Farrar & Rinehart, 1933)

Vaughan, H. M., *Studies in the Italian Renaissance* (Methuen & Co., Ltd., 1930)

CERVANTES

Translations: Cohen, J. M., *Don Quixote* (Penguin Books, Inc., 1950); Fishman, F., *Don Quijote* (Barron's Educational Series, Inc., 1950); Jarvis, C., *The Life and Exploits of the Ingenious Gentleman Don Quixote de la Mancha* (Harper & Brothers, 1923), Motteux, P., *Don Quixote* (Everyman's Library, E. P. Dutton & Co., 1906; The Modern Library, 1930, Modern Library College Edition, 1950, Random House); Ormsby, J., *The Ingenious Gentleman Don Quixote of La Mancha* (A. A. Knopf, 1926)

Bell, A. F., *Cervantes* (University of Oklahoma Press, 1947)

Bernadete, M. J. (ed.), *The Anatomy of Don Quixote* (The Dragon Press, 1932)

Calvert, A. F., *The Life of Cervantes* (J. Lane, 1905)

Crooks, E. J., *The Influence of Cervantes in France in the Seventeenth Century* (Johns Hopkins Press, 1931)

Entwistle, W. J., *Cervantes* (Clarendon Press, 1940)

Fitzmaurice-Kelly, J., *The Life of Miguel de Cervantes Saavedra* (Chapman & Hall, 1892), *Miguel de Cervantes Saavedra* (Clarendon Press, 1913)

Flores, A. (ed.), *Cervantes across the Centuries* (Dryden Press, 1947)

Frank, B., *A Man Called Cervantes* (Cassell & Co., Ltd., 1934)

Gregory, I. A., Lady, *Three Last Plays* (G. P. Putnam's Sons, 1928)

Krutch, J. W., *Five Masters* (J. Cape & H. Smith, 1930)

Lussky, A. E., *Tieck's Romantic Irony* (University of North Carolina Press, 1932)

Madariaga, S., *Don Quixote* (Clarendon Press, 1935)

Rosenkranz, H., *El Greco and Cervantes* (R. M. McBride & Co., 1932)

Schevill, R., *Cervantes* (Duffield & Co., 1919)
Smith, J. R., *The Life of Cervantes* (E. P. Dutton & Co., 1914)
Trachman, S. E., *Cervantes' Women of Literary Tradition* (Instituto de las Españas en los Estados Unidos, 1932)
Turkevitch, L. B., *Cervantes in Russia* (Princeton University Press, 1950)
Woodberry, G. E., *Great Writers* (The Macmillan Co., 1912), *Literary Essays* (Harcourt, Brace & Howe, 1920)

CINTHIO

Translation: *A Discourse of Civill Life* (Edward Blount, 1606)
Taylor, J. E., *The Moor of Venice, Cinthio's Tale and Shakespeare's Tragedy* (Chapman & Hall, 1855)

DU BARTAS

Translations: Haight, T. W. (ed.), *The Divine Weeks of Josuah Sylvester* (H. M. Youmans, 1908); Sylvester, J., *Du Bartas His Deuine Weekes and Workes Translated* (Humfrey Lownes, 1611; Robert Young, 1633)
Taylor, G. C., *Milton's Use of Du Bartas* (Harvard University Press, 1934)

DU BELLAY

Translations: Gottfried, R., *Six Sonnets from Les Regrets* (Corydon Press, 1944); Spenser, E., *Ruins of Rome, Visions of Bellay* in Spenser's *Works* (Any Edition); Turquet, G. M., *The Defence and Illustration of the French Language* (J. M. Dent & Sons, Ltd., 1939)
Belloc, H., *Avril* (Sheed & Ward, 1945)
Cameron, A. V., *The Influence of Ariosto's Epic and Lyric Poetry on Ronsard and His Group* (The Johns Hopkins Press, 1930)
Clements, J. J., *Critical Theory and Practice of the Pléiade* (Harvard University Press, 1942)
Levengood, S. L., *The Use of Color in the Verse of the Pléiade* (Les Presses Universitaires de France, 1927)
Merrill, R. V., *The Platonism of Joachim du Bellay* (The University of Chicago Press, 1925)

D'URFÉ

Fischer, W. P., *The Literary Relations between La Fontaine and the "Astrée" of Honore d'Urfé* (Publications of the University of Pennsylvania, 1913)
McMahon, M. C., *Aesthetics and Art in the Astrée of Honore d'Urfé* (The Catholic University of America, 1925)

ERASMUS

Translations: *Erasmus in Praise of Folly* (Reeves & Turner, 1870; P. Eckler Publishing Co., 1922; The Truth Seeker Co., 1929); Bailey, N., *All the Familiar Colloquies of D. Erasmus* (J. Darby, 1725; J. J. & P. Knapton, 1733), *The Whole Familiar Colloquies of Desiderius Erasmus* (Hamilton, Adams & Co., 1877); Carter, H., *Moriae Encomium* (Limited Editions Club, 1943); Chaloner, T., *The Praise of Folie* (Edward Arnold, 1901); Hudson, H. H., *The Praise of Folly* (Princeton University Press, 1941); Kennet, W., *Moriae Encomium* (J. Woodward, 1709; J. Wilford, 1735); Knox, V., *The Complaint of Peace* (London, 1795); L'Estrange, R., *Twenty Select Colloquies* (H. Brome, 1680; Abbey Classics, Chapman & Dodd, 1923), *Twenty-two Select Colloquies* (R. Bentley, 1689; R. Gare & H. Hindmarsh, 1699; D. Brown, 1711); Tauerner, R., *Proverbes or Adagies* (W. Myddylton, 1550; Agathynian Club, 1867); Udall, N., *The Apophthegmes of Erasmus* (R. Roberts, 1877); Whitcomb, M. (ed.), *Select Colloquies of Erasmus* (Sixteenth Century Classics, University of Pennsylvania, 1902); Wilson, J., *The Praise of Folly* (Clarendon Press, 1913)

Abbott, L. F., *Twelve Great Modernists* (Doubleday, Page & Co., 1927)

Allen, P. S., *Erasmus* (Clarendon Press, 1934), *The Age of Erasmus* (Clarendon Press, 1914)

Elliott-Binns, L. E., *Erasmus, the Reformer* (Methuen & Co., Ltd., 1923)

Emerton, E., *Desiderius Erasmus of Rotterdam* (G. P. Putnam's Sons, 1899)

Froude, J. A., *Life and Letters of Erasmus* (C. Scribner's Sons, 1894)

Hearnshaw, F. J. C. (ed.), *The Social and Political Ideas of Some Great Thinkers of the Renaissance and the Reformation* (G. G. Harrap & Co., Ltd., 1925)

Hollis, C., *Erasmus* (Eyre & Spottiswoode, 1933)

Huizinga, J., *Erasmus* (C. Scribner's Sons, 1924)

Hyma, A., *Erasmus and the Humanists* (F. S. Crofts & Co., 1930), *The Youth of Erasmus* (University of Michigan Press, 1930)

Mangan, J. J., *Life, Character and Influence of Desiderius Erasmus of Rotterdam* (The Macmillan Co., 1927)

Seebohm, F., *The Oxford Reformers* (Everyman's Library, E. P. Dutton & Co., 1914)

Smith, P., *Erasmus* (Harper & Brothers, 1923), *A Key to the Colloquies of Erasmus* (Harvard University Press, 1927)

Wilkinson, M., *Erasmus of Rotterdam* (P. J. Kenedy & Sons, 1921)

Woodward, W. H., *Desiderius Erasmus* (Cambridge University Press, 1904)

Zweig, S., *Erasmus of Rotterdam* (The Viking Press, 1934; Garden City Publishing Co., 1937)

FROISSART

Translations: Bouchier, J., *The Chronicle of Froissart* (The Tudor Translations, D. Nutt, 1901-03), *Froissart's Cronycles* (Basil Blackwell, 1927-28); Thomas, J., *Sir John Froissart's Chronicles* (Longman, Hurst, Rees, and Orme, 1805-06; W. Smith, 1839; J. Winchester, 1843; H. G. Bohn, 1849; Leavitt & Allen, 1855; G. Routledge & Sons, 1868)

Coulton, G. G., *The Chronicler of European Chivalry* (The Studio, 1930)

Ker, W. P., *Essays on Medieval Literature* (The Macmillan Co., 1905)

Read, H. E., *The Sense of Glory* (Cambridge University Press, 1929)

Shears, F. S., *Froissart; Chronicler and Poet* (G. Routledge & Sons, Ltd., 1930)

Smith, R. M., *Froissart and the English Chronicle Play* (Columbia University Press, 1915)

GRAZZINI

Translation: Lawrence, D. H., *The Story of Doctor Manente* (G. Orioli, 1929)

GUARINI

Translation: Fanshawe, R., *Il Pastor Fido* (H. Moseley, 1648)

THE HUMANISTS

Bush, D., *The Renaissance and English Humanism* (University of Toronto Press, 1939)

Emerton, E., *Humanism and Tyranny* (Harvard University Press, 1925)

Gilmore, M. P., *The World of Humanism, 1453-1517* (Harper & Brothers, 1952)

Hyma, A., *Erasmus and the Humanists* (F. S. Crofts & Co., 1930)

Mackail, J. W., *Studies in Humanism* (Longmans, Green & Co., 1938)

Mahood, M. M., *Poetry and Humanism* (Yale University Press, 1950)

Panofsky, E., *Studies in Iconology* (Oxford University Press, 1939)

Robertson, J. M., *Pioneer Humanists* (Watts & Co., 1907)

Schevill, F., *The First Century of Italian Humanism* (F. S. Crofts & Co., 1928)

Taylor, H. D., *Thought and Expression in the Sixteenth Century* (Macmillan Co., 1920)

Thorndike, L., *Science and Thought in the Fifteenth Century* (Columbia University Press, 1939)

Trinkhaus, C. E., *Adversity's Noblemen* (Columbia University Press, 1940)

Walsh, G. G., *Medieval Humanism* (Macmillan Co., 1942)

Weiss, R., *Humanism in England during the Fifteenth Century* (B. Blackwell, 1941)

Woodward, W. H., *Vittorino da Feltre and Other Humanist Educators* (Cambridge University Press, 1921), *Studies in Education during the Age of the Renaissance, 1400-1600* (Cambridge University Press, 1906)

JODELLE

Cameron, A. V., *The Influence of Aristo's Epic and Lyric Poerty on Ronsard and His Group* (The Johns Hopkins Press, 1930)

Clements, J. H., *Critical Theory and Practice of the Pléiade* (Harvard University Press, 1942)

Levengood, S. L., *The Use of Color in the Verse of the Pléiade* (Les Presses Universitaires de France, 1927)

LABÉ

Translation: Prokosch, F., *The Love Sonnets* (New Directions Publications, 1947)

LOPE DE VEGA

Translations: *The Father Outwitted* (M. Carey, No. 122 Market Street, 1811); *The Pilgrim* (D. Farmer, 1738); *Romeo and Juliet* (W. Griffin, 1770); Brewster, W. T., *The New Art of Writing Plays* (The Dramatic Museum of Columbia University, 1914); Jagendorf, M., *Doctors All* (S. French, 1937); Longfellow, H. W., *Coplas de don Jorge Manrique* (Allen & Ticknor, 1833); Price, E. R., *Peribanez* (Valley Press, 1937); Rennart, H. A., *Arte Nuevo de Hacer Comedias* in his *Life of Lope de Vega* (Gowans & Gray, Ltd., 1904); Thomas, H., *The Star of Seville* (Gregynog, 1935); Underhill, J. G., *Four Plays, by Lope de Vega* (C. Scribner's Sons, 1936)

Buchanan, M. A., *The Chronology of Lope de Vega's Plays* (Toronto University Library, 1922)

Fichter, W. L., *Lope de Vega's El Castigo del Discreto, together with a Study of Conjugal Honor in His Theater* (Instituto de las Españas en los Estados Unidos, 1925)

Fitzmaurice-Kelly, J., *Lope de Vega and the Spanish Drama* (R. B. Johnson, 1902)

Flores, A., *Lope de Vega, Monster of Nature* (Brentano's, 1930)

Holland, H. R., *Account of the Lives and Writings of Lope Felix de Vega Carpio and Guillen de Castro* (London, 1817), *Some Account of the Life and Writings of Lope Felix de Vega Carpio* (Longman, Hurst, 1806)

Lincoln, J. N., *Saint Ursula, the Infanta Isabel, and Lope de Vega* (University of Michigan Press, 1947)

Moore, J. A., *The Romancero in the Chronicle Legends of Lope de Vega* (University of Pennsylvania Press, 1940)

Morley, S. G., and Bruerton, C., *The Chronology of Lope de Vega's Comedias* (The Modern Language Association of America, 1940)

Morley, S. G., *Lope de Vega's Peregrino Lists* (University of California Press, 1930)

Peers, E. A. (ed.), *Liverpool Studies in Spanish Literature* (Institute of Hispanic Studies, 1946)

Perry, H. T. E., *Masters of Dramatic Comedy and Their Social Themes* (Harvard University Press, 1939)

Rennart, H. A., *The Life of Lope de Vega* (Gowans & Gray, Ltd., 1904)

Schevill, R., *The Dramatic Art of Lope de Vega* (University of California Press, 1918)

Stevens, C. H., *Lope de Vega's El Palacio Confuso, together with a Study of the Menaechmi Theme in Spanish Literature* (Instituto de las Españas en los Estados Unidos, 1939)

LORENZO DE' MEDICI

Armstrong, E., *Lorenzo de' Medici and Florence in the Fifteenth Century* (G. P. Putnam's Sons, 1896)

Carpenter, E., *Lorenzo de' Medici* (G. P. Putnam's Sons, 1893)

Horsburgh, E. L. S., *Lorenzo the Magnificent, and Florence in Her Golden Age* (G. P. Putnam's Sons, 1908)

Lipari, A., *The Dolce Stil Novo According to Lorenzo de' Medici* (Yale University Press, 1936)

Loth, D., *Lorenzo the Magnificent* (Brentano's, 1929)

Maguire, Y., *The Private Life of Lorenzo the Magnificent* (A. Ouseley, Ltd., 1936)

Paget, V., *Euphorion* by Vernon Lee (pseud.) (T. F. Unwin, 1899)

Rascoe, W., *The Life of Lorenzo de' Medici* (A. Strahan, 1797; Bronson & Chauncey, 1803; The European Library, D. Bogue, 1846; Bohn's Standard Library, H. G. Bohn, 1847)

Santayana, G., *Interpretations of Poetry and Religion* (C. Scribner's Sons, 1900)

THE LUSIADS

See Camoens

MACHIAVELLI

Translations: *The Art of War* (H. C. Southwick, 1815); *History of Florence* (The World's Great Classics, The Colonial Press, 1901); *The Florentine History* (G. Harper, 1674); *The History of Florence . . . together with The Prince and Various Historical Tracts* (Bohn's Standard Library, H. G. Bohn, 1847; Universal Classics Library, M. W. Dunne, 1901); *Machiavelli* (Tudor Translations, D. Nutt, 1905); *The Prince; an Elizabethan Translation* (The University of

North Carolina Press, 1944); *The Prince and The Discourses* (Modern Library College Editions, The Modern Library, Random House, 1950); *The Works of the Famous Nicholas Machiavel* (A. Churchill, 1720); T. B., esq., *The Florentine Historie* (W. P., 1595); Bergin, T. G., *The Prince* (Crofts Classics, F. S. Crofts & Co., 1947); Dacres, E., *The Prince* (The De La More Press, Alexander Moring, Ltd., 1929); Detmold, C. E., *The Historical, Political, and Diplomatic Writings of Machiavelli* (J. R. Osgood & Co., 1882); Dukes, A., *Mandragola* (The Bloomsbury Publishing Co., Ltd., 1940); Farnesworth, E., *The Works of N. Machiavel* (T. Davies, J. Dodsley, 1775); Gilbert, A. H., *The Prince and Other Works* (University Classics, Packard & Co., 1941); Lester, C. E., *The Florentine Histories* (New York, 1845); Marriott, W. K., *Florentine History* (Everyman's Library, J. M. Dent & Sons, Ltd., 1912), *The Prince* (Everyman's Library, E. P. Dutton & Co., 1908); Ricci, L., *The Prince* (World's Classics, Oxford University Press, 1903), *The Prince and the Discourses* (The Modern Library and Modern Library College Edition, 1940); Ricci, L. and Vincent, E. R. P., *The Prince* (Mentor Books, The New American Library of World Literature, Inc., 1931); Thomson, N. H., *Discourses on the First Decade of Titus Livius* (K. Paul, Trench & Co., 1883); Young, S., *Mandragola* (The Macaulay Co., 1927)

Beck, N. W., *The Political Science of Niccolo Machiavelli* (Chicago, Ill., 1944)

Butterfield, H., *The Statecraft of Machiavelli* (G. Bell & Sons, Ltd., 1940)

Crawford, R. M., *The Renaissance, and Other Essays* (Melbourne University Press, 1947)

Derieux, S. A., *Machiavelli and Bacon* (Chicago, 1910)

Eliot, T. S., *For Lancelot Andrewes* (Doubleday Doran & Co., Inc., 1929)

Eshleman, L. W., *Moulders of Destiny* (Covici-Friede, 1938)

Ferrara, O., *The Private Correspondence of Nicolo Machiavelli* (Oxford University Press, 1929)

Gilbert, A. H., *Machiavelli's Prince and Its Forerunners* (Duke University Press, 1938)

Hearnshaw, F. J. C. F. (ed.), *The Social and Political Ideas of Some Great Thinkers of the Renaissance and the Reformation* (G. G. Harrap & Co., Ltd., 1925)

Jann, E., *Machiavelli* (G. G. Harrap & Co., Ltd., 1930)

Marcu, V., *Accent on Power* (Farrar & Rinehart, 1939)

Maugham, W. S., *Then and Now* (Doubleday & Co., 1946)

Meyer, E., *Machiavelli and the Elizabethan Drama* (E. Felber, 1897)

Muir, D. E., *Machiavelli and His Times* (W. Heinemann, Ltd., 1936)

Olschki, L., *Machiavelli the Scientist* (The Gillick Press, 1945)

Powys, L., *Rats in the Sacristy* (Watts & Co., 1937)

Prezzolini, G., *Nicolo Machiavelli, the Florentine* (Brentano's, 1928)
Pulver, J., *Machiavelli; the Man, His Work and His Times* (H. Joseph, Ltd., 1937)
Robertson, J. M., *Pioneer Humanists* (Watts & Co., 1907)
Roeder, R., *The Man of the Renaissance* (The Viking Press, 1933)
Stearns, F. P., *Napoleon and Machiavelli* (Riverside Press, 1903), *Politics and Metaphysics* (R. G. Badger, 1915)
Valeriu, M., *Accent on Power; The Life and Times of Machiavelli* (Farrar & Rinehart, Inc., 1939)
Vaughan, H. M., *Studies in the Italian Renaissance* (Methuen & Co., Ltd., 1930)
Villari, P., *The Life and Times of Niccolò Machiavelli* (T. F. Unwin, 1892)
Whitfield, J. H., *Machiavelli* (B. Blackwell, 1947)

MALHERBE

Belloc, H., *Avril* (Sheed & Ward, 1945)
Gosse, E. W., *Malherbe and the Classical Reaction in the Seventeenth Century* (Clarendon Press, 1920)
Humiston, C. C., *A Comparative Study of the Metrical Technique of Ronsard and Malherbe* (University of California Press, 1941)
Watson, P. B., *Tales of Normandie* (Marshall Jones Co., 1930)

MARGUERITE OF NAVARRE

Translations: Machen, A., *The Heptameron* (The Bibliophilist's Library, G. Barrie, 189-?; The Borzoi Classics, A. A. Knopf, 1924); Saintsbury, G., *The Heptameron of the Tales of Margaret, Queen of Navarre* (The Navarre Society, Ltd., 1928)
Freer, M. W., *The Life of Marguerite d'Angoulême* (Hurst & Blackett, 1854)
Neely, R. S., *Marguerite, the Sister and Wife of Kings* (The University of Georgia Press, 1939)
Putnam, S., *Marguerite of Navarre* (Coward-McCann, Inc., 1935)
Robinson, A. M. F., *Margaret of Angoulême, Queen of Navarre* (Roberts Bros., 1887)
Ryley, M. B., *Queens of the Renaissance* (Methuen & Co., 1907)
Williams, H. N., *The Pearl of Princesses; the Life of Marguerite d'Angoulême* (Brentano's, 1916)

MARINO

Translation: Crashaw, R., *The Suspicion of Herod* (Bournes, Jr. Bros., 1834)

MAROT

Bailey, J. C., *The Claims of French Poetry* (M. Kennerley, 1904)
Belloc, H., *Avril* (Sheed & Ward, 1945)
Borland, L., *The Influence of Marot on English Poetry of the Sixteenth Century* (Chicago, 1913)
Morley, H., *Clement Marot, and Other Studies* (Chapman & Hall, 1771)

MASUCCIO

Translation: Waters, W. G., *The Novellino of Masuccio* (Lawrence & Bullen, 1895)

MICHELANGELO

Translations: Carden, R. W., *Michelangelo; a Record of His Life as Told in His Own Letters and Papers* (A. Constable & Co., Ltd., 1913); Cheney, E. D. (ed.), *Selected Poems from Michelangelo Buonarroti* (C. T. Dillingham, 1885); Newell, W. W., *Sonnets and Madrigals of Michelangelo Buonarroti* (Houghton Mifflin & Co., 1900); Symonds, J. A., *The Sonnets of Michael Angelo Buonarroti* (Old World Series, B. Mosher, 1901; G. P. Putnam's Sons, 1902; J. Murray, 1926), *The Sonnets of Michael Angelo Buonarrote and Tommaso Campanella* (Smith, Elder, & Co., 1878)
Acker, H., *Five Sons of Italy* (Nelson, 1950)
Brion, M., *Michelangelo* (The Greystone Press, 1940)
Condivi, A., *The Life of Michelagnolo Bvonarroti* (D. B. Updike, 1904)
De Tolnay, C., *The Youth of Michelangelo* (Princeton University Press, 1947)
Finlayson, D. L., *Michelangelo, the Man* (Thomas Y. Crowell Co., 1935)
Gobineau, J. A., Count de, *The Renaissance* (G. P. Putnam's Sons, 1927)
Harper, G. M., *John Morley and Other Essays* (Princeton University Press, 1920)
Lerman, L., *Michelangelo, a Renaissance Profile* (A. A. Knopf, 1942)
Ludwig, E., *Three Titans* (G. P. Putnam's Sons, 1930)
Papini, G., *Michelangelo* (L. Murnane, tr.) (Dutton, 1952)
Rolland, R., *Michelangelo* (Duffield & Co., 1915; Bonibooks, A. & C. Boni, 1935)
Rose, G. B., *Renaissance Masters* (G. P. Putnam's Sons, 1908)
Ruskin, J., *Lectures on Landscape* (Library Edition, 1906, Vol. XXII)
Santayana, G., *Interpretations of Poetry and Religion* (C. Scribner's Sons, 1900)
Symonds, J. A., *The Life of Michelangelo* (C. Scribner's Sons, 1893; Macmillan & Co., Ltd., 1911; The Modern Library, 1928; Carlton House, 1936)
Trollope, T. A., *Life of Vittoria Colonna* (American Book Exchange, 1879)

MONTAIGNE

Translations: *Of the Education of Children & other Selected Essays* (The Great Books Foundation, n. d.); *The Essays of Montaigne* (S. & E. Ballad, 1759; J. Pote, 1776; W. Miller, 1811); Carmody, F., *Essays of Montaigne* (The L-D. Allen Press, 1948); Colton, C., *Essays* (T. Basset, 1685-93; Reeves & Turner, 1877, 1902; A. L. Burt, 1892), *Montaigne's Essays* (B. & B. Barker, 1743; Ward, Lock & Co., 1875), *The Works of Michel de Montaigne* (E. C. Hill, 1910); Colton, C. and Hazlitt, W. C., *Selected Essays* (The Modern Library, 1949); Florio, J., *The Essayes of Michael, Lord of Montaigne* (G. Routledge & Sons, 1885; The Temple Classics, J. M. Dent & Co., 1897-1905; Everyman's Library, J. M. Dent & Sons, 1910; Tudor Translations, D. Nutt, 1892-93; Houghton, Mifflin & Co., 1902-04; The Scott Library, W. Scott, Ltd., 1903; The World's Classics, Oxford University Press, 1904; The Nonesuch Press, 1931), *Essays Written in French by Michael Lord of Montaigne* (E. Blount & W. Barrett, 1613); Frame, D. M., *Selections from the Essays of Montaigne* (Crofts Classics, Appleton-Century-Crofts, Inc., 1948); Gide, A. (ed.), *The Living Thoughts of Montaigne* (Longmans, Green & Co., 1939); Hazlitt, W. C., *The Works of Michael de Montaigne* (C. Templeman, 1945; J. W. Moore, 1849; Riverside Press, 1864; Hurd & Houghton, 1864, 1872-75; W. T. Amies, 1879); How, L., *Montaigne's Essay on Friendship, and XXIX Sonnets by Estienne de La Boetie* (Houghton Mifflin Co., 1915); Ives, G. B., *The Essays of Montaigne* (Harvard University Press, 1925), *The Essays of Michael de Montaigne* (The Limited Editions Club, 1946; The Heritage Press, 1947); Lowenthal, M., *The Autobiography of Michel de Montaigne* (Houghton Mifflin Co., 1935); Trenchmann, E. J., *The Diary of Montaigne's Journey to Italy* (L. & V. Woolf, 1929); *The Essays of Montaigne* (Oxford University Press, 1946; The Modern Library, 1946); Waters, W. G., *The Journal of Montaigne's Travels in Italy* (J. Murray, 1903); Zeitlin, J., *The Essays of Michel de Montaigne* (A. A. Knopf, 1934-36)

Abercrombie, N., *Saint Augustine and French Classical Thought* (Clarendon Press, 1938)

Boase, A. M., *The Fortunes of Montaigne; a History of the Essays in France, 1580-1669* (Methuen & Co., Ltd., 1935)

Compayré, G., *Montaigne and Education of the Judgment* (T. Y. Crowell & Co., 1908)

Dowden, E., *Michel de Montaigne* (J. B. Lippincott Co., 1905)

Emerson, R. W., *Representative Men* (Phillips, Sampson & Co., 1849; H. G. Bohn, 1850; Riverside Library, Houghton, Mifflin & Co., 1930)

Feis, J., *Shakspere and Montaigne* (K. Paul, Trench, & Co., 1884)

Frame, D. M., *Montaigne in France, 1812-1852* (Columbia University Press, 1940)

Gide, A. P. G., *Montaigne* (Blackamore Press, 1929)

Lamandé, A., *Montaigne, Grave and Gay* (H. Holt & Co., 1928)

Lowndes, M. E., *Michel de Montaigne* (Cambridge University Press, 1898)

Mauzey, J. V., *Montaigne's Philosophy of Human Nature* (St. Stephen's College, 1933)

Murry, J. M., *Heaven—and Earth* (J. Cape, 1938), *Heroes of Thought* (J. Messner, Inc., 1938)

Norton, G., *The Early Writings of Montaigne* (The Macmillan Co., 1904), *Montaigne. His Personal Relations to Some of His Contemporaries, and His Literary Relations to Some Later Writers* (Houghton, Mifflin & Co., 1908), *The Spirit of Montaigne* (Houghton, Mifflin & Co., 1908), *Studies in Montaigne* (The Macmillan Co., 1904)

Powys, J. C., *Suspended Judgments* (G. A. Shaw, 1916)

Powys, L., *Thirteen Worthies* (American Library Service, 1923; G. Richards, Ltd., 1923)

Robertson, J. M., *Montaigne and Shakespeare* (A. & C. Black, 1909)

St. John, B., *Montaigne, the Essayist* (Chapman & Hall, 1858)

Sarafian, K. A., *French Educational Theorists* (University of Southern California, 1933)

Sichel, E. H., *Michel de Montaigne* (E. P. Dutton & Co., 1911)

Taylor, G. C., *Shakspere's Debt to Montaigne* (Harvard University Press, 1925)

Taylor, J. S., *Montaigne and Medicine* (P. B. Hoeber, 1922)

Vinet, A. R., *Montaigne* (M. W. Dodd, 1850)

Whibley, C., *Literary Portraits* (A. Constable & Co., Ltd., 1904)

Willis, J. C., *Montaigne* (A. A. Knopf, 1927)

Windsor, A. L., *Ethica* (Smith Elder & Co., 1860)

Woodberry, G. E., *Great Writers* (The Macmillan Co., 1912), *Literary Essays* (Harcourt, Brace & Howe, 1920)

Young, C. L., *Emerson's Montaigne* (The Macmillan Co., 1941)

MONTEMAYOR

Translations: *The Pilgrim by Lopez de Vega Carpio. Also, Diana* (D. Farmer, 1738); Yong, B., *Diana Of George Of Montemayor* (E. Bollifant, J. G. Bishop, 1598)

PELETIER

Cameron, A. V., *The Influence of Ariosto's Epic and Lyric Poetry on Ronsard and His Group* (The Johns Hopkins Press, 1930)

Clements, J. J., *Critical Theory and Practice of the Pléiade* (Harvard University Press, 1942)

Levengood, S. L., *The Use of Color in the Verse of the Pléiade* (Les Presses Universitaires de France, 1927)

PETRARCH

Translations: *Certain Sonnets to Laura in Life and Death* (The Marion Press, 1905); *Eighteen Sonnets of Francis Petrarch* (Kahoe & Co., 1929); *The Sonnets, Triumphs, and Other Poems of Petrarch* (Bohn's Illustrated Library, H. G. Bohn, 1859, G. Bell & Sons, 1879); Armi, A. M., *Sonnets & Songs* (Pantheon, 1946); Auslander, J., *The Sonnets of Petrarch* (Longmans, Green & Co., 1931); Cosenza, M. E., *Petrarch's Letters to Classical Authors* (The University of Chicago Press, 1910); Dobson, Mrs., *Petrarch's View of Human Life* (J. Stockdale, 1791; Vernor & Hood, 1797); Foulke, W. D., *Some Love Songs of Petrarch* (Oxford University Press, 1915); Higginson, T. W., *Fifteen Sonnets of Petrarch* (Houghton, Mifflin & Co., 1903); Ibbett, W. J., *Some Sonnets & Songs of the Divine Poet M. Francesco Petrarca* (High House Press, 1926); Le Mesurier, T., *Translations Chiefly from the Italian of Petrarch and Metastasio* (J. Cooke, 1795); Lohse, J., *Thoughts from the Letters of Petrarch* (J. M. Dent & Co., 1901; G. Giannini & Son, 1911); Nott, J., *Petrarch Translated* (Inskeep & Bradford, 1809); Parker, H., *The Triumphs of Petrarch* (Nichols & Sons, 1887); Robinson, J. H., *Petrarch, the First Modern Scholar and Man of Letters* (G. P. Putnam's Sons, 1898); Synge, J. M., *With Petrarch* (Peter Pauper Press, 1928); Tobin, A., *Love's Crucifix* (W. Heinemann, 1902), *On the Death of Madonna Laura* (J. W. Luce & Co., 1907); Zeitlin, J., *The Life of Solitude, by Francis Petrarch* (University of Illinois Press, 1924)

Borghesi, P., *Petrarch and His Influence on English Literature* (N. Zanichelli, 1906)

Campbell, T., *Life of Petrarch* (H. Colburn, 1841), *Life and Times of Petrarch* (H. Colburn, 1843)

Cosenza, M. E., *Francesco Petrarca and the Revolution of Cola di Rienzo* (University of Chicago Press, 1913)

Dole, N. H., *A Teacher of Dante, and Other Studies in Italian Literature* (Moffat, Yard & Co., 1908)

Foscolo, U., *Essays on Petrarch* (J. Murray, 1823)

Hollway-Calthrop, H. C., *Petrarch, His Life and Times* (Methuen & Co., 1907)

Hubbard, E., *Petrarch and Laura* (The Roycrofters, 1906)

Jerrold, M. F., *Francesco Petrarca* (J. M. Dent & Co., 1909)

Mills, E. J., *The Secret of Petrarch* (T. F. Unwin, 1904)

Nolhac, P. de, *Petrarch, and the Ancient World* (Merrymount Press, 1907)

Pearson, Mrs. L. E., *Elizabethan Love Conventions* (University of California Press, 1933)

Phelps, R. S., *The Earlier and Later Forms of Petrarch's Canzoniere* (The University of Chicago Press, 1925)

Potter, M. A., *Four Essays* (Harvard University Press, 1917)

Rearden, T. H., *Petrarch, and Other Essays* (W. Doxey, 1897)

Robinson, J. H. and Rolfe, H. W., *Petrarch: the First Modern Man of Letters* (G. P. Putnam's Sons, 1914)

Sade, J. F. P. A. de, *The Life of Petrarch* (Vernor & Hood, 1803; S. A. Mitchell & H. Ames, 1817)

Severs, J. B., *The Literary Relationships of Chaucer's Clerkes Tale* (Modern Language Association of America, 1942)

Silber, G. R., *The Influence of Dante and Petrarch on Certain of Boccaccio's Lyrics* (George Banta Publishing Co., 1940)

Tatham, E. H. R., *Francesco Petrarca, the First Modern Man of Letters* (The Sheldon Press, 1925-26)

Wilkins, E. H., *Modern Discussions of the Dates of Petrarch's Prose Letters* (The University of Chicago Press, 1929), *A Tentative Chronological List of Petrarch's Prose Letters* (The University of Chicago Press, 1929)

Woodhouselee, A. F. T., *An Historical and Critical Essay on the Life and Character of Petrarch* (J. Ballantyne & Co., 1810)

THE PLÉIADE

Cameron, A. V., *The Influence of Ariosto's Epic and Lyric Poetry on Ronsard and His Group* (The Johns Hopkins Press, 1930)

Clements, J. J., *Critical Theory and Practice of the Pléiade* (Harvard University Press, 1942)

Levengood, S. L., *The Use of Color in the Verse of the Pléiade* (Les Presses Universitaires de France, 1927)

POLIZIANO

Translations: Greswell, W. P., *Memoirs of Angelus Politianus* (Cadell & Davies, 1801); Lord, L. E., *A Translation of the Orpheus of Angelo Politian and the Aminta of Torquato Tasso* (Oxford University Press, 1931); Symonds, J. A., *Poliziano's Orfeo* in his *Sketches and Studies in Italy* (Smith, Elder & Co., 1879; J. Murray, 1914)

PULCI

Translations: Byron, Lord, *The Morgante Maggiore of Pulci* in Byron's *Works* (Any Edition); Hunt, L., *The Italian Poets Translated into English Prose* (H. W. Derby, 1861)

Grillo, G., *Two Aspects of Chivalry, Pulci and Boiardo* (The Excelsior Press, Inc., 1942)

Hunt, L., *Stories from the Italian Poets* (Chapman & Hall, 1846)
Shulters, J. R., *Luigi Pulci and the Animal Kingdom* (J. H. Furst Co., 1920)

QUEVEDO

Translations: *The Works of Don Francisco de Quevedo* (Mundell & Sons, 1798); R. L., *The Visions of Don Francisco de Quevedo Villegas* (Methuen & Co., 1904); L'Estrange, R., Stevens, J., et al., *Quevedo, the Choice, Humorous and Satirical Works* and Duff, J., *A Version of the Life of the Great Rascal* (Broadway Translations, G. Routledge & Sons, Ltd., 1926); Stevens, J., *The Comical Works of Don Francisco de Quevedo* (J. Woodward, 1709; C. Ward, R. Chandler, & W. Sandby, 1742), *Fortune in Her Wits, or, The Hour of All Men* (R. Sare, F. Saunders, & T. Bennet, 1697); Watts, H. E., *Pablo de Segovia, the Spanish Sharper* (T. F. Unwin, 1892; Blue Jade Library, A. A. Knopf, 1926)

RABELAIS

Translations: *All the Extant Works of François Rabelais* (Covici-Friede, 1929); *Gargantua and Pantagruel* (J. Washburn, 1930); *The Heroic Deeds of Gargantua and Pantagruel* (Everyman's Library, E. P. Dutton & Co., 1928); Le Clercq, J., *The Complete Works of Rabelais* (The Modern Library, Random House, 1928), *Gargantua & Pantagruel* (The Limited Editions Club; The Heritage Press, 1942); Putnam, S., *The Portable Rabelais* (The Viking Press, 1946); Smith, W. F., *The Five Books and Minor Writings* (Cambridge University Press, 1934); Urquhart, T. and Motteux, P. A., *The Complete Works of Dr. Francis Rabelais* (Boni & Liveright, 1933), *Five Books of the Lives, Heroic Deeds and Sayings of Gargantua and His Son Pantagruel* (A. H. Bullen, 1904), *Gargantua and Pantagruel* (The Tudor Translations, D. Nutt, 1900; Everyman's Library, E. P. Dutton & Co., Inc., 1932-33; The World's Classics, Oxford University Press, 1934), *Gargantua and Pantagruel*, I. & II. (The Great Books Foundation, 1949), *The Lives, Heroic Deeds & Sayings of Gargantua and His Son Pantagruel* (Simon & Schuster, Inc., 1928), *The Urquhart-Le Motteux Translation of the Works of Francis Rabelais* (Harcourt, Brace & Co., 1931), *The Works of Mr. Francis Rabelais* (J. B. Lippincott Co., 1912), *The Works of Rabelais* (London, n. d., J. Brindley, 1750; H. G. Bohn, 1859; Chatto & Windus, 1902)
Besant, W., *Rabelais* (J. B. Lippincott & Co., 1879)
Brown, H., *Rabelais in English Literature* (Harvard University Press, 1933)
Chappell, A. F., *The Enigma of Rabelais* (Cambridge University Press, 1924)

Clement, N. H., *The Influence of the Arthurian Romances on the Five Books of Rabelais* (University of California Press, 1926)

Fetzer, H., *The Book of Rabelais* by Jake Falstaff (pseud.) (Doubleday Doran & Co., 1928)

France, A., *Rabelais* (H. Holt & Co., 1929)

Nock, A. J. and Wilson, C. R., *Francis Rabelais, the Man and His Work* (Harper & Brothers, 1929), *A Journey into Rabelais's France* (W. Morrow & Co., 1934)

Plattard, J., *The Life of Rabelais* (G. Routledge & Sons, Ltd., 1930)

Powys, J. C., *Rabelais, His Life* (Bodley Head, 1948)

Powys, L., *Rats in the Sacristy* (Watts & Co., 1937)

Putnam, S., *François Rabelais, Man of the Renaissance* (J. Cape & H. Smith, 1929)

Sarafian, K. A., *French Educational Theorists* (University of Southern California, 1933)

Smith, W. F., *Rabelais in His Writings* (Cambridge University Press, 1918)

Tilley, A. A., *François Rabelais* (J. B. Lippincott Co., 1907), *Studies in the French Renaissance* (Cambridge University Press, 1922)

Van Loon, H. W., *The Story of Rabelais and Voltaire* (Bantam Books, Bantam Publications, Inc., 1925)

Watson, F., *Laughter for Pluto; a Book about Rabelais* (L. Dickson, Ltd., 1933)

Whibley, C., *Literary Portraits* (A. Constable & Co., Ltd., 1904)

RONSARD

Translations: Graves, C., *Selected Poems of Pierre de Ronsard* (The Porpoise Press, 1924); Page, C. H., *Songs & Sonnets of Pierre de Ronsard* (Houghton, Mifflin, & Co., 1903); Silver, I., *The Pindaric Odes of Ronsard* (Paris, 1937); Wolfe, H., *Sonnets pour Helene* (Eyre & Spottiswoode, 1934)

Bailey, J. C., *The Claims of French Poetry* (W. Kennerley, 1909)

Belloc, H., *Avril* (Sheed & Ward, 1945)

Bishop, M., *Ronsard; Prince of Poets* (Oxford University Press, 1940)

Cameron, A. V., *The Influence of Ariosto's Epic and Lyric Poetry on Ronsard and His Group* (The Johns Hopkins Press, 1930)

Clements, J. J., *Critical Theory and Practice of the Pléiade* (Harvard University Press, 1942)

Cornelia, W. B., *The Classical Sources of the Nature References in Ronsard's Poetry* (Publications of the Institute of French Studies, Inc., Columbia University, 1934)

Humiston, C. C., *A Comparative Study of the Metrical Techniques of Ronsard and Malherbe* (University of California Press, 1941)

Levengood, S. L., *The Use of Color in the Verse of the Pléiade* (Les Presses Universitaires de France, 1927)

Lewis, D. B. W., *Ronsard* (Coward-McCann & Sheed & Ward, 1944)

Silver, I., *The Pindaric Odes of Ronsard* (Privately Printed, 1937)

Storer, W. H., *Virgil and Ronsard* (E. Champion, 1923)

Wolfe, H., *Ronsard and French Romantic Poetry* (Clarendon Press, 1935)

SANNAZARO

Translations: *Sannazarius on the Birth of Our Saviour* (W. Lewis, 1736); Greswell, W. P., *Memoirs of Angelus Politianus . . . etc.* (Cadell & Davies, 1805); Rooke, J., *Select Translations from the Works of Sannazarius* (J. Milton, 1726)

Grillo, G., *Two Aspects of Chivalry, Pulci and Boiardo* (The Excelsior Press, 1942)

STRAPAROLA

Translations: *The Story of the Two Lovers of Pisa* in J. P. Collier, *Shakespeare's Library* (T. Rodd, 1850); Armin, R., *The Italian Taylor, and His Boy* (R. Triphook, 1810)

TASSO

Translations: *Godfrey Of Bulloigne* (Christopher Hunt of Exceter, 1594); Fairfax, F., *Godfrey of Bulloigne; or, The Recovery of Jerusalem* (R. Bentley, T. Sawbridge & G. Wells, 1687; Knight & Son, 1817; R. Triphook, 1817; J. G. Routledge & Sons, Ltd., 1819; C. Knight & Co., 1844; G. Cox, 1844-53; Wiley & Putnam, 1845-46; G. Routledge & Co., 1858; Colonial Press, 1901); Grillo, E., *Aminta* (J. M. Dent & Sons, Ltd., 1924); Hoole, J., *Jerusalem Delivered* (J. Dodsley, 1772; J. Johnson, 1802; T. Bensley, 1803; Edward Little & Co., 1810; Johnson & Co., 1811; Suttaby, Evance & Fox, 1819); Hunt, L., *The Italian Poets Translated into English Prose* (H. W. Derby, 1861); Lord, L. E., *A Translation of the Orpheus of Angelo Politian and the Aminta of Torquato Tasso* (Oxford University Press, 1931); Whitmore, F., *Amyntas* (The Ridgewood Press, 1930); Wiffen, J. H., *Jerusalem Delivered* (J. Murray, 1826; Longman, Rees, Orme, Brown, & Green, 1830; D. Appleton & Co., 1846; Bell & Daldy, 1867; S. W. Green's Sons, 1882)

Black, J., *Life of Torquato Tasso* (Edinburgh, 1810)

Boulting, W., *Tasso and His Times* (G. P. Putnam's Sons, 1907)

Bowra, C. M., *From Virgil to Milton* (Macmillan & Co., Ltd., 1945)

Hunt, L., *Stories from the Italian Poets* (Chapman & Hall, 1846)

Milman, R., *The Life of Torquato Tasso* (H. Colburn, 1850)

Woodberry, G. E., *Inspiration of Poetry* (The Macmillan Co., 1910)

TYARD

Cameron, A. V., *The Influence of Ariosto's Epic and Lyric Poetry on Ronsard and His Group* (The Johns Hopkins Press, 1930)

Clements, J. J., *Critical Theory and Practice of the Pléiade* (Harvard University Press, 1942)

Levengood, S. L., *The Use of Color in the Verse of the Pléiade* (Les Presses Universitaires de France, 1927)

CHAPTER FOUR

NEOCLASSICISM
FRENCH LITERATURE OF THE SEVENTEENTH CENTURY

(GENERAL)

Bagley, C. R., *An Introduction to French Literature of the Seventeenth Century* (D. Appleton-Century Co., Inc., 1937)

Bungener, F., *The Preacher and the King* (Gould & Lincoln, 1854)

Cauldwell, H., *Introduction to French Classicism* (The Macmillan Co., 1931)

Crump, P. E., *Nature in the Age of Louis XIV* (G. Routledge & Sons, Ltd., 1928)

Guizot, F. P. G., *Corneille and His Times* (Harper & Brothers, 1852)

Nussbaum, F. I., *The Triumph of Science and Reason, 1660-1685* (Harper & Brothers, 1953)

Sainte-Beuve, C. A., *Portraits of the Seventeenth Century* (K. Wormeley, tr.) (G. P. Putnam's Sons, 1904)

Stewart, H. F. and Tilley, A. A., *The Classical Movement in French Literature* (Cambridge University Press, 1923)

Tilley, A. A., *From Montaigne to Molière* (Cambridge University Press, 1923)

Wright, C. H. C., *French Classicism* (Harvard University Press, 1920)

FRENCH LITERATURE OF THE EIGHTEENTH CENTURY

(GENERAL)

Barante, A. G. P., *A Tableau of French Literature during the Eighteenth Century* (London, 1833)

Becker, C. L., *The Heavenly City of the Eighteenth Century Philosophers* (Yale University Press, 1932)

Brooks, G., *Dames and Daughters of the French Court* (T. F. Unwin, 1905)

Green, F. C., *Eighteenth-Century France* (J. M. Dent & Sons, Ltd., 1929), *Minuet* (J. M. Dent & Sons, Ltd., 1935)

Michell, R. B., *French Literature before 1800* (F. S. Crofts & Co., 1935)

Mornet, D., *French Thought in the Eighteenth Century* (L. L. Levin, tr.) (Prentice-Hall, 1929)

Tilley, A. A., *The Decline of the Age of Louis XIV* (Cambridge University Press, 1929)

Vinet, A. R., *History of French Literature in the Eighteenth Century* (Edinburgh, 1854)

ITALIAN LITERATURE OF THE EIGHTEENTH CENTURY

(GENERAL)

Paget, V., *Studies of the Eighteenth Century in Italy* (T. F. Unwin, 1907)

BAYLE

Translation: Des Maiseaux, M., *A General Dictionary, Historical and Critical* (J. Roberts, 1734-41, 10 v.)

Courtines, L. P., *Bayle's Relations with England and the English* (Columbia University Press, 1938)

Cowdrick, R. E., *The Early Reading of Pierre Bayle* (Mennonite Publishing House, 1939)

Robinson, H., *Bayle, the Sceptic* (Columbia University Press, 1931), *Essays in Intellectual History* (New York, 1929)

Smith, H. E., *The Literary Criticism of Pierre Bayle* (Brandow Printing Co., Albany, 1912)

BEAUMARCHAIS

Translations: *The Barber of Seville* (S. French, Ltd., 1939); Holcroft, T., *The Marriage of Figaro* (G. G. & J. J. Robinson, 1785)

Beck, J. M., *May It Please the Court* (New York, 1930)

Bigelow, J., *Beaumarchais the Merchant* (C. Scribner & Co., 1870)

Clements Library of American History, *Beaumarchais and the American Revolution* (Michigan University, 1925)

Dalsème, R., *Beaumarchais* (G. P. Putnam's Sons, 1929)

Frischauer, P., *Beaumarchais, Adventurer in the Century of Women* (The Viking Press, 1935)

Hazard, B. E., *Beaumarchais and the American Revolution* (E. L. Slocomb, 1910)

Jones, F. N., *Beaumarchais and Plautus* (Scott, Foresman & Co., 1908)

Kite, E. S., *Beaumarchais and the War of American Independence* (R. G. Badger, 1918)

Lemaître, G. E., *Beaumarchais* (A. A. Knopf, 1949)

Loménie, L. L., de, *Beaumarchais and His Times* (Addey & Co., 1856)

Rivers, J., *Figaro, the Life of Beaumarchais* (Hutchinson & Co., 1922)

Tallentyre, S. G., *The Friends of Voltaire* (Smith, Elder & Co., 1906)

BOILEAU

Translation: Cook, A. S., (ed.), *The Art of Poetry: The Poetical Treatises of Horace, Vida, and Boileau* (G. E. Stechert & Co., 1926)

Astie, J. F., *Louis XIV and the Writers of His Age* (J. P. Jewett & Co., 1855)

Clark, A. F. B., *Boileau and the French Classical Critics in England* (E. Champion, 1925)

Haley, M. P., *Racine and the Art Poétique of Boileau* (The Johns Hopkins Press, 1938)

BOSSUET

Translations: *An Exposition of the Doctrine of the Catholic Church* (W. Clowes, 1815); *History of the Variations of the Protestant Churches* (J. Doyle, 1836-42); Ephilstone, J., *An Universal History* (R. Moore, 1821)

Butler, C., *Some Account of the Life and Writing of J. B. Bossuet* (London, 1812)

Bungener, F., *The Preacher and the King* (Gould & Lincoln, 1854)

Currier, A. H., *Nine Great Preachers* (The Pilgrim Press, 1912)

Lear, H. L., *Bossuet and His Contemporaries* (Rivingtons, 1877)

Simpson, W. J. S., *A Study of Bossuet* (The Macmillan Co., 1937)

BUFFON

Translations: *The System of Natural History* (J. Ruthven & Sons, 1800); Barr, J. S., *Natural History* (H. D. Symonds, 1797); Clarke, B., *The Book of Birds* (R. Tyas, 1841)

Butler, S., *Evolution, Old and New* (Hardwicke & Bogue, 1879)

Duclaux, A. M. F., *The French Ideal* (Chapman & Hall, Ltd., 1911)

Jardine, W., *Mammalia* (H. G. Bohn, 1866)

CORNEILLE

Translations: Cibber, C., *Cinna's Conspiracy* (B. Lintot, 1713); Cotton, C., *Horace* (H. Brome, 1671); Feltenstein, R., *Le Cid* (Barron's Educational Series, Inc., 1953); Felix, M. R., *Horace* (Darcie & Corbyn, 1855); Foote, S., *The Liar* (W. Simpkin & R. Marshall, 1822); Landis, P., *Six Plays* [Corneille and Racine] (The Modern Library, Random House, 1931); Whitehead, W., *The Roman Father* (R. Dodsley, 1750)

Astie, J. F., *Louis XIV and the Writers of His Age* (J. P. Jewett & Co., 1885)

Croce, B., *Ariosto, Shakespeare, and·Corneille* (H. Holt & Co., 1920)
Fisher, D. F., *Corneille and Racine in England* (The Macmillan Co., 1904)
Frye, P. H., *Corneille: the Neo-classic Tragedy and the Greek* (Nebraska University, 1906)
Guizot, F. P. G., *Corneille and His Times* (Harper & Brothers, 1852)
Riddle, L. M., *The Genesis and Sources of Corneille's Tragedies* (The Johns Hopkins Press, 1926)
Stoll, E. E., *Shakespeare and Other Masters* (Harvard University Press, 1940)
Turnell, M., *The Classical Moment* (H. Hamilton, 1947)
Van Roosbroeck, G. L., *The Purpose of Corneille's "Cid"* (Pioneer Printers, 1921)
Vincent, L. H., *Corneille* (Houghton, Mifflin & Co., 1901)
Watson, P. B., *Tales of Normandie* (Marshall Jones Co., 1930)

CRÉBILLON

Translations: Murphy, A., *Zenobia* (W. Griffin, 1768); Sinnett, E., *Atreus and Thyestes* (H. Baldwyn, 1822)

CYRANO DE BERGERAC

Translations: Aldington, R., *Voyages to the Moon and the Sun* (G. Routledge & Sons, Ltd., 1923); Lovell, A., *The Comical History of the States and Empires of the Worlds of the Moon and the Sun* (Doubleday & McClure Co., 1899); Bourland, B. P., *Satyrical Characters* (Cleveland Rowfant Club, 1914)
Ayres, R. F., *Romance of Cyrano de Bergerac* (F. T. Neely, 1899)
Nevill, Ralph H., *Echoes Old and New* (Chatto & Windus, 1919)
Rogers, C., *Cyrano* (Doubleday, Doran & Co., Inc.)

D'ALEMBERT

Translations: *Hell Destroyed* (J. W. Trust, 1823); *Miscellaneous Pieces* (C. Henderson, 1764); Aiken, J. (ed.), *Select Eulogies of the French Academy* (London, 1799)
DeFord, M. A., *Love-Children* (The Dial Press, 1931)
Tallentyre, S. G., *The Friends of Voltaire* (Smith, Elder & Co., 1906)

DANCOURT

Translations: Shadwell, C., *The Humors of the Army* (James Knapton, 1713); Vanbrugh, J., *The City Wives' Confederacy* (Harrison & Co., 1779)

DIDEROT

Translations: *Dorval* (London, 1767); *Historical and Literary Memoirs and Anecdotes* (H. Colburn, 1814); *Thoughts on Religion* (R. Carlyle, 1819); Allison, J. M. S., *Concerning the Education of a Prince* (Yale University Press, 1941); Birrell, F., *Dialogues* (G. Routledge & Sons, Ltd., 1927), *Memoirs of a Nun* (G. Routledge & Sons, Ltd., 1928); Burgoyne, J., *The Heiress* (Chamberlaine, 1786); Freese. J. H., *The Memoirs and Correspondence of Mme. d'Épinay* (H. S. Nichols, Ltd., 1899); Hardaker, W., *Old Thoughts for New Thinkers* (Progressive Publishing Co., 188?); Jackson, Mrs. W., *Rameau's Nephew and Other Works* (Chapman & Hall, 1926); Jourdain, M., *Diderot's Early Philosophical Works* (The Open Court Publishing Co., 1916); La Fontainerie, F. de, *French Liberation and Education in the Eighteenth Century* (McGraw-Hill Book Co., Inc., 1932); Lee, S., *The Chapter of Accidents* (T. Cadell, 1780); Pollock, W. H., *The Paradox of Acting* (Chatto & Windus, 1883)

Babbitt, I., *Spanish Character and Other Essays* (Houghton Mifflin Co., 1940)

Barker, J. E., *Diderot's Treatment of the Christian Religion* (King's Crown Press, 1941)

Cru, R. L., *Diderot as a Disciple of English Thought* (Columbia University Press, 1913)

Ellis, H., *The New Spirit* (Houghton, Mifflin Co., 1929)

Morley, J., *Diderot and the Encyclopedists* (The Macmillan Co., 1923)

Palache, J. G., *Four Novelists of the Old Régime* (The Viking Press, 1926)

Reed, H. E., *In Defence of Shelley, and Other Essays* (W. Heinemann, Ltd., 1936), *Reason and Romanticism* (Faber & Gwyer, 1926)

Steel, Eric M., *Diderot's Imagery* (The Corporate Press, 1941)

Tallentyre, S. G., *The Friends of Voltaire* (Smith, Elder & Co., 1906)

Vexler, F., *Studies in Diderot's Esthetic Naturalism* (Columbia University Press, 1922)

THE ENCYCLOPEDISTS

Translation: Diderot and D' Alembert, *The Plan of the French Encyclopedia* (London, 1752)

Gordon, D. H., *The Censorship of Diderot's Encyclopédie* (Columbia University Press, 1947)

Oliver, A. R., *The Encyclopedists as Critics of Music* (Columbia University Press, 1947)

Roustan, M., *The Pioneers of the French Revolution* (E. Benn, Ltd., 1926)

Wade, I. O., *The "Philosophe" in the French Drama of the Eighteenth Century* (Princeton University Press, 1926)

Wadia, P. A., *The Philosophers and the French Revolution* (S. Sonnenschein & Co., Ltd., 1904)

FÉNELON

Translations: *Apples of Gold, Gathered by Fénelon* (J. B. Lippincott & Co., 1856); *Selections from Fénelon* (Little, Brown & Co., 1906); Hawkesworth, J., *Adventures of Telemachus* (Hurd & Houghton, 1864); Lear, H. L. S., *The Spiritual Letters of Archbishop Fénelon* (Longmans, Green, & Co., 1909)

Astie, J. F., *Louis XIV and the Writers of His Age* (J. P. Jewett & Co., 1855)

Bausset, L. F., *Life of Fénelon* (London, 1810)

Benson, Arthur C., *Men of Might* (E. Arnold, 1921)

Bradford, G., *Saints and Sinners* (Houghton Mifflin Co., 1932)

Butler, C., *The Life of Fénelon* (P. H. Nicklin & Co., 1811)

Duclaux, A. M. F., *The French Ideal* (Chapman & Hall, Ltd., 1911)

Janet, P. A. R., *Fénelon; His Life and Works* (Sir Isaac Pitman & Sons, Ltd., 1914)

Lamartine, A. M., *Memoirs of Celebrated Characters* (Harper & Brothers, 1854)

Mudge, J., *Fénelon the Mystic* (Eaton & Mains, 1906)

Sanders, E. K., *Fénelon, His Friends and Enemies* (Longmans, Green & Co., 1901)

Sarafian, K. A., *French Educational Theorists* (University of Southern California, 1933)

FONTENELLE

Translations: *Conversations on the Plurality of Worlds* (Lackington, Allen & Co., 1809); *The Northern Worthies* (E. Mory, 1728); Glanvill, J., *A Plurality of Worlds* (Nonesuch Press, 1929); Ozell, Mr., *Letters of Gallantry* (J. Brown & J. Watts, 1715); Pound, E., *Dialogues of Fontenelle* (The Egoist, 1917); Whitehead, W., *The School for Lovers* (J. Dodsley, 1770)

Behn, Mrs. A., *A Discovery of New Worlds* (William Canning, 1688), *The History of Oracles* (1688)

Feuillerat, A. (ed.), *Studies by Members of the French Department* (Yale University Press, 1941)

Thorold, A. L., *Six Masters in Disillusion* (A. Constable & Co., Ltd., 1909)

FRÉRON

Green, F. C., *Eighteenth Century France* (J. M. Dent & Sons, Ltd., 1929)

GOLDONI

Translations: Aldington, R., *The Good-Humored Ladies* (C. W. Beaumont, 1922); Black, J., *Memoirs of Carlo Goldoni* (A. A. Knopf,

1926); Coleman, A. J. du P., *Inquisitive Women* (G. Schirmer's 1911); Dent, E. J., *The Servant of Two Masters* (Cambridge University Press, 1928); Dibdin, C., *The Wedding Ring* (T. Becket, 1773); Fraser, C. L., *The Liar* (Selwyn & Blount, Ltd., 1922); Fuller, H. B., *The Coffee-House* (S. French, 1925), *The Fan* (S. French, 1925); Gregory, Lady, *Mirandolina* (G. P. Putnam's Sons, 1924); Hollister, R. D. T., *A Curious Mishap* (Ann Arbor, 1924); Lloyd, C., *Three Comedies by Carlo Goldoni* (The National Alumni, 1907); Shadwell, C., *The Humors of the Army* (James Knapton, 1713); Steenderen, F. C. L. van, *Goldoni on Playwriting* (Columbia University Dramatic Museum, 1919); Vanbrugh, J., *The City Wives' Confederacy* (Harrison & Co., 1779)

Chatfield-Taylor, H. C., *Goldoni* (Duffield & Co., 1913)

Copping, E., *Alfieri and Goldoni* (Addey & Co., 1857)

Dole, N. H., *A Teacher of Dante and Other Studies* (Moffat, Yard, & Co., 1908)

Grillo, E. N. G., *Studies in Modern Italian Literature* (Jackson, Wylie & Co., 1930)

Kennard, Joseph S., *Goldoni and the Venice of His Time* (The Macmillan Co., 1920)

Perry, H. T. E., *Masters of Dramatic Comedy* (Harvard University Press, 1939)

GRESSET

Mahony, F. S., *The Reliques of Father Prout* (Bell & Daldy, 1866)

LA BRUYÈRE

Translation: Van Laun, H., *The Characters of Jean de la Bruyère* (G. Routledge & Sons, Ltd., 1929)

Gosse, E. W., *Three French Moralists* (W. Heinemann, 1918)

LA FAYETTE, MME. DE

Translations: *The Death of Madame* (Harrison of Paris, 1931); Ashton, H., *The Princess of Clèves* (G. Routledge & Sons, Ltd., 1925); Perry, T. S., *The Princess of Clèves* (Little, Brown & Co., 1911); Shelmerdine, J. M., *The Secret History of Henrietta* (E. P. Dutton & Co., 1929)

Brooks, G., *Dames and Daughters of the French Court* (T. F. Unwin, 1905)

Maurois, A., *Seven Faces of Love* (Didier, 1944)

Ravenel, F., *Women and the French Tradition* (The Macmillan Co., 1918)

Rea, L., *The Life and Times of Marie Madeleine, Countess of Lafayette* (Methuen & Co., 1905)

LA FONTAINE

Translations: Auslander, J. and Le Clercq, J., *The Fables of Jean de La Fontaine* (Limited Editions Club, 1930); Marsh, E., *The Fables of Jean de La Fontaine* (W. Heinemann, Ltd., 1931), *La Fontaine's Fables* (Everyman's Library, E. P. Dutton & Co., 1952); Thornbury, Walter, *The Fables of La Fontaine* (Cassell & Co., Ltd., 1868); Wright, E., Jr., *Fables of La Fontaine* (W. P. Hazard, 1863)

Bailey, J. C., *The Claims of French Poetry* (M. Kennerley, 1909)

Hamel, F., *Jean de la Fontaine* (S. Paul & Co., 1911)

Sutherland, M., *La Fontaine: The Man and His Work* (Jonathan Cape, 1953)

LA HARPE

Translations: Francklin, T., *The Earl of Warwick* (T. Davies, 1766); Swettenham, F., *Three Gifts* (J. Lane, Ltd., 1928)

LA ROCHEFOUCAULD

Translations: Heard, J., *Maxims* (Houghton Mifflin Co., 1917); Kronenberger, L., *The Maxims* (Stackpole Sons, 1936); Pratt, K., *Maxims* (The Haworth Press, 1931); Stevens, F. G., *The Maxims* (H. Milford, 1939)

Bishop, M., *The Life and Adventures of La Rochefoucauld* (Cornell University Press, 1951)

Gosse, E. W., *Three French Moralists* (W. Heinemann, 1918)

Grubbs, H. A., *The Originality of La Rochefoucauld's Maxims* (Paris, 1929)

Harvey, F. B., *Church, State, and Letters* (The Epworth Press, 1943)

LE SAGE

Translations: Clark, B. H., *Crispin* (S. French, 1915); Gowans, A. L., *A Day of the Fates* (Gowans & Gray, 1922); Smollett, T., *The Adventures of Gil Blas* (G. Routledge & Sons, 1891; World's Classics, Oxford University Press, 1907); Thomas, J., *Asmodeus* (J. Thomas, 1841); Townsend, J., *The Bachelor of Salamanca* (Worthington Co., 1890)

Saintsbury, G. E. B., *A Short History of the Life and Writings of Alain René le Sage* (Ballantyne, Hanson & Co., n. d.)

MAINTENON, MME. DE

Translations: *The Secret Correspondence of Madame de Maintenon* (G. B. Whittaker, 1827); Wormeley, K. P., *The Correspondence of Madame, Princess Palatine* (Hardy, Pratt & Co., 1899)

Barnard, H. C., *Madame de Maintenon and Saint-Cyr* (A. & C. Black, Ltd., 1934)

Blennerhasset, C. J., *Louis XIV and Madame de Maintenon* (G. Allen & Sons, 1910)

Crutwell, M., *Madame de Maintenon* (J. M. Dent & Sons, Ltd., 1930)

MALHERBE

Belloc, H., *Avril* (Sheed & Ward, 1945)

Gosse, E. W., *Malherbe and the Classical Reaction* (Clarendon Press, 1920)

Watson, P. B., *Tales of Normandie* (Marshall Jones Co., 1930)

MARIVAUX

Translations: Aldington, R., *The Game of Love and Chance* in *French Comedies of the Eighteenth Century* (London, 1923); Ford, H., & Le Verrier, M. L., *Love in Livery* (S. French, 1907); Jones, W. K., *The Test* (Poet Lore, 1924)

Jamieson, R. K., *Marivaux* (King's Crown Press, 1941)

Tilley, A. A., *Three French Dramatists* (Cambridge University Press, 1933)

MARMONTEL

Translations: *The Incas* (J. Nourse, P. Elmsly, etc., 1777); Howells, W. D., *Autobiography* (Houghton, Osgood & Co., 1898); Morrison, G. F., *Belizarius* (R. M. De Witt, 1857); Patmore, B., *Memoirs of Marmontel* (G. Routledge & Sons, Ltd., 1930); Saintsbury, G., *Moral Tales* (G. Allen, 1895)

MOLIÈRE

Translations: *Plays* (The Modern Library, 1924); Baker, H. and Miller, J., *Comedies* (Everyman's Library, E. P. Dutton & Co., 1929); Bishop, M., *The Would-Be-Invalid* (Crofts Classics, Appleton-Century-Crofts, Inc., 1950); Frank, W. (ed.), *Plays by Molière* (Boni & Liveright, 1924); Gregory, Lady, *The Kiltartan Molière* (Maunsel & Co., Ltd., 1910); Morley, H. (ed.), *Plays from Molière by English Dramatists* (G. Routledge & Sons, 1885); Van Laun, H., *The Dramatic Works of Molière* (W. Paterson, 1875-76); Wall, C. H., *The Dramatic Works of Molière* (G. Bell & Sons, 1876-77)

Ashton, H., *Molière* (G. Routledge & Sons, Ltd., 1930)

Chapman, P. A., *The Spirit of Molière* (Princeton University Press, 1940)

Chatfield-Taylor, H. C., *Molière* (Duffield & Co., 1906)

Mantzius, K., *A History of Theatrical Art, Vol. IV* (Duckworth & Co., 1905)

Matthews, B., *Molière, His Life and Works* (C. Scribner's Sons, 1926)

Palmer, J. L., *Molière* (Brewer & Warren, Inc., 1930)

Perry, H. T. E., *Masters of Dramatic Comedy* (Harvard University Press, 1939)

Pierce, W. T., *The Bourgeois from Molière to Beaumarchais* (Johns Hopkins University, 1907)

Tilley, A. A., *Molière* (Cambridge University Press, 1921)

Trollope, H. M., *The Life of Molière* (E. P. Dutton & Co., 1905)

Turnell, M., *The Classical Moment* (H. Hamilton, 1947)

Stoll, E. E., *Shakespeare and Other Masters* (Harvard University Press, 1940)

Vincent, L. H., *Molière* (Houghton, Mifflin & Co., 1902)

Wheatley, K. E., *Molière and Terence* (The University of Texas Press, 1931)

Wilcox, J., *The Relation of Moliere to Restoration Comedy* (Columbia University Press, 1938)

MONTESQUIEU

Translations: Baker, J., *Considerations on the Causes of the Grandeur and Decadence of the Romans* (D. Appleton & Co., 1894); Davidson, J., *Persian Letters* (M. W. Dunne, 1901); Nugent, T., *The Spirit of the Laws* (G. Bell & Sons, 1878); Uzanne, O. (ed.), *The Temple of Gnidus* (Vizetelly & Co., 1889)

Collins, J. C., *Voltaire, Montesquieu and Rousseau in England* (E. Nash, 1908)

Fletcher, F. T. H., *Montesquieu and English Politics* (E. Arnold & Co., 1939)

Levin, L. M., *The Political Doctrine of Montesquieu's Esprit des Lois* (Columbia University Press, 1936)

Sorel, A., *Montesquieu* (A. C. McClurg & Co., 1892)

MOTTEVILLE, MME. DE

Translation: Wormeley, K. P., *Memoirs of Mme. de Motteville* (Hardy, Pratt & Co., 1901)

PARINI

Translation: Bower, H. M., *The Day* (G. Routledge & Sons, Ltd., 1927)

Grillo, E. N. G., *Studies in Modern Italian Literature* (Jackson, Wylie & Co., 1930)

PASCAL

Translations: Mauriac, F. (ed.), *The Living Thoughts of Pascal* (Longmans, Green & Co., 1940); M'Crie, T., *The Provincial Letters* (Houghton, Osgood & Co., 1880); Paul, C. K., *The Thoughts of Blaise Pascal* (G. Bell & Sons, 1905); Rawlings, G. B., *Pascal's Pensées* (The Peter Pauper Press, 1946); Stewart, H. F., *The Heart of Pascal* (Cambridge University Press, 1945), *Pascal's Apology for Religion* (Cambridge University Press, 1942); Trotter, W. F., *Pensées* (Everyman's Library, E. P. Dutton & Co., 1908), *Thoughts* (P. F. Collier & Son, 1910); Trotter, W. F. and M'Crie, T., *Pensées and the Provincial Letters* (The Modern Library, Random House, 1941)

Abercrombie, N., *Saint Augustine and French Classical Thought* (Clarendon Press, 1938)

Babbitt, I., *Spanish Character and Other Essays* (Houghton Mifflin Co., 1940)

Belloc, H., *Pascal's Provincial Letters* (Catholic Truth Society, 1921)

Bishop, M. G., *Pascal, The Life of Genius* (Reynal & Hitchcock, 1936)

Bradshaw, M. J., *Philosophical Foundations of Faith* (Columbia University Press, 1941)

Calliet, E., *The Clue to Pascal* (The Westminster Press, 1943); *Pascal* (The Westminster Press, 1945)

Chevalier, J., *Pascal* (Longmans, Green & Co., 1930)

Clark, W., *Pascal and the Port Royalists* (C. Scribner's Sons, 1902)

Duclaux, A. M. F., *The French Ideal* (Chapman & Hall, Ltd., 1911), *Portrait of Pascal* (T. F. Unwin, Ltd., 1927)

Eastwood, D., *The Revival of Pascal* (Clarendon Press, 1936)

Leavenworth, I. F., *The Physics of Pascal* (Institute of French Studies, 1930)

Maritain, J., *Ransoming the Time* (C. Scribner's Sons, 1941)

Mesnard, J., *Pascal* (Philosophical Library, 1952)

Morgan, C., *Reflections in a Mirror* (The Macmillan Co., 1944)

Powys, J. C., *Suspended Judgments* (G. A. Shaw, 1916)

Saint-Cyres, S. H. N., *Pascal* (J. Murray, 1909)

Soltan, R. H., *Pascal* (Blackie & Son, Ltd., 1927)

Stewart, H. F., *The Secret of Pascal* (Cambridge University Press, 1941)

Vinet, A. R., *Studies on Pascal* (T. & T. Clark, 1859)

Waterman, M., *Voltaire, Pascal, and Human Destiny* (King's Crown Press, 1942)

Webb, C. C. J., *Pascal's Philosophy of Religion* (Clarendon Press, 1929)

PRÉVOST

Translations: Gribble, G. D., *Manon Lescaut* (G. Routledge & Sons, Ltd., 1925); Moylan, D. C., *History of Manon Lescaut* (Masterpieces of French Literature, Société des Beaux-Arts, 1910), *Manon Lescaut and Carmen* (Everyman's Library, E. P. Dutton & Co., 1929); Robertson, M. E. I., *Adventures of a Man of Quality* (G. Routledge & Sons, Ltd., 1930); Waddell, H., *The Story of Manon Lescaut* (The Heritage Club, 1938)

Havens, G. R., *The Abbé Prévost and English Literature* (The Johns Hopkins Press, 1921)

Wilcox, F. H., *Prévost's Translations of Richardson's Novels* (University of California Press, 1927)

RACINE

Translations: Boswell, R. B., *Dramatic Works* (G. Bell & Sons, Ltd., 1918), *Phaedra* (F. Rullman, 1880); Dunstan, W. R., *The Litigants* (Oxford University Press, 1928); Fontaine, E., *Andromache* (College Translations, 1929); Landis, P., *Six Plays* [Corneille and Racine] (The Modern Library, Random House, 1931); Masefield, J., *Berenice* (W. Heinemann, 1922); Spoerl, H. D., *Mithridates* (The Tufts College Press, 1926)

Babbitt, I., *Spanish Character, and Other Essays* (Houghton Mifflin Co., 1940)

Clark, A. F. B., *Jean Racine* (Harvard University Press, 1939)

Duclaux, A. M. F., *The Life of Racine* (T. F. Unwin, Ltd., 1925)

Eccles, F. Y., *Racine in England* (Clarendon Press, 1922)

Fisher, D. F., *Corneille and Racine in England* (The Macmillan Co., 1904)

Giraudoux, J., *Racine* (G. Fraser, 1938)

Haley, M. P., *Racine and the Art Poétique of Boileau* (The Johns Hopkins Press, 1938)

Orgel, V., *A New View of the Plays of Racine* (The Macmillan Co., 1948)

Savory, D. L., *Jean Racine* (Oxford University Press, 1940)

Spitzer, L., *Linguistics and Literary History* (Princeton University Press, 1948)

Stoll, E. E., *Shakespeare and Other Masters* (Harvard University Press, 1940)

Strachey, L., *Books and Characters* (Harcourt, Brace & Co., 1922)

Tilley, A. A., *Three French Dramatists* (Cambridge University Press, 1933)

Turnell, M., *The Classical Moment* (H. Hamilton, 1947)

REGNARD

Translation: Fielding, H., *The Intriguing Chambermaid* (Modern British Drama, 1811)

RETZ

Translation: *Memoirs* (E. Earle, 1817)

Ogg, D., *Cardinal de Retz* (Methuen & Co., 1912)

ROHAN

Translation: Bridges, G., *The Memoirs* (G. Bedell & J. Collins, 1660)

SAINT-ÉVREMOND

Translations: *The Works* (J. Churchill, 1714); Hayward, J., *The Letters of St. Évremond* (G. Routledge & Sons, Ltd., 1930), *Miscellanea* (S. Holford, 1686)

SAINT-SIMON

Translations: Arkwright, F., *The Memoirs* (Brentano's, 1915); St. John, B., *The Memoirs* (Chatto & Windus, 1876)

Collins, C. W., *Saint Simon* (J. B. Lippincott & Co., 1880)

SÉVIGNÉ, MME. DE

Translations: Aldington, R. (ed.), *Letters of Mme de Sévigné* (E. P. Dutton & Co., 1937); Anderson, E. P. (ed.), *The Best Letters of Mme de Sévigné* (A. C. McClurg & Co., 1898); Newton, A. E., *The Letters of Mme de Sévigné* (J. P. Horn & Co., 1927)

Aldis, J., *The Queen of Letter-Writers* (Methuen & Co., 1907)

Boissier, G., *Madame de Sévigné* (G. Routledge & Sons, 1887)

Bradford, G., *Portraits of Women* (Houghton Mifflin Co., 1916)

Brooks, G., *Dames and Daughters of the French Court* (T. F. Unwin, 1905)

Fitzgerald, E., *Dictionary of Mme. de Sévigné* (The Macmillan Co., 1914)

Hunt, L., *Men, Women, and Books* (Smith, Elder & Co., 1847)

Irvine, L. L., *Ten Letter Writers* (L. & V. Woolf, 1932)

Lemaître, J., *Literary Impressions* (D. O'Connor, 1921)

Ravenel, F., *Women and the French Tradition* (The Macmillan Co., 1918)

Tallentyre, S. G., *The Women of the Salons* (G. P. Putnam's Sons, 1926)

Tilley, A. A., *Madame de Sévigné* (Cambridge University Press, 1936)

Tuckerman, H. T., *Characteristics of Literature, Second Series* (Lindsay & Blakiston, 1851)

VOLTAIRE

Translations: *An Essay upon the Civil Wars* (The Georgian Press, 1928); *The History of Charles XII* (E. Duyckinck, 1803); *The History of the Misfortunes of John Calas* (T. Sherlock, 1772); *The History of the Russian Empire* (G. Dearborn, 1835); *Memoirs of the Life of Voltaire. Written by Himself* (G. Robinson, 1784); *The Princess of Babylon* (The Nonesuch Press, 1927); *Voltaire's Romances* (P. Eckler Publishing Co., 1922); Aldington, R., *Candide* (The Nonesuch Press, 1939), *Letters of Voltaire and Frederick the Great* (G. Routledge & Sons, Ltd., 1927); Cameron, N., *Candide* (The Novel Library, 1947); Dowson, E., *La Pucelle* (The Lutetian Society, 1899); Fleming, W. S., *Philosophical Dictionary* (The Great Books Foundation, 1949); Havens, G. R., *Selections from Voltaire* (The Century Co., 1925); Hill, A., *Merope* (J. Wenmann, 1777); Jones,

C. L. S., *The Henriad* (S. Smith, 1834); Littell, P. (ed.), *Candide* (Boni & Liveright, 1918); McCabe, J., *Selected Works* (Watts & Co., 1921), *Toleration* (G. P. Putnam's Sons, 1912); Maurois, A. (ed.), *The Living Thoughts of Voltaire* (Longmans, Green & Co., 1939); Miller & Hoadly, *Mahomet* (T. Lowndes, 1766); Morley J. (ed.), *Candide* (G. Routledge & Sons, 1886), *The Works* (St. Hubert Guild, 1901-03); Pollack, M. P., *The Age of Louis XIV* (Everyman's Library, E. P. Dutton & Co., 1926); Redman, B. R. (ed.), *The Portable Voltaire* (Viking Press, 1949); Smollett, T. and Thornton, J. C., *Candide and Other Tales* (Everyman's Library, E. P. Dutton & Co., 1937); Tallentyre, S. G., *Voltaire in His Letters* (G. P. Putnam's Sons, 1919); Todhunter, W., *Voltaire's History of Charles XII* (J. M. Dent & Co., 1908); Torrey, M. L., (ed.), *Candide* (Crofts Classics, Appleton-Century-Crofts, Inc., 1946); Torrey, M. L., *Voltaire and the Enlightenment* (F. S. Crofts & Co., 1931); Whibley, C. (ed.), *Letters concerning the English Nation* (P. Davies, 1926); Woolf, H. I., *Voltaire's Philosophical Dictionary* (A. A. Knopf, 1924), *Zadig* (E. P. Dutton & Co., 1923)

Aldington, R., *Voltaire* (G. Routledge & Sons, Ltd., 1925)

Ballantyne, A., *Voltaire's Visit to England* (Murray, 1919)

Barr, M. M. H., *Voltaire in America* (The Johns Hopkins Press, 1941)

Black, J. B., *The Art of History* (Methuen & Co., Ltd., 1926)

Bradford, G., *Bare Souls* (Harper & Brothers, 1924)

Brailsford, H. N., *Voltaire* (T. Butterworth, Ltd., 1935)

Brandes, G. M. C., *Voltaire* (A. & C. Boni, 1930)

Chase, C. B., *The Young Voltaire* (Longmans, Green & Co., 1926)

Collins, J. C., *Voltaire, Montesquieu and Rousseau in England* (E. Nash, 1908)

Crist, C. M., *The Dictionnaire Philosophique* (S. J. Clark's Sons, Inc., 1934)

Espinasse, F., *Life of Voltaire* (Walter Scott Publishing Co., 1892)

Feuillerat, A. (ed.), *Studies by Members of the French Department* (Yale University Press, 1941)

Fitch, R. E., *Voltaire's Philosophic Procedure* (The News-Times Publishing Co., 1935)

Guérard, A. L., *French Prophets of Yesterday* (D. Appleton & Co., 1913)

Ingersoll, R. G., *Voltaire* (C. P. Farrell, 1907)

Jusserand, J. A. J., *English Essays from a French Pen* (T. F. Unwin, 1895)

Lancaster, H. C., *French Tragedy in the Time of Louis XV and Voltaire* (Johns Hopkins Press, 1950)

Lounsbury, T. R., *Shakespeare and Voltaire* (D. Nutt, 1902)

Lowenstein, R., *Voltaire as an Historian of Seventeenth-Century French Drama* (The Johns Hopkins Press, 1935)

Ludwig, E., *Genius and Character* (Harcourt, Brace & Co., 1927)

Macdonald, F., *Studies in the France of Voltaire and Rousseau* (T. F. Unwin, 1895)

Maurel, A., *The Romance of Mme. du Châtelet and Voltaire* (Hutchinson & Co., Ltd., 1930)

Meyer, A. E., *Voltaire; Man of Justice* (Howell, Soskin, 1945)

Morley, J., *Voltaire* (The Macmillan Co., 1903)

Noyes, A., *Voltaire* (Sheed & Ward, 1936)

Powys, J. C., *Suspended Judgments* (G. A. Shaw, 1916)

Robertson, J. M., *Voltaire* (Watts & Co., 1922)

Russell, T. W., *Voltaire, Dryden, and Heroic Tragedy* (Columbia University Press, 1946)

Schilling, B. N., *Conservative England and the Case against Voltaire* (Columbia University Press, 1950)

Stoll, E. E., *Shakespeare and Other Masters* (Harvard University Press, 1940)

Strachey, L., *Books and Characters* (Harcourt, Brace & Co., 1922)

Tallentyre, S. G., *The Friends of Voltaire* (Smith, Elder & Co., 1906), *The Life of Voltaire* (G. P. Putnam's Sons, 1905)

Thaddeus, V., *Voltaire, Genius of Mockery* (Brentano's, 1928)

Torrey, N. L., *The Spirit of Voltaire* (Columbia University Press, 1938), *Voltaire and the English Deists* (Yale University Press, 1930)

Wade, I. O., *Studies in Voltaire* (Princeton University Press, 1947), *Voltaire and Mme. du Châtelet* (Princeton University Press, 1941)

Waterman, M., *Voltaire, Pascal, and Human Destiny* (King's Crown Press, 1942)

Part II

THE ROMANTIC MOVEMENT TO THE TWENTIETH CENTURY

GENERAL

Barnes, H. E., *An Intellectual and Cultural History of the Western World* (Random House, 1937)

Brandes, G., *Main Currents in Nineteenth Century Literature* (Boni & Liveright, 1923)

Clark, B. H. (ed.), *European Theories of the Drama* (D. Appleton & Co., 1929)

Clark, B. H. and Freedley, G. (eds.), *A History of Modern Drama* (D. Appleton-Century Co., 1947)

Croce, B., *European Literature in the Nineteenth Century* (A. A. Knopf, 1924)

Drinkwater, J., *The Outline of Literature* (G. P. Putnam's Sons, 1931)

Guérard, A., *Preface to World Literature* (H. Holt & Co., 1940)

Henderson, A., *European Dramatists* (Stewart & Kidd Co., 1926)

Horton, R. W. and Hopper, V. F., *Backgrounds of European Literature* (Horton & Hopper, 1948)

Knowlton, E. C., *An Outline of World Literature* (Ronald Press Co., 1929)

Laird, C. (ed.), *The World through Literature* (Appleton-Century-Crofts, Inc., 1951)

Macy, J., *The Story of the World's Literature* (Boni & Liveright, 1925)

Magnus, L., *Dictionary of European Literature* (E. P. Dutton & Co., 1927), *A History of European Literature* (Nicholson, 1934)

Moulton, R. G., *World Literature and its Place in General Culture* (The Macmillan Co., 1911)

Nicoll, A., *World Drama: From Aeschylus to Anouilh* (Harcourt, Brace & Co., 1950)

Powys, J. C., *The Enjoyment of Literature* (Simon & Schuster, 1938)

Rascoe, B., *Titans of Literature* (G. P. Putnam's Sons, 1932)

Roubiczek, P., *The Misinterpretation of Man; Studies in European Thought of the Nineteenth Century* (C. Scribner's Sons, 1947)

Smith, H. (ed.), *Columbia Dictionary of Modern European Literature* (Columbia University Press, 1947)

Townsend, A. H., *Good Reading* (Mentor Books, New American Library, 1947-48), *A Guide to Good Reading* (Hendricks House, Farrar Straus, 1935-48)

Von Tieghem, P., *Outline of Literary History of Europe since the Renaissance* (Century Co., 1930)

Wordsworth, J. C., *Adventures in Literature* (Heath Cranton, 1929)

DUTCH LITERATURE

Bowring, J., *Batavian Anthology* (Taylor & Hessey, 1824), *Sketch of the Language and Literature of Holland* (Diederichs Bros., 1829)

Gosse, Sir E. W., *Studies in the Literature of Northern Europe* (C. K. Paul & Co., 1879)

Greshoff, J., *Harvest of the Lowlands* (Querido, 1945)

FRENCH LITERATURE

Aldington, R., *Literary Studies and Reviews* (Allen, 1924)

Babbitt, I., *French Literature* (American Library Assn., 1928), *The Masters of Modern French Criticism* (Houghton Mifflin Co., 1921)

Besant, W., *The French Humorists* (Roberts & Bros., 1874)

Brèmond, H., *A Literary History of Religious Thought in France* (The Macmillan Co., 1928)

Brogan, D. W., *French Personalities and Problems* (H. Hamilton, 1946)

Brunetière, F., *Essays in French Literature* (C. Scribner's Sons, 1898)

Butler, K. T., *A History of French Literature* (E. P. Dutton & Co., 1923)

Cohn, A., *French Literature* (Columbia University Press, 1911)

Demogeot, J. C., *History of French Literature* (Rivingtons, 1874)

Des Granges, C. M., *An Illustrated History of French Literature* (Hatier, 1921)

Dowden, E., *A History of French Literature* (D. Appleton & Co., 1897)

Duhamel, G., *In Defense of Letters* (E. F. Bozman, tr.) (Greystone Press, 1939)

Ellis, H., *From Rousseau to Proust* (Houghton Mifflin Co., 1935)

Faguet, E., *A Literary History of France* (T. F. Unwin, 1907)

Gosse, Sir E. W., *French Profiles* (Heinemann, 1905)

Guyer, F. E., *The Main Stream of French Literature* (D. C. Heath & Co., 1932)

Hatzfeld, H., *Literature through Art* (Oxford University Press, 1952)

Jensen, E. M., *The Influence of French Literature on Europe* (R. G. Badger, 1919)

Konta, Mrs. A., *The History of French Literature* (D. Appleton & Co., 1910)

Mauriac, F., *Men I Hold Great* (E. Pell, tr.) (Philosophical Library, 1951)

Maurois, A., *Seven Faces of Love* (Didier, 1944)

Nitze, W. A. and Dargan, E. P., *A History of French Literature* (H. Holt & Co., 1927)

Ritchie, R. L. G., *France: A Companion to French Studies* (Methuen & Co., Ltd., 1937)

Saintsbury, G., *French Literature and Its Masters* (A. A. Knopf, 1946), *A Short History of French Literature* (Clarendon Press, 1901)

Schiefley, W. H., *Essays on French Literature* (Wetzel Publishing Co., Inc., 1930)

Smith, M. S., *The Spirit of French Letters* (The Macmillan Co., 1912)

Smith, M. A., *Short History of French Literature* (H. Holt & Co., 1924)

Strachey, L., *Landmarks in French Literature* (H. Holt & Co., 1912), *Books and Characters* (Harcourt, Brace & Co., 1926)

Van Laun, H., *History of French Literature* (Chatto & Windus, 1883)

Waite, V., *An Approach to French Literature* (G. G. Harrap, 1947)

Wright, C. H. C., *A History of French Literature* (Oxford University Press, 1912)

ITALIAN LITERATURF

De Sanctis, F., *History of Italian Literature* (Harcourt Brace & Co., 1931)

Flamini, F. A., *A History of Italian Literature* (E. M. O'Connor, tr.) (The National Alumni, 1906)

Foligno, C., *Epochs of Italian Literature* (Clarendon Press, 1920)

Foster, M. A., *Italian Literature* (W. & R. Chambers, 1853)

Gardner, E. G., *The Arthurian Legend in Italian Literature* (J. M. Dent & Sons, Ltd., 1930), *A History of Italian Literature* (D. Appleton & Co., 1898), *Italy, a Companion to Italian Studies* (Methuen & Co., Ltd., 1934), *The Story of Italian Literature* (Harper & Brothers, 1927)

Herbert, C., *Italy and Italian Literature* (Gilbert & Piper, 1835)

Kennard, J. S., *A Literary History of the Italian People* (The Macmillan Co., 1941)

Marshall, R., *Italy in English Literature* (Columbia University Press, 1934)

Robertson, J. G., *Studies in the Genesis of Romantic Theory in the Eighteenth Century* (Cambridge University Press, 1923)

Sanctis, F. de, *History of Italian Literature* (J. Redfern, tr.) (Harcourt, Brace & Co., 1931)

Trail, F., *A History of Italian Literature* (V. Ciocia, 1903-04), *The Scholar's Italy* (Williams & Wilkins Co., 1923)

GERMAN LITERATURE

Bithell, J., *Germany* (Methuen & Co., 1947)

Bruford, W. H., *Germany in the Eighteenth Century* (Cambridge University Press, 1935)

Butler, E. M., *The Tyranny of Greece over Germany* (Cambridge University Press, 1935)

Francke, K., *A History of German Literature as Determined by Social Forces* (H. Holt & Co., 1901)

Gostwick, J., *German Literature* (Lippincott, Grambo & Co., 1854)

Gostwick, J. and Harrison, R., *Outlines of German Literature* (Schönhof & Möller, 1873)

Hosmer, J. K., *A Short History of German Literature* (C. Scribner's Sons, 1899)

Menzel, W., *German Literature* (D. A. Talboys, 1840)

Metcalfe, F., *History of German Literature* (Longman, Brown, Green, Longmans, & Roberts, 1858)

Moore, R. W., *History of German Literature* (Bay View Reading Club, 1903)

Moschyisker, F. A., *A Guide to German Literature* (London, 1850)

Priest, G. M., *A Brief History of German Literature* (C. Scribner's Sons, 1909)

Robertson, J. G., *A History of German Literature* (W. Blackwood & Sons, 1902), *The Literature of Germany* (Home University Library of Modern Knowledge, H. Holt & Co., 1913), *Outlines of the History of German Literature* (G. P. Putnam's Sons, 1911)

Rose, W., *Men, Myths, and Movements in German Literature* (G. Allen & Unwin, Ltd., 1931)

Scherer, W., *History of German Literature* (C. Scribner's Sons, 1886)

Staël-Holstein, A. L. G., *Germany* (Houghton, Mifflin & Co., 1882)

Taylor, B., *Studies in German Literature* (G. P. Putnam's Sons, 1879)

Thomas, C., *A History of German Literature* (Appleton Dollar Library, D. Appleton & Co., 1928)

Waterhouse, G., *A Short History of German Literature* (Methuen & Co., 1942)

Zeydel, E. H., *The Holy Roman Empire in German Literature* (Columbia University Press, 1918)

PORTUGUESE LITERATURE

Bell, A. F. G., *Portuguese Literature* (Oxford University Press, 1922)

Young, G. (ed.), *Portugal, an Anthology* (Clarendon Press, 1916)

SCANDINAVIAN LITERATURE

Blankner, F., *The History of the Scandinavian Literatures* (Dial Press, 1938)

Horn, F. W., *History of the Literature of the Scandinavian North* (S. C. Griggs & Co., 1884)

Jorgenson, T., *History of Norwegian Literature* (The Macmillan Co., 1933)

Larsen, H. A., *Scandinavian Literature* (American Library Association, 1930)

SPANISH LITERATURE

Adams, N. B., *The Heritage of Spain* (H. Holt & Co., 1949)

Bell, A. F. G., *Castilian Literature* (Clarendon Press, 1938), *Contemporary Spanish Literature* (A. A. Knopf, 1925)

Bouterwek, F., *History of Spanish and Portuguese Literature* (London, 1823)

Brenan, G., *The Literature of the Spanish People from Roman Times to the Present Day* (Cambridge University Press, 1951)

Clarke, H. B., *Spanish Literature* (G. Allen & Unwin, Ltd., 1921)

Fitzmaurice-Kelly, J., *Chapters on Spanish Literature* (A. Constable & Co., 1908), *A History of Spanish Literature* (D. Appleton & Co., 1920), *A New History of Spanish Literature* (H. Milford, 1926), *Some Masters of Spanish Verse* (Oxford University Press, 1924)

Ford, J. D. M., *Main Currents of Spanish Literature* (H. Holt & Co., 1919)

Foster, A. F., *Hand-book of Spanish Literature* (W. & R. Chambers, 1851)

Laborde, E. D., *A History of Spanish Literature* (W. Heinemann, Ltd., 1931)

Madariaga, S. de, *The Genius of Spain* (Clarendon Press, 1933)

McClelland, I. L., *The Origins of the Romantic Movement in Spain* (Institute of Hispanic Studies, 1937)

Mérimée, E., and Morley, S. G., *A History of Spanish Literature* (H. Holt & Co., 1930)

Northrup, G. T., *An Introduction to Spanish Literature* (The University of Chicago Press, 1936)

Peers, E. A. (ed.), *Spain; a Companion to Spanish Studies* (Dodd, Mead & Co., 1929), *A History of the Romantic Movement in Spain* (Cambridge University Press, 1940)

Perrier, J. L., *A Short History of Spanish Literature* (J. L. Perrier, 1925)
Sedgwick, H. D., *Spain* (Little, Brown & Co., 1937)
Ticknor, G., *History of Spanish Literature* (Harper & Brothers, 1849)

CHAPTER FIVE

THE ROMANTIC MOVEMENT: FRANCE AND ITALY

GENERAL

Abercrombie, L., *Romanticism* (M. Secker, 1926)
Addison, A. E., *Romanticism and the Gothic Revival* (R. R. Smith, 1938)
Auden, W. H., *The Enchafed Flood* (Random House, 1950)
Babbitt, I., *Rousseau and Romanticism* (Houghton Mifflin Co., 1919)
Barzun, J., *Romanticism and the Modern Ego* (Little, Brown & Co., 1944)
Brandes, G., *Main Currents in Nineteenth Century Literature* (Boni & Liveright, 1923)
Carr, P., *Days with the French Romantics* (Methuen & Co., Ltd., 1932)
Cippico, A., *The Romantic Age in Italian Literature* (P. L. Warner, 1918)
Clement, N. H., *Romanticism in France* (Modern Language Assn., 1939)
Comfort, A., *Art and Social Responsibility* (Falcon Press, 1946)
Davies, T. R., *French Romanticism and the Press* (Cambridge University Press, 1906)
Dawson, C. H., *Medieval Religion and Other Essays* (Sheed & Ward, 1934)
Dodds, A. E., *The Romantic Theory of Poetry* (Longmans, Green, & Co., 1926)
Draper, F. W. M., *The Rise and Fall of French Romantic Drama* (Constable & Co., Ltd., 1923)
Finch, M. B., *The Origins of French Romanticism* (Constable & Co., Ltd., 1920)
Frye, P. H., *Romance and Tragedy* (Marshall Jones Co., 1902)
Gribble, F. H., *The Passions of the French Romantics* (Chapman & Hall, 1910)
Grierson, H. J. C., *Classical and Romantic* (Cambridge University Press, 1923)
Jones, P. M., *Tradition and Barbarism* (Faber & Faber, 1930)
Lavrin, J., *Studies in European Literature* (Constable & Co., 1929)
Lounsbury, T. R., *Shakespeare and Voltaire* (D. Nutt, 1902)
Lucas, F. L., *The Decline and Fall of the Romantic Ideal* (Cambridge University Press, 1936)
Magnus, L. A., *A General Sketch of European Literature in the Centuries of Romance* (K. Paul, Trench, Trubner & Co., 1918)

Mowat, R. B., *The Romantic Age* (G. G. Harrap & Co., 1937)
Omond, T. S., *The Romantic Triumph* (C. Scribner's Sons, 1900)
Osterweis, R. G., *Romanticism and Nationalism* (Yale University Press, 1949)
Praz, M., *The Romantic Agony* (Oxford University Press, 1933)
Robertson, J. G., *Studies in the Genesis of Romantic Theory* (Cambridge University Press, 1923)
Stewart, H. F., *The Romantic Movement in French Literature* (Cambridge University Press, 1916)
Vaughan, C. E., *The Romantic Revolt* (C. Scribner's Sons, 1907)

ALFIERI

Translations: *Memoirs of the Life & Writings of Victor Alfieri* (H. Colburn, 1810); *Saul* (T. Cadell, 1821); Bowring, E. A., *Myrrha* (A. Bates, 1902), *The Tragedies of Vittorio Alfieri* (G. Bell & Sons, 1876); Howells, W. D. (ed.), *Autobiography* (J. R. Osgood & Co., 1877); Lester, C. E., *Autobiography* (Paine & Burgess, 1845); Lloyd, C., *The Tragedies of Vittorio Alfieri* (Longman, Hurst, Rees, Orme, & Brown, 1815); McAnally, Sir H., *The Life of Vittorio Alfieri* (University of Kansas Press, 1953)
Copping, E., *Alfieri and Goldoni* (Addey & Co., 1857)
Dole, N. H., *A Teacher of Dante* (Moffat, Yard & Co., 1908)
Grillo, E. N. G., *Studies in Modern Italian Literature* (Jackson, Wylie, & Co., 1930)
Lee, V., *The Countess of Albany* (Roberts Bros., 1897)
Megaro, G., *Vittorio Alfieri* (Columbia University Press, 1930)
Miller, C. R. D., *Alfieri* (The Bayard Press, 1936)
Vaughan, H. M., *The Last Stuart Queen* (Brentano's, 1911)

BÉRANGER

Translations: *Love Songs of France* (New Amsterdam Book Co., 1896); Ashburton, R. O., *Gleanings from Béranger* (Privately Printed, 1889); Betts, C. L., *Songs from Béranger* (F. A. Stokes & Bro., 1888); Brough, D. B., *Béranger's Songs* (Addey & Co., 1856); Canby, M. T., *Songs of France* (W. F. Fell & Co., 1894); Griswold, R. W., *The Songs of Béranger in English* (Carey & Hart, 1844); Thornby, G. W., *The Legend of the Wandering Jew* (Addey & Co., 1857); Walsh, W. S. (ed.), *Béranger's Poems* (J. B. Lippincott Co., 1889); Young, W., *One Hundred Songs* (Chapman & Hall, 1847), *Two Hundred Lyrical Poems* (G. P. Putnam, 1850)
Bagehot, W., *Literary Studies* (Longmans, Green & Co., 1879)
Gautier, T., *Famous French Authors* (R. Worthington, 1879)

CHATEAUBRIAND

Translations: *Atala* (Tegg & Castleman, 1803); *The Martyrs* (Whiting & Watson, 1811); *The Natchez* (H. Colburn, 1827); *Of Buonaparte* (H. Colburn, 1814); *Portrait of Bonaparte* (Eastburn, Kirk & Co., 1814); *Recollections of Italy, England, and America* (M. Carey, 1816); *Travels in America and Italy* (London, 1828); Bingham, C., *Atala* (S. T. Armstrong, 1814); Harry, J. S., *Atala* (Belford, Clarke & Co., 1886); Shoberl, F., *Travels in Greece, Palestine, Egypt, and Barbary* (Van Winkle & Wiley, 1814); Smead, M. J. and Levebre, H. P., *Atala* (H. G. Langley, 1844); Ward, N., *The Interesting History of Atala* (Oram & M. H., 1818); White, C. I., *The Genius of Christianity* (J. B. Lippincott & Co., 1868); Wright, O. W. (ed.), *The Martyrs* (Derby & Jackson, 1859)

Babbitt, I., *The Masters of Modern French Criticism* (Houghton Mifflin Co., 1912)

Boyle, E., *Biographical Essays* (Oxford University Press, 1936)

Carrère, J., *Degeneration in the Great French Masters* (Brentano's, 1922)

Evans, J., *Chateaubriand* (Macmillan & Co., 1939)

Gambier-Parry, M., *Studies of Childhood and Youth* (Heath Cranton, Ltd., 1925)

Gribble, F. H., *Chateaubriand and His Court of Women* (C. Scribner's Sons, 1909)

Hart, C. R., *Chateaubriand and Homer* (The Johns Hopkins Press, 1928)

Huneker, J., *The Pathos of Distance* (C. Scribner's Sons, 1913)

Lynes, C., *Chateaubriand as a Critic of French Literature* (Oxford University Press, 1946)

Maurois, A., *Chateaubriand* (Harper & Brothers, 1938)

Miller, M. H., *Chateaubriand and English Literature* (The Johns Hopkins Press, 1925)

Naylor, L. H., *Chateaubriand and Virgil* (The Johns Hopkins Press, 1930)

Paléologue, G. M., *The Romantic Diplomat* (Hutchinson & Co., Ltd., 1926)

Prescott, W. H., *Biographical and Critical Miscellanies* (J. B. Lippincott & Co., 1892)

Rudwin, M. J., *Supernaturalism and Satanism in Chateaubriand* (The Open Court Publishing Co., 1922)

Sedgwick, H. D., *Madame Récamier* (Bobbs-Merrill Co., 1940)

Spring, H. P., *Chateaubriand at the Crossways* (Columbia University Press, 1924)

Walker, T. C., *Chateaubriand's Natural Scenery* (Oxford University Press, 1946)

CHÉNIER

Translation: *Love Songs of France* (New Amsterdam Publishing Co., 1896)
Bailey, J. C., *The Claims of French Poetry* (M. Kennerley, 1909)
Morton, J. B., *For Hilaire Belloc* (Sheed & Ward, 1942)

CONDILLAC

Translation: Carr, G., *Treatise on the Sensations* (University of Southern California, 1930)
Schaupp, Z., *The Naturalism of Condillac* (University of Nebraska, 1926)

CONDORCET

Translations: *The Life of Voltaire* (G. G. J. & J. Robinson, 1790); Vickery, A. D., *The First Essay on the Political Rights of Women* (Garden City Press, Ltd., 1912)
Burlingame, A. E., *Condorcet* (The Stratford Co., 1930)
Frazer, Sir J. G., *Condorcet on the Progress of the Human Mind* (Clarendon Press, 1933)
La Fontainerie, F. de, *French Liberalism in the Eighteenth Century* (McGraw-Hill, 1932)
Morley, J. M., *Biographical Studies* (Macmillan & Co., 1923)
Schapiro, J. S., *Condorcet and the Rise of Liberalism* (Harcourt, Brace & Co., 1934), *Essays in Intellectual History* (New York, 1929)

CONSTANT

Translations: *Adolphe* (The Novel Library, 1948); Cameron, N., *Cecile* (New Directions Publications, 1953); Hookham, P., *Adolphe* (A. M. Philpot, 1924); Lippmann, H. B., *Prophecy from the Past* (Reynal & Hitchcock, 1941); Maccall, W., *On the Human Causes Which Have Concurred toward the Establishment of Christianity* (J. Robertson, 185-?); May, J. L., *Adolphe* (S. Paul & Co., Ltd., 19—?); Ripley, G., *Philosophical Miscellanies* (Hilliard, Gray, & Co., 1838)
Bennet, W. H., *Select Biographical Sketches* (G. Routledge & Sons, 1867)
Cecil, Lord D., *Poets and Story-tellers* (Macmillan & Co., 1949)
Schermerhorn, E. W., *Benjamin Constant* (W. Heinemann, Ltd., 1924)
Scott, G., *The Portrait of Zélide* (C. Scribner's Sons, 1927)

DELAVIGNE

Translations: Markwell, W. R., *Louis XI* (P. J. Kenedy & Sons, 1913); Oxenford, J., *The Monastery of St. Just* (T. H. Lacy, 185-?)

DELILLE

Translations: Maunde, J., *The Rural Philosopher* (Franklin & Garrow, 1804); Montolieu, Mrs., *The Gardens* (T. Bensley, 1805)
Drake, N., *Noontide Leisure* (T. Cadell, 1824)

DUMAS, PÈRE

Translations: *The Black Tulip* (Everyman's Library, E. P. Dutton & Co., 1906); *Celebrated Crimes* (Chapman & Hall, 1843); *Celebrated Crimes* (P. F. Collier & Son, 1910); *The Collected Works* (Little, Brown & Co., 1898-99); *The Count of Monte Cristo* (Everyman's Library, E. P. Dutton & Co., 1909); *Marguerite de Valois* (Everyman's Library, E. P. Dutton & Co., 1908); *The Three Musketeers* (Everyman's Library, E. P. Dutton & Co., 1906); *Twenty Years After* (Everyman's Library, E. P. Dutton & Co., 1907); *The Works* (A. L. Burt Co., 1901); *The Works* (P. F. Collier, 1893); Burnham, I. G., *Celebrated Crimes* (H. S. Nichols, 1895); LeClercq, J., *The Three Musketeers* (The Modern Library, Random House, 1928)

Capes, R., *Punchinello* (J. Crowther, 1947)

Castelar y Ripoli, E., *Life of Lord Byron and Other Sketches* (Harper & Brothers, 1876)

Cook, M., *Five French Negro Authors* (Associated Publishers, Inc., 1943)

Davidson, A. F., *A. Dumas Père; His Life and Works* (J. B. Lippincott & Co., 1902)

Fitzgerald, P., *Famous French Authors* (R. Worthington, 1879)

Fitzgerald, P. H., *Life and Adventures of Alexander Dumas* (Tinsley Bros., 1873)

Gorman, H. S., *The Incredible Marquis* (Farrar & Rinehart, Inc., 1929)

Gribble, F. H., *Dumas, Father and Son* (E. P. Dutton & Co., 1930)

Grierson, F., *Parisian Portraits* (J. Lane, 1913)

Lang, A., *Essays in Little* (C. Scribner's Sons, 1891)

Lucas-Dubreton, J., *The Fourth Musketeer* (Coward-McCann, Inc., 1928)

Saintsbury, G. E. B., *Essays in English Literature, 1780-1860, Second Series* (C. Scribner's Sons, 1895)

Spurr, H. A., *The Life and Writings of Alexandre Dumas* (Fred A. Stokes Co., 1902)

Todd, R., *The Laughing Mulatto* (Rich & Cowan, Ltd., 1940)

GAUTIER

Translations: *The Evil Eye* (W. B. Conkley Co., 1893); *Famous French Authors* (R. Worthington, 1879); *Love Songs of France* (New Amsterdam Book Co., 1896); *Mademoiselle de Maupin* (A. A. Knopf, 1920); *Mademoiselle de Maupin and One of Cleopatra's Nights* (The Modern Library, Random House, 1921); *Spirite* (D. Appleton & Co., 1877); Arrington, L., *Four Destinies* (Worthington Co., 1892); Beaumont, C. W., *The Ballet Called Giselle* (C. W. Beaumont, 1914), *The Romantic Ballet* (C. W. Beaumont, 1932); Berthon, H. E. (ed.), *Nine French Poets* (Macmillan & Co., Ltd., 1930); Bessie, A., *Mademoiselle de Maupin* (C. Kendall, 1930); Bierstadt, O. A., *The Sign Board* (Rand, McNally & Co., 1891);

Gould, R. H., *Constantinople* (H. Holt & Co., 1875); Hall, A. D., *Spirite* (Rand, McNally & Co., 1890); Hearn, L., *One of Cleopatra's Nights* (R. Worthington, 1882); Ives, G. B., *Theophile Gautier's Short Stories* (G. P. Putnam's Sons, 1909); L—, M. de, *Three Romances* (Brentano's, 1888); Loranger, A., *Fortunio* (L. Lipkind, 1890); Mathers, R. and E. P., *Mademoiselle de Maupin* (Golden Cockerel Press, 1938); Monkshood, G. F., *Captain Fracasse* (Brentano's, 1910); Phillips, A., *A Romantic in Spain* (A. A. Knopf, 1926); Ripley, M. M., *A Winter in Russia* (H. Holt & Co., 1874); Thorne, G., *Charles Baudelaire* (Greening & Co., 1915); Tyson, F. Mac I., *Russia* (The J. C. Winston Co., 1905); Verelst, M., *Tales before Supper* (Brentano's, 1887); Wright, A. Mc C., *The Romance of a Mummy* (J. B. Lippincott, 1882); Young, M., *The Romance of a Mummy* (J. & R. Maxwell, 1886)

Dillingham, L. B., *The Creative Imagination of Théophile Gautier* (Psychological Review Co., 1927)

Dowden, E., *Studies in Literature, 1789-1877* (K. Paul, Trench & Co., 1902)

Huneker, J., *The Pathos of Distance* (C. Scribner's Sons, 1913)

Palache, J. G., *Gautier and the Romantics* (The Viking Press, 1926)

Vincent, L. H., *The Bibliotaph* (Houghton, Mifflin & Co., 1899)

GÉRARD DE NERVAL

Translations: Aldington, R., *Aurelia* (Chatto & Windus, 1932); Elphinstone, C., *The Women of Cairo* (G. Routledge & Sons, 1929); Gunsbourg, R., *The Damnation of Faust* (F. Rullman, 1906); Halévy, L. (ed.), *Sylvie* (G. Routledge & Sons, 1887); Holland, V., *Dreams and Life* (The First Editions Club, 1933); O'Sullivan, S., *Nicolas Flamel* (Dublin Magazine, 1924); Page, L., *Sylvie* (T. B. Mosher, 1896)

Mutridge, A., *Critical Ventures in Modern French Literature* (C. Scribner's Sons, 1924)

HELVÉTIUS

Translations: *De l'Esprit* (J. M. Richardson, 1809); Hooper, W., *A Treatise on Man* (J. Cundee, 1810)

Bradlaugh, C. (ed.), *Biographies of Ancient and Modern Celebrated Freethinkers* (J. P. Mendum, 1871)

Grossman, M., *The Philosophy of Helvétius* (Columbia University Press, 1926)

Hazlitt, W., *Essays on the Principles of Human Action* (J. Miller, 1835)

Plekhanov, G. V., *Essays in the History of Materialism* (J. Lane, 1934)

Tallentyre, S. G., *The Friends of Voltaire* (Smith, Elder & Co., 1906)

HOLBACH

Translations: *Common Sense* (Isaiah Thomas, 1795); *Good Sense* (R. Carlile, 1826); *A Letter from Thrasybulus* (R. Carlile, 1826); Kroop, A., *Superstition in All Ages* (P. Eckler, 1890); Mirabaud, M., *The System of Nature* (G. Kearsley, 1797); Robinson, H. D., *Good Sense* (G. Vale, 1850), *The System of Nature* (G. W. & A. J. Matsell, 1835)

Bradlaugh, C., *Biographies of Ancient and Modern Celebrated Freethinkers* (J. P. Mendum, 1871)

Cushing, M. P., *Baron d'Holbach* (Columbia University Press, 1914)

Plekhanov, G. V., *Essays in the History of Materialism* (J. Lane, 1934)

Tallentyre, S. G., *The Friends of Voltaire* (Smith, Elder & Co., 1906)

Wickwar, W. H., *Baron d'Holbach* (G. Allen & Unwin, Ltd., 1935)

HUGO

Translations: *The Battle of Waterloo* (J. Bradburn, 1863); *Bug-Jargal* (Athenaeum Society, 1894); *By Order of the King* (A. L. Burt Co., 190-?); *Cosette* (Little, Brown & Co., 1887); *The Destroyer of the Second Republic* (Sheldon & Co., 1870); *Dramas* (University Press Co., 18—?); *Dramatic Works* (Athenaeum Society, 1909); *Hans of Iceland* (Athenaeum Society, 1894); *Hans of Iceland* (J. Robins & Co., 1825); *Hernani* (Chickering & Sons, 1881); *The History of a Crime* (Athenaeum Society, 1909); *The Hunchback* (DeWitt & Davenport, 1848); *The Idyll and the Epic* (Little, Brown & Co., 1887); *The Laughing Man* (T. Nelson & Sons, 1920); *Les Miserables* (G. Munro, 1878); *Love Songs of France* (New Amsterdam Book Co., 1896); *Lucretia Borgia* (Metropolitan Print, 1875); *The Man Who Laughs* (University Press Co., 1869); *Marius* (Little, Brown & Co., 1887); *Napoleon the Little* (Vizetelly & Co., 1852); *Notre Dame de Paris* (University Press Co., 1831; Everyman's Library, E. P. Dutton & Co., 1910); *Notre-Dame* (G. Routledge & Sons, 188-?); *The Novels Complete* (G. Barrie & Son, 1892-94); *The Novels* (P. F. Collier & Son, 1877-1901); *The Novels and Poems* (E. R. Dumont, 1887-96); *The Poems* (Athenaeum Society, 1909); *The Romances of Victor Hugo* (G. D. Sproul, 1896); *Ruy Blas* (W. Winter, 1876); *Sketches and Legends of the Rhine* (Cornish, Lamport & Co., 1845); *The Toilers of the Sea* (Harper & Brothers, 1866); *Victor Hugo's Letter on John Brown* (J. P. Beadle & Co., 1860); *The Works* (W. J. Black, Inc., 1928); *Works* (Estes & Lauriat, 191-?); Aird, D., *The Rhine* (D. Aird, 1843); Alger, A. L., *Notre-Dame de Paris* (Estes & Lauriat, 1888); Anderson, M. B., *Wm. Shakespeare* (A. A. McClurg & Co., 1887); Artois, M. W., *The Toilers of the Sea* (G. Barrie, 1892); Baillot, A., *Wm. Shake-*

speare (Hurst & Blackett, 1864); Benedict, F. L., *Ninety-Three* (Harper & Brothers, 1874); Berthon, H. E. (ed.), *Nine French Poets* (Macmillan & Co., Ltd., 1930); Blair, E. T. and E., *Amy Robsart* (The Christopher Publishing House, 1933); Burleigh, G. S., *The Legend of the Centuries* (Privately Printed, 1874); Byrne, C. A., *Angelo* (F. Rullman, 1905); C. R., *Angelo* (H. Lacy, 185-?); Davidson, G. H., *Angelo* (G. H. Davidson, 1855); Davidson, J., *A Queen's Romance* (G. Richards, 1904); Davidson, Lady T., *The Love Letters of Juliette Drouet* (McBride, Nast & Co., 1914); Delano, Mrs. A., *Ninety-Three* (Athenaeum Society, 1888); Denby, E. H., *Ecce! France* (Coq D'Or Press, 1942); Dole, H. B., *Ninety-Three* (T. Y. Crowell & Co., 1888); Dole, N. H., *Victor Hugo's Letters to His Wife and Others* (Estes & Lauriat, 1895); Dowden, E., and Others, *The Literary Life and Poetical Works* (Hurst & Co., 1883); Felix, M. R., *Angelo* (Darcie & Corbyn, 1855); Fetridge, F., *The History of a Crime* (Harper & Brothers, 1878); Fitzball, E., *Esmeralda* (S. French, 186-?); Fleetwood, Sir P. H., *The Last Days of a Condemned* (Smith, Elder, & Co., 1840); Halliday, A., *Notre Dame* (R. M. de Witt, n.d.); Hapgood, I. F., *Les Misérables* (T. Y. Crowell & Co., 1887), *Notre-Dame de Paris* (T. Y. Crowell & Co., 1888), *The Toilers of the Sea* (T. Y. Crowell & Co., 1888); Harding, J. W., *The Memoirs* (G. W. Dillingham Co., 1899); Haynes, J., *Notre Dame de Paris* (P. F. Collier & Son, 1902); Hooker, B., *Ruy Blas* (H. Holt & Co., 1931); Ives, G. B., *Napoleon the Little* (Athenaeum Society, 1909); Kenny, J., *Hernani* (T. H. Lacy, 183-?); Latimer, E. W., *The Love Letters of Victor Hugo* (Harper & Brothers, 1901); Lazarus, E., *Poems and Translations* (Privately Printed, 1886); Lyster, F., *Ruy Blas* (F. Rullman, 1894); Manson, J., *The Alps and Pyrenees* (Bliss, Sands & Co., 1898); Meurice, P. (ed.), *The Letters of Victor Hugo from Exile* (Houghton, Mifflin & Co., 1898), *The Letters of Victor Hugo to His Family* (Houghton, Mifflin & Co., 1896); O'Rourke, L., *Victor Hugo's Intellectual Autobiography* (Funk & Wagnalls Co., 1907); Parton, J., *Victor Hugo's Oration on Voltaire* (Private-Printed, 1899); Phillips, B., *The Laughing Man* (G. H. Richmond & Co., 1894); Shoberl, F., *The Hunchback of Notre Dame* (R. Bentley, 1849); Slous, F. L. and Crosland, Mrs. N., *Dramatic Works* (P. F. Collier, 1887); Weston, J. M., *Lucretia Borgia* (J. French & Son, 1855); Wilbour, C. E., *The Hunchback of Notre Dame* (The Modern Library, Random House, 1941), *Jargal* (Carleton, 1866), *Les Misérables* (Carleton, 1862; Everyman's Library, E. P. Dutton & Co., 1909; The Modern Library, Random House, 1931); Wraxall, L., *Les Misérables* (W. I. Pooley & Co., 18—?; G. Routledge & Sons, 188-?; Little, Brown & Co., 1887; Heritage Press, 1938); Young, Sir G., *Poems from Victor*

Hugo (Macmillan & Co., Ltd., 1901); Young, W., *The Man Who Laughs* (D. Appleton & Co., 1869)

Amicis, E. de, *Studies of Paris* (G. P. Putnam's Sons, 1879)

Bailey, J. C., *The Claims of French Poetry* (M. Kennerley, 1909)

Barbow, A., *Victor Hugo* (S. C. Griggs & Co., 1881), *Victor Hugo and His Time* (Harper & Brothers, 1882)

Baring, M., *Goethe and Victor Hugo* (The Tucker Publishing Co., 1900)

Boyle, E., *Biographical Essays (1790-1890)* (Oxford University Press, 1936)

Bruner, J. D., *Studies in Victor Hugo's Dramatic Characters* (Ginn & Co., 1908)

Caldwell, S. B., *Gospels of Courage* (The Roycrofters, 1936)

Daudet, L., *Cloudy Trophy* (W. Morrow & Co., 1938)

Dowden, E., *Studies in Literature, 1789-1877* (K. Paul, Trench & Co., 1902)

Duclaux, A. M. F., *Victor Hugo* (Constable & Co., Ltd., 1921)

Escholier, R., *Victor Hugo* (Payson & Clarke, Ltd., 1930)

Giese, W. F., *Victor Hugo* (The Dial Press, 1926)

Gladden, W., *Witnesses of the Light* (Houghton, Mifflin & Co., 1903)

Grant, E. M., *The Career of Victor Hugo* (Harvard University Press, 1945), *Victor Hugo during the Second Republic* (Smith College Publications, 1935)

Haggard, A. C. P., *Victor Hugo* (Hutchinson & Co., 1923)

Harper, G. McL., *John Morley and Other Essays* (Princeton University Press, 1920)

Hillis, N. D., *Great Books as Life-Teachers* (F. H. Revell Co., 1899)

Hooker, K. W., *The Fortunes of Victor Hugo in England* (Columbia University Press, 1938)

Hugo, A., *Victor Hugo* (Carleton, 1863)

Josephson, M., *Victor Hugo* (Doubleday, Doran & Co., 1942)

Kohnt, G. A., *Victor Hugo and the Jews* (Cameron Co., 1902)

Latrobe, J. H. B., *Colonization* (J. D. Tory, 1851)

Marzials, F. T., *Life of Victor Hugo* (W. Scott, 1888)

Mirecourt, E. de, *Famous French Authors* (R. Worthington, 1879)

Morley, J., *Biographical Studies* (Macmillan & Co., Ltd., 1923)

Noel, R. B. W., *Essays on Poetry and Poets* (K. Paul, Trench & Co., 1886)

O'Connor, M. D., *A Study of the Sources of Han D'Islande* (The Catholic University of America Press, 1942)

Pendell, W. D., *Victor Hugo's Acted Dramas* (The Johns Hopkins Press, 1947)

Stevenson, R. L., *Familiar Studies of Men and Books* (C. Scribner's Sons, 1902)

Swinburne, A. C., *Studies in Prose and Poetry* (Chatto & Windus, 1894),
  A Study of Victor Hugo (Chatto & Windus, 1886)
Towle, G. M., *Certain Men of Mark* (Roberts Bros., 1880)
Wack, H. W., *The Romance of Victor Hugo and Juliette Drouet* (G. P.
  Putnam's Sons, 1905)

LAMARTINE

Translations: *Biographies and Portraits of Some Celebrated People*
  (Tinsley Bros., 1866); *Heroic Characters of the Revolution* (H. G.
  Clarke & Co., 1848); *History of Turkey* (D. Appleton & Co.,
  1855-7); *Lamartine on Atheism* (Phillips, Sampson & Co., 1850);
  The Life and Times of Christopher Columbus (E. & G. Goldsmid,
  1887); *The Life and Voyages of Christopher Columbus* (P. O'Shea,
  1870); *Life of Mary, Queen of Scots* (Sheldon & Co., 1860); *Life
  of Oliver Cromwell* (Delisser & Procter, 1859); *Love Songs of
  France* (New Amsterdam Book Co., 1896); *Memoirs of Celebrated
  Characters* (Harper & Brothers, 1854); *Memoirs of My Youth*
  (Harper & Brothers, 1849); *The Past, Present, and Future of the
  Republic* (Harper & Brothers, 1850); *Pictures of the First French
  Revolution* (Simms & McIntyre, 1850); *A Pilgrimage to the Holy
  Land* (Carey, Lea, & Blanchard, 1838); *Raphael* (A. C. McClurg
  & Co,. 1890); *The Stone-Mason of St. Point* (Harper & Brothers,
  1873); *Travels in the East* (W. & R. Chambers, 1839); *The Wan-
  derer and His Home* (Simms & McIntyre, 1851); Anstruther, R.,
  Jocelyn (London, 1844); Bromwell, H. P. H., *The Dying Poet*
  (H. E. Bromwell, 1918); Durivage, F. A. and Chase, W. S., *History
  of the French Revolution of 1848* (Phillips, Sampson & Co., 1849);
  Grinke, S. M., *Joan of Arc* (Adams & Co., 1867); Helper, M. L.,
  My Mother's Manuscript (Philadelphia, 1877); Lamartine, A., *The
  History of the Restoration of Monarchy in France* (Harper &
  Brothers, 1851-3), *Narrative of the Residence of Fatalla Sayeghir*
  (Carey, Lea, 1836); Ousely, C., *England in 1850* (W. C. Bryant &
  Co., 1851); Ryde, H. T., *History of the Girondists* (H. G. Bohn,
  1847-8); Robinson, F., *Genevieve* (Stringer & Townsend, 1850);
  Scoble, A. R., *Genevieve* (Harper & Brothers, 1852)
Berthon, H. E. (ed.), *Nine French Poets* (Macmillan & Co., Ltd., 1930)
Cormenin, de, *The Polity of Reason* (H. G. Clarke & Co., 1848)
Duclaux, A. M. F., *The French Ideal* (Chapman & Hall, Ltd., 1911)
Gambier-Parry, M., *Studies of Childhood* (Heath Cranton, Ltd., 1925)
Gautier, T., *Famous French Authors* (R. Worthington, 1879)
George, A. J., *Lamartine and Romantic Unanimism* (Columbia Univer-
  sity Press, 1940)
Grierson, F., *Parisian Portraits* (J. Lane, 1913)

Lacretelle, H. de, *Lamartine and His Friends* (G. P. Putnam's Sons, 1880)

Mérimée, P., *Letters to an Incognita* (Scribner, Armstrong & Co., 1874)

Pirazzini, A., *The Influence of Italy on the Literary Career of Alphonse de Lamartine* (Columbia University Press, 1917)

Schmidt, I., *The Life and Writings of Alphonse de Lamartine* (G. Davidson, 1853)

Whitehouse, H. R., *The Life of Lamartine* (Houghton Mifflin Co., 1918)

LA METTRIE

Translation: *Man a Machine* (W. Owen, 1749)

Luzac, E., *Man More than a Machine* (W. Owen, 1752)

LEOPARDI

Translations: Bickersteth, G. L., *The Poems* (Cambridge University Press, 1923); Edwardes, C., *Essays and Dialogues* (Trübner & Co., 1882); Heath-Stubbs, J., *Poems* (J. Lehmann, 1946); Maxwell, P., *Essays, Dialogues, and Thoughts* (W. Scott, 1893); Morrison, J. M., *The Poems* (Gay & Bird, 1900); Smith, W. F., *Masterpieces of Giacomo Leopardi* (Geo. Banta Publishing Co., 1939); Trevelyan, C., *Translations from Leopardi* (Cambridge University Press, 1941)

Bickersteth, G. L., *Leopardi and Wordsworth* (British Academy, 1927)

Dege, F., *Life and Leopardi* (E. MacDonald, Ltd., 1920)

Origo, I., *Leopardi* (Oxford University Press, 1935)

Robb, N. A., *Four in Exile* (Hutchinson, 1948)

Van Horne, J., *Studies on Leopardi* (University of Iowa, 1916)

MAISTRE, JOSEPH DE

Translations: *Essay on the Generative Principle of Political Constitutions* (Little & Brown, 1847); O'Flaherty, T. J., *Letters on the Spanish Inquisition* (W. Smith, 1830); Salter, R. H., *The Divine Origin of Government* (J. D. Lockwood, 1850)

Caponigri, A. R., *Some Aspects of the Philosophy of Joseph de Maistre* (University of Chicago, 1945)

Maccall, W., *Foreign Biographies* (Wm. Maccall, 1873)

Mary Alphonsus, Mother, *The Influence of Joseph de Maistre on Beaudelaire* (Bryn Mawr, 1943)

Morley, J., *Biographical Studies* (Macmillan & Co., Ltd., 1923), *Critical Miscellanies* (Chapman & Hall, 1871-77)

MAISTRE, XAVIER DE

Translations: *Prasca Loupouloff* (J. Burns, 1845); Goldsmid, E., *A Journey Round My Room* (Goldsmid, 1885); H. A., *A Journey Round My Room* (Hurd & Houghton, 1871); J. A. S., *The Leper of Aoste* (Valpey, Angel & Co., 1873); Outhwaite, Mrs. D., *A Journey Round My Room* (W. Smith, 18—?); Wallenstein, J., *The Leper of Aosta* (Cummings, Hilliard & Co., 1825)

MANZONI

Translations: *The Betrothed* (Burns, Bates & Co., 1867); *I Promessi Sposi* (J. Burns, 1844; G. Bell & Sons, 1883); *A Vindication of Catholic Morality* (Keating & Brown, 1836)

Tuckerman, H. T., *Characteristics of Literature* (Lindsay & Blakiston, 1851)

Wall, B., *Manzoni* (Bowes, 1953)

MUSSET

Translations: *Barberine and Other Comedies* (C. H. Sergel & Co., 1892); *The Beauty-Spot* (Brentano's, 1888); *A Good Little Wife* (T. H. Lacy, 18—?); *Love Songs of France* (New Amsterdam Book Co., 1896); Baring, M., *Fantasio* (The Pleiad, 1929); Clark, B. H., *The Green Coat* (S. French, 1915); Clarke, M. A. and Others, *The Complete Writings of Alfred de Musset* (E. C. Hill Co., 1905); Gwynn, S. L., *Comedies* (W. Scott, 1890); Vermont, E. de V., *Three Novelettes* (Brentano's, 1888); W. P. C., *All is Fair in Love and War* (Sampson, 1868); Wagstaff, B. S., *Atys* (M. Kinnerley, 1909); Wirt, A. G., *A Caprice* (Poet Lore, 1922)

Berthon, H. E. (ed.), *Nine French Poets* (Macmillan & Co., Ltd., 1930)

Besant, Sir W., *Essays and Historiettes* (Chatto & Windus, 1903)

Carrère, J., *Degeneration in the Great French Masters* (Brentano's, 1922)

Hetzel, P. J., *Public and Private Life of Animals* (S. Low, Marston, Searle & Rivington, 1887)

Musset, P. de, *Famous French Authors* (R. Worthington, 1879)

Sedgwick, H. D., *Alfred de Musset* (The Bobbs-Merrill Co., 1931)

Swinburne, A. C., *Miscellanies* (Chatto & Windus, 1886)

Tilley, A. A., *Three French Dramatists* (Cambridge University Press, 1933)

Vincens, C., *The Life of Alfred de Musset* (E. C. Hill Co., 1906)

Winwar, F., *The Life of the Heart* (Harper & Brothers, 1945)

NODIER

Translations: *Bean Flower and Pea Blossom* (D. Appleton & Co., 1952); *Genius Goodfellow* (D. Appleton & Co., 1852); *History of the Secret Societies of the Army* (Longman & Co., 1815); *The Luck of the Bean-Rows* (D. O'Connor, 1921); Dole, N. H., *Trilby* (Estes & Lauriat, 1895); Fraser, C. L., *The Woodcutter's Dog* (D. O'Connor, 1921); Percival, G., *Giovanni Sbogarro* (C. S., Van Winkle, 1870); Koch, T. W., *Francesco Colonna* (Privately Printed, 1929); Smith,

M. C., *Trilby* (Lamson, Wolffe & Co., 1895); Wright, M. O., *The Bibliomaniac* (J. O. Wright & Co., 1894)

QUESNAY

Translations: *The OEconomical Table* (W. Owen, 1766); Maverick, L. A., *China, a Model for Europe* (Paul Anderson Co., 1946); McCulloch, J. R., *Treatises and Essays* (A. & C. Black, 1859)

RACINE, LOUIS

Translation: John, K., *Life of Milton* (L. & V. Woolf, 1930)

ROUSSEAU, JEAN-BAPTISTE

Translation: Miller, J., *The Coffee-House* (J. Watts, 1737)
Grubbs, H. A., *Jean-Baptiste Rousseau* (Oxford University Press, 1941)

ROUSSEAU, JEAN JACQUES

Translations: *A Concise and Genuine Account of the Dispute between Mr. Hume and R—* (T. Becket, 1766); *The Confessions* (J. Bew, 1783; A. W. Lovering, 190-?; Aldus Society, 1903; Everyman's Library, E. P. Dutton & Co., 1931; The Modern Library, Random House, 1946); *A Discourse [on the Arts and Sciences]* (G. Burnet, 1760); *A Discourse on the Origin and Foundation of the Inequalities among Mankind* (London, 1761); *A Dissertation on Political Economy* (Barber & Southwick, 1797); *Eloisa* (London, 1784; J. Harding, Longman, Hurst, Reese & Orme, 1810); *Julia; or the New Eloisa* (J. Bell, J. Dickson, & C. Elliot, 1773); *A Letter to M. d'Alembert on Theatrical Entertainments* (J. Nourse, 1759); *Origin of Inequality on Political Economy* (The Great Books Foundation, 1949); *Original Correspondence* (J. Johnson, 1804); *Original Letters* (D. Symonds, 1799); *A Treatise on the Social Contract* (T. Becket, 1764); Akerley, J. (ed.), *Voltaire and Rousseau against the Atheists* (Wiley & Putnam, 1845); Barker, Sir E. (ed.), *Social Contract* (Oxford University Press, 1947); Bell, R. (ed.), *Illuminations for Legislators* (Robert Bell, 1784); Burney, C., *The Cunning Man* (T. Becket & P. A. de Hondt, 1766); Cohn, J. M., *Confessions* (Penguin Books, Inc., 1953); Cole, G. D. H., *The Social Contract and Discourses* (Everyman's Library, E. P. Dutton & Co., 1913); Feltenstein, R., *Emile*, Vol. I. (Barron's Educational Series, Inc., 1950); Fletcher, J. G., *The Reveries of a Solitary* (G. Routledge & Sons, Ltd., 1927); Foxley, B., *Emile* (J. M. Dent & Sons, 1933), *Emile, or Education* (Everyman's Library, E. P. Dutton & Co., 1911); Freese, J. H., *Memoirs and Correspondence of Mme d'Épinay* (H. S. Nichols, Ltd., 1889); Glover, A. J. B., *The Confessions* (The Nonesuch Press, 1938); Harrington, R. M., *The Social Contract*

(G. P. Putnam's Sons, 1906); Hendel, C. W. (ed.), *Citizens of Geneva* (Oxford University Press, 1937); Hopkins, G., *The Social Contract* (World's Classics, Oxford University Press, 1947); Martyn, T., *Letters on the Elements of Botany* (B. & J. White, 1796); Nugent, Mr., *Emilius* (J. Nourse & P. Vaillant, 1763); Payne, W. H., *Emile* (D. Appleton & Co., 1887); Schreiner, O., *Profession of Faith of a Savoyard Vicar* (P. Eckler, 1889); Tozer, H. J., *The Social Contract* (G. Allen & Unwin, Ltd., 1924); Vaughan, C. E., *The Political Writings* (Cambridge University Press, 1915); Vaughan, C. F., *A Lasting Peace* (Constable & Co., Ltd., 1917); Waring, W., *A Dictionary of Music* (J. French, 177-?); Worthington, E., *Emile* (D. C. Heath & Co., 1886)

Amiel, H. F., *Jean Jacques Rousseau* (Van W. Brooks, tr.) (B. W. Huebsch, 1922)

Babbitt, I., *Rousseau and Romanticism* (Houghton Mifflin Co., 1919), *Spanish Character and Other Essays* (Houghton Mifflin Co., 1940)

Boyd, W., *The Educational Theory of Jean Jacques Rousseau* (Longmans, Green & Co., 1911)

Brougham, H. P., *Lives of Men of Letters* (Carey & Hart, 1845)

Buchner, M. L., *A Contribution to the Study of the Descriptive Technique of Jean Jacques Rousseau* (The Johns Hopkins Press, 1937)

Carlyle, T., *On Heroes and Hero-Worship* (Wiley & Putnam, 1846)

Carrère, J., *Degeneration in the Great French Masters* (Brentano's, 1922)

Cassirer, E., *Rousseau, Kant, Goethe* (Princeton University Press, 1945)

Charpentier, J., *Rousseau* (L. MacVeagh, 1931)

Cobban, A. B. C., *Rousseau and the Modern State* (G. Allen & Unwin, Ltd., 1934)

Collins, J. C., *Voltaire, Montesquieu & Rousseau in England* (E. Nash, 1908)

Davidson, T., *Rousseau and Education* (C. Scribner's Sons, 1898)

Ellis, M., *Julie* (University of Toronto Press, 1949)

Fisher, H. A. L., *Studies in History and Politics* (Oxford University Press, 1920)

Fuseli, H., *Remarks on the Writings and Conduct of J. J. Rousseau* (T. Cadell, 1767)

Graham, H. G., *Rousseau* (J. B. Lippincott & Co., 1883)

Gran, G. von der L., *J. J. Rousseau* (W. Blackwood & Sons, 1912)

Green, F. C., *Rousseau and the Idea of Progress* (Clarendon Press, 1950)

Greene, E. B., *A Defence of Mr. Rousseau* (S. Bladon, 1766)

Gribble, F. H., *Rousseau and the Women He Loved* (C. Scribner's Sons, 1908)

Hendel, C. W., *J. J. Rousseau, Moralist* (Oxford University Press, 1934)

Höffding, H., *J. J. Rousseau and His Philosophy* (Yale University Press, 1930)

Josephson, M., *J. J. Rousseau* (Harcourt, Brace & Co., 1931)

Lemaître, J., *J. J. Rousseau* (The McClure Co., 1907)

Lowell, J. R., *The English Poets* (W. Scott, 1888)

Macdonald, Mrs. F., *J. J. Rousseau, a New Criticism* (G. P. Putnam's Sons, 1906), *Studies in the France of Voltaire and Rousseau* (T. Fisher Unwin, 1895)

Macmurray, J. (ed.), *Some Makers of the Modern Spirit* (Methuen & Co., 1933)

Maritain, J., *Three Reformers* (Sheed & Ward, 1929)

Maurois, A., *Seven Faces of Love* (Didier, 1944)

Morley, J., *Rousseau* (Macmillan & Co., 1886)

Murry, J. M., *Heaven—and Earth* (J. Cape, 1938), *Heroes of Thought* (J. Messner, Inc., 1938)

Neil, T. P., *Makers of the Modern Mind* (Bruce Publishing Co., 1949)

Osborn, A. M., *Rousseau and Burke* (Oxford University Press, 1940)

Sarafian, K. A., *French Educational Theorists* (University of Southern California, 1933)

Sells, A. L., *The Early Life and Adventures of J. J. Rousseau* (W. Heffer & Sons, Ltd., 1929)

Strachey, L., *Books and Characters* (Harcourt, Brace & Co., 1922)

Texte, J., *J. J. Rousseau and the Cosmopolitan Spirit in Literature* (Duckworth & Co., 1899)

Vulliamy, C. E., *Rousseau* (G. Bles, 1931)

Walpole, H., *Reminiscences* (J. Sharpe, 1819)

Williams, A. T., *The Concept of Equality in the Writings of Rousseau, Bentham, and Kant* (Columbia University, 1907)

Wright, E. H., *The Meaning of Rousseau* (Oxford University Press, 1929)

SAINT-PIERRE

Translations: *The History of the Adventures, Love, and Constancy, of Paul and Virginia* (J. B. Moore, 1824); Anderson, M. B., *Paul and Virginia* (A. C. McClurg & Co., 1894); Bell, C., *Paul and Virginia* (W. S. Gottsberger, 1888); Clarke, E., *The Works* (H. G. Bohn, 1846); Cobb, J., *Paul and Virginia* (J. Cumberland, 1828); Hunter, H., *Botanical Harmony Delineated* (J. Nancrede, 1797), *Paul and Virginia* (E. Goodale, 1799), *Studies of Nature* (J. Nancrede, 1797), *A Vindication of Divine Providence* (J. Nancrede, 1797); Kendall, E. A., *The Beauties of Saint Pierre* (Vernor & Hood, 1799); M. M., *Voyages of Amasis* (I. Thomas & E. T. Andrews, 1795); Malthus, D., *Paul and Mary* [sic] (J. Dodsley, 1789); Parish, J., *A Voyage to the Island of Mauritius* (W. Griffin, 1775); Rede, L. T., *Studies of Nature* (T. Lovewell, 1803); Shoberl, F., *The Works* (J. Cundee,

1807); Williams, H. M., *Paul and Virginia* (Longman, Hurst, Rees, Orme, & Brown, 1814)

Vincens, C., *Bernardin de St. Pierre* (A. C. McClurg & Co., 1893)

Ware, J. N., *The Vocabulary of Bernardin de St. Pierre* (The Johns Hopkins Press, 1927)

SAINTE-BEUVE

Translations: *English Portraits* (H. Holt & Co., 1875); *Famous French Authors: Gautier* (R. Worthington, 1879); Benthon, H. E., (ed.), *Nine French Poets* (Macmillan & Co., Ltd., 1930); Lee, E., *Essays* (W. Scott, 1892); Maceuen, M., *Celebrities of the Past and Present* (Porter & Coates, 1874); Mathews, W., *Monday-Chats* (S. C. Griggs & Co., 1882); Preston, H. W., *Memoirs of Mme Desbordes-Valmore* (Roberts Bros., 1873), *Portraits of Celebrated Women* (Roberts Bros., 1868); Sharp, W., *Portraits of Men* (A. C. McClurg & Co., 1891); Trechmann, E. J., *Causeries du Lundi* (World's Classics, Oxford University Press, 1933); Wormely, K. P., *Illustrious Dames of the Court of the Valois Kings* (Lamb Publishing Co., 1912), *Portraits of the Eighteenth Century* (G. P. Putnam's Sons, 1905), *Portraits of the Seventeenth Century* (G. P. Putnam's Sons, 1904)

Babbitt, I., *The Masters of Modern French Criticism* (Houghton Mifflin Co., 1912)

Birrell, A., *Res Judicatae* (C. Scribner's Sons, 1892)

Faguet, E., *Politicians and Moralists of the Nineteenth Century* (E. Benn, Ltd., 1928)

Giese, W. F., *Sainte-Beuve* (University of Wisconsin Press, 1931)

Harper, G. McL., *Charles-Augustin Sainte-Beuve* (J. B. Lippincott Co., 1909)

MacClintock, L., *Sainte-Beuve's Critical Theory* (University of Chicago Press, 1920)

Mirecourt, E. de, *Famous French Authors* (R. Worthington, 1879)

Mott, L. F., *Sainte-Beuve* (D. Appleton & Co., 1925)

Pollak, G., *International Minds* (The Nation Press, 1919), *International Perspective in Criticism* (Dodd, Mead & Co., 1914)

Whitridge, A., *Critical Ventures in Modern French Literature* (C. Scribner's Sons, 1924)

SENACOUR

Translations: Frothingham, J. P., *Obermann* (The Riverside Press, 1901); Waite, A. E., *Obermann* (Brentano's, 1903)

Brooks, Van W., *The Malady of the Ideal* (A. C. Fifield, 1913)

Jones, P. M., *French Introspectives* (Cambridge University Press, 1937)

SOUMET

Translations: *The Gladiator* (J. J. Little & Co., 1883); *Jeanne d'Arc* (Darcie & Corbyn, 1855)

STAËL, MME DE

Translations: *Considerations on the Principal Events of the French Revolution* (J. Eastburn & Co., 1818); *Corinna* (Longworth, Sargeant, and M. & W. Ward, 1808); *Germany* (J. Murray, 1813); *The Influence of Literature upon Society* (S. Andrus & Son, 1844); *Memoirs of the Private Life of My Father* (H. Colburn, 1818); *Napoleon Bonaparte* (New School for Social Research, 1934); *Ten Years' Exile* (Collins & Co., 1821); Hill, I., *Corinne* (H. C. Baird, 1854); L. E. L., *Corinne* (H. G. Langley, 1844); Wright, O. W., *Germany* (Houghton, Mifflin & Co., 1882)

Blennerhassett, C. J., *Mme de Staël* (Chapman & Hall, 1889)

Boelte, A., *Mme de Staël* (G. P. Putnam & Son, 1869)

Brooks, G., *Dames and Daughters of the French Court* (T. F. Unwin, 1905)

Chapman, E. R., *A Comtist Lover* (T. F. Unwin, 1886)

Child, L. M., *The Biographies of Mme de Staël and Mme Roland* (Carter & Hendee, 1832)

Clarke, I. C., *Six Portraits* (Hutchinson & Co., Ltd., 1935)

Dark, S., *Twelve More Ladies* (Hodder & Stoughton, Ltd., 1932)

Duffy, B., *Mme de Staël* (Roberts Bros., 1887)

Goldsmith, M. L., *Mme de Staël* (Longmans, Green & Co., 1938)

Gribble, F. H., *Mme de Staël and Her Lovers* (Eveleigh Nash, 1907)

Haggard, A. C. P., *Mme de Staël* (Hutchinson & Co., 1922)

Hawkins, R. L., *Mme de Staël and the United States* (Harvard University Press, 1930)

Jaeck, E. G., *Mme de Staël and the Spread of German Literature* (Oxford University Press, 1915)

McKay, R. E., *The Influence of Rousseau on Mme de Staël* (University of Chicago, 1909)

Pope-Hennessy, N., *Secret Societies and the French Revolution* (John Lane Co., 1911)

Ravenel, F., *Women and the French Tradition* (Macmillan & Co., 1918)

Rich, H., *Mme de Staël* (Stone & Kimball, 1895)

Roux, A. A., *Louise Necker* (Bérard & Mondon, 1858)

Sorel, A., *Mme de Staël* (A. C. McClurg & Co., 1891)

Stevens, A., *Mme de Staël* (J. Murray, 1881)

Tallentyre, S. G., *The Women of the Salons* (G. P. Putnam's Sons, 1926)

Watson, P. B., *Some Women of France* (Coward-McCann, Inc., 1936)

Whitford, R. C., *Mme de Staël's Literary Reputation in England* (University of Illinois Press, 1918)
Wilson, R. McN., *Germaine de Staël* (Eyre & Spottiswoode, 1931)

TURGOT

Translations: *Reflections on the Formation and the Distribution of Riches* (Macmillan & Co., 1898); Stephens, W. W., *The Life and Writings of Turgot* (Longmans, Green & Co., 1895)
Barnard, J. M., *A Sketch of Anne Robert Jacques Turgot* (G. H. Ellis, 1899)
Dakin, D., *Turgot and the Ancien Régime* (Methuen & Co., Ltd., 1939)
Hodgson, W. B., *Turgot* (Trübner & Co., 1870)
La Fontainerie, F. de, *French Liberalism and Education in the Eighteenth Century* (McGraw-Hill Book Co., 1932)
Lodge, E. C., *Sully, Colbert, and Turgot* (Methuen & Co., Ltd., 1931)
Mirabeau, H. G. R., *Considerations on the Order of Cincinnatus* (J. Johnson, 1785)
Morley, J., *Biographical Studies* (Macmillan & Co., Ltd., 1923), *Critical Miscellanies* (Chapman & Hall, 1871-77)
Pinkerton, M. B., *The Right to Work versus Slavery* (M. B. Pinkerton, 1942)
Price, R., *Observations on the Importance of the American Revolution* (Powars & Willis, 1784)
Say, L., *Turgot* (A. C. McClurg & Co., 1888)
Shepherd, R. P., *Turgot and the Six Edicts* (Columbia University Press, 1903)
Tallentyre, S. G., *The Friends of Voltaire* (Smith, Elder & Co., 1906)
White, A. D., *Seven Great Statesmen* (The Century Co., 1912)

VIGNY

Translations: Berthon, H. E. (ed.), *Nine French Poets* (Macmillan & Co., Ltd., 1930); Hazlitt, W., *Cinq-Mars* (Little, Brown & Co., 1899); Huard, F. W., *Military Servitude and Grandeur* (G. D. Doran Co., 1919); Hare, H., *The Military Necessity* (Cresset Press, 1953)
Bird, C. W., *Alfred de Vigny's Chatterton* (Lymanhouse, 1941)
Whitridge, A., *Alfred de Vigny* (Oxford University Press, 1933)

VOLNEY

Translations: *The Law of Nature* (D. I. Eaton, 1796); *Lectures on History* (J. Ridgway, 1800); *New Researches on Ancient History* (J. P. Mendum, 1874); *Ruins* (Dixon & Sickels, 1828; C. B. Blanchard, 1858); *Travels through Syria and Egypt* (G. G. J. & J. Robinson, 1787); *View of the Climate and Soil of the United States of America*

(J. Johnson, 1804); *Volney's Answer to Dr. Priestley* (Philadelphia, 1797)

Bradlaugh, C., *Biographies of Ancient and Modern Celebrated Freethinkers* (P. Eckler, 18—?)

CHAPTER SIX

THE GOLDEN AGE OF GERMAN LITERATURE

GENERAL

Andreen, G. A., *Studies in the Idyll in German Literature* (Lutheran Augusta Book Concern, Printers, 1902)

Bennett, E. K., *A History of the German Novelle* (Cambridge University Press, 1934)

Bithell, J. (ed.), *Germany, a Companion to German Studies* (Methuen & Co., Ltd., 1937)

Boyesen, H. H., *Essays on German Literature* (C. Scribner's Sons, 1892)

Braun, W. A., *Types of Weltschmerz in German Poetry* (The Macmillan Co., 1905)

Bruford, W. H., *Germany in the Eighteenth Century* (Cambridge University Press, 1935)

Butler, E. M., *The Tyranny of Greece over Germany* (Cambridge University Press, 1935)

Eloesser, A., *Modern German Literature* (C. A. Phillips, tr.) (A. A. Knopf, 1933)

Francke, K., *A History of German Literature* (H. Holt & Co., 1916)

Gode-von-Aesch, A., *Natural Science in German Romanticism* (Columbia University Press, 1941)

Gooch, G. P., *Germany and the French Revolution* (Longmans, Green & Co., 1920)

Hedge, F. H., *Prose Writers of Germany* (Carey & Hart, 1848)

Hentschel, C., *The Byronic Teuton; Aspects of German Pessimism, 1800-1933* (Methuen & Co., Ltd., 1940)

Hook, S., *From Hegel to Marx* (Reynal & Hitchcock, 1936)

Kahn, L. W., *Social Ideals in German Literature, 1770-1830* (Columbia University Press, 1938)

Klenze, C. von, *From Goethe to Hauptmann* (Viking Press, 1926)

Legge, J. G., *Rhyme and Revolution in Germany* (Constable & Co., Ltd., 1918)

Lewisohn, L., *The Spirit of Modern German Literature* (B. W. Huebsch, 1916)

Mowat, R. B., *The Romantic Age* (G. G. Harrap & Co., 1937)

Perlman, L., *The Jew in Retrospect; a Sociological Inquiry into the Nature and Origin of Literary Patterns in German Literature* (New York, 1942)

Porterfield, A. W., *An Outline of German Romanticism, 1766-1866* (Ginn & Co., 1914)

Robertson, J. G., *A History of German Literature* (G. P. Putnam's Sons, 1925), *Outlines of the History of German Literature* (G. P. Putnam's Sons, 1925)

Rose, W., *From Goethe to Byron; the Development of 'Weltschmerz' in German Literature* (G. Routledge & Sons, Ltd., 1924)

Scherer, W., *A History of German Literature* (C. Scribner's Sons, 1912)

Silz, W., *Early German Romanticism* (Harvard University Press, 1929)

Thomas, C., *A History of German Literature* (W. Heinemann, 1909; D. Appleton & Co., 1913)

Thomas, R. H., *German Perspectives* (W. Heffer & Sons, Ltd., 1940)

Viereck, P. R. E., *Metapolitics* (A. A. Knopf, 1941)

Walzel, O., *German Romanticism* (G. P. Putnam's Sons, 1932)

Wernaer, R. M., *Romanticism and the Romantic School in Germany* (D. Appleton & Co., 1910)

Willoughby, L. A., *The Classical Age of German Literature, 1740-1805* (Oxford University Press, 1926), *The Romantic Movement in Germany* (Oxford University Press, 1926)

ARNDT

Translations: *Ardnt's* [sic] *Spirit of the Times* (W. M. Thiselton, 1808); Dabis, A., *Fairy Tales from the Isle of Rügen* (D. Nutt, 1896)

Anderson, E. N., *Nationalism and the Cultural Crisis in Prussia, 1806-1815* (Farrar & Rinehart, Inc., 1939)

Pundt, A. G., *Arndt and the Nationalist Awakening in Germany* (Columbia University Press, 1935)

Seeley, J. R., *The Life and Adventures of E. M. Arndt, the Singer of the German Fatherland* (Roberts Bros., 1879)

ARNIM

Liedke, H. R., *Literary Criticism and Romantic Theory in the Work of Achim von Arnim* (Columbia University Press, 1937)

BODMER

Scenna, A., *The Treatment of Ancient Legend and History in Bodmer* (Columbia University Press, 1937)

Viles, G. B., *Comparison of Bodmer's Translation of Milton's Paradise Lost with the Original* (Cornell University, 1902)

BÜRGER

Translations: *The Lass of Fair Wone* (Schaw & Pillans, 1796); Brooks, C. T., *Schiller's Homage of the Arts* (J. Munroe & Co., 1847; J. Miller, 1864); Cameron, J. M., *Leonora* (Longman, Brown, Green & Longmans, 1847); Lukens, C. J., *The Wild Huntsman* (Philadelphia, 1870), *Lean 'Nora; a Resurrection* (C. S., Clarke, Jr., 1878); Rosetti, D. G., *Lenore* (Ellis & Elvey, 1900); Scott, W., *The Wild Huntsman, William and Helen* in Scott's *Works* (Any Edition); Spencer, W. R., *Leonora* (London, 1796), *Poems* (T. Cadell & W. Davies, 1811); Stanley, J. T., *Leonora* (W. Miller, 1796)

Blenkensop, E. S., *Bürger's Originality* (B. Backwell, 1936)

Emerson, O. F., *The Earliest English Translations of Bürger's Leonore* (Western Reserve University Press, 1915)

Retzsch, F. A. M., *Outlines to Bürger's Ballads* (Roberts Bros., 1873)

Smith, A. R., *Wild Oats and Dead Leaves* (Chapman & Hall, 1860)

Whyte, S., *Miscellanea Nova* (Dublin, 1800)

CHAMISSO

Translations: *Peter Schlemihl* (J. Knight Co., 1893); *A Sojourn at San Francisco Bay 1816* (The Book Club of California, 1936); *The Shadowless Man; or the Wonderful History of Peter Schlemihl* (J. Burns, 1845); Bolton, T., *The Wonderful History of Peter Schlemihl* (B. W. Huebsch, Inc., 1923); Bowring, J., *Peter Schlemihl* (London, 1824); H. Hardwicke, 1861); Hedge, F. H., *The Wonderful History of Peter Schlemihl* (Ginn & Co., 1899); Hewitt, W., *The Wonderful History of Peter Schlemihl* (Burgess & Stringer, 1844); Phillips, Jr., H., *Faust* (Philadelphia, 1881)

Mahr, A. A., *The Visit of the "Rurik" to San Francisco in 1816* (Stanford University Press, 1932)

Mann, T., *Essays of Three Decades* (A. A. Knopf, 1947)

CRAMER

Translation: Mrs. Douglas, *The Life of Professor Gellert* (J. Hatchard, 1805)

EICHENDORFF

Translations: Rossy, M., *The Happy Wanderer and Other Poems by Josef von Eichendorff* (R. G. Badger, 1925); Wister, Mrs. A. L., *Leaves from the Life of a Good-for-Nothing* (J. B. Lippincott Co., 1889)

Heinzelmann, J. H., *The Influence of the German Volkslied on Eichendorff's Lyric* (G. Fock, 1910)

Wrenn, M. E., *A Comparative Study of the Ballads and Lyrics of Heine and Eichendorff* (Chicago, 1910)

FOUQUÉ

See La Motte Fouqué

GELLERT

Translations: *The Tender Sisters* (London, 1805); *The Life of the Swedish Countess de G——*, (J. Donaldson, 1776)
Trust in God; or, Three Days in the Life of Gellert (R. Carter & Bros., 1875)
Auerbach, B., *Christian Gellert, and Other Sketches* (S. Low, Son, & Co., 1858)
Cramer, J. A., *The Life of Professor Gellert* (J. Hatchard, 1805)
Oertel, P. F. W., *Three Days of Gellert's Life* (The Christopher Publishing House, 1932)

GOETHE

Translations: *Clavigo* (I. Johnson, 1798); *Dramatic Works of Goethe: Comprising Faust, Iphigenia in Tauris, Torquato Tasso, Egmont, tr. by Anna Swanwick. And Goetz von Berlichingen, tr. by Sir Walter Scott* (H. G. Bohn, 1850; Bell & Daldy, 1872; J. D. Williams, 1882); *Elective Affinities* (D. W. Niles, 1872); *Goethe's Correspondence with a Child* (Ticknor & Fields, 1861); *Goethe's Stella as Translated in 1798* in Morley, H. (ed.), *Parodies and Other Burlesque Pieces* (G. Routledge & Sons, 1890); *Goethe's Works* (G. Barrie, 1885); *Goethe's Works* (Bohn's Standard Library, G. Bell & Sons, 1848); *Goetz of Berlingen* (J. Stockdale, 1799); *The Letters of Charlotte, during her Connexion with Werter* (W. A. Davis, 1797); *Memoirs of Göethe* [sic] (Collins & Hannay, 1824); *Memoirs of Goethe* (H. Colburn, 1824); *The Sorrows of Werter* (Nathaniel Bell, 1796; H. Chamberlaine, 18—?); *The Sorrows of Werter* (Thomas Collier, 1789; S. Andrus, 1824); *The Sorrows of Werter; Elective Affinities; and a Nouvelette* (J. D. Williams, 1882); *Wilhelm Meister's Apprenticeship* (Wells & Lilly, 1828); Adler, G. J., *Iphigenia in Tauris* (D. Appleton & Co., 1850); Andrews, W. P., *Goethe's Faust* (Princeton University Press, 1929); Anster, J., *Faust* (J. C. Yorston & Co., 1888; Frederick A. Stokes Co., 1890; Dingwall-Rock, Ltd., 1925), *Faustus* [Part I.] (Longman, Rees, 1835); *The First Part of Goethe's Faust* (G. Routledge & Sons, 1887), *Faustus; the Second Part* (Longman, Green, & Green, 1864; G. Routledge & Sons, 1886), *Goethe's Faust* (Morley's Universal Library, G. Routledge & Sons, 1886; Dodd, Mead & Co., 1894); Arnold, T. J., *Reynard the Fox* (Naltali & Bond, 1855; D. Appleton & Co., 1860; T. Stroefer, 1870; J. C. Nimmo, 1887); Aytoun, W. E. and Martin, T., *Poems and Ballads of Goethe* (W. Blackwood & Sons, 1859; Delisser & Procter, 1859; W. Gowans, 1863); Bannan, M. R., *The Fisher Maiden, and the Lover's*

Caprice (The John C. Yorston Publishing Co., 1899); Bell, *Faust, Part II* (London, 1842); Biermann, B., *Goethe's World as Seen in Letters and Memoirs* (New Directions, 1949); Birch, J., *Faust* (Black & Armstrong, 1839); Blackie, J. S., *The Wisdom of Goethe* (W. Blackwood & Sons, 1883); Bowring, E. A., *Hermann and Dorothea* J. B. Lippincott Co., 1889), *The Poems of Goethe* (J. W. Parker & Son, 1853); Bowring, E. A., Aytoun, W. E., Martin, T., *The Poems of Goethe* (J. D. Williams, 1882); Boylan, R. D., *Novels and Tales* (Bohn's Standard Library, H. G. Bohn, 1854), *Wilhelm Meister's Apprenticeship* (London, 1855; H. G. Bohn, 1861; Bell & Daldy, 1868); Brooks, C. T., *Faust* [Part I.] (Ticknor & Fields, 1856); Calvert, G. H., *Correspondence between Schiller and Goethe, from 1794 to 1805* (Wiley & Putnam, 1845); Carlyle, T., *Wilhelm Meister's Apprenticeship and Travels* (Ticknor & Fields, 1865; Chapman & Hall, 187-?; Scribner, Welford & Co., 1874; J. R. Osgood & Co., 1876; American Book Exchange, 1881; Wm. L. Allison & Son, 1882; J. D. Williams, 1882), *Wilhelm Meister* (Everyman's Library, J. M. Dent & Son, Ltd., 1930); Coleridge, A. D., *Goethe's Letters to Zelter* (G. Bell & Sons, 1887); Cookson, G. M., *Faust, Part One* (Broadway Translations, G. Routledge & Sons, Ltd., 1927); Coxwell, C. F., *Goethe's Tragedy of Faust* (The C. W. Daniel Co., 1932); Dale, H., *Hermann and Dorothea* (Stroefer & Kirchner, 189-?); Dowden, E., *West-Eastern Divan* (J. M. Dent & Sons, Ltd., 1914); Dwight, J. S., *Select Minor Poems, translated from the German of Goethe and Schiller* (Hilliard, Gray & Co., 1839); Dyrsen, P., *Goethe's Poems* (F. W. Christern, 1878); Eastlake, C. L., *Theory of Colours* (London, 1840); Filmore, L., *Faust* [Part I.] (W. Smith, 1847); Frothingham, E., *Hermann and Dorothea* (Roberts Bros., 1870); Gibson, W., *The Poems of Goethe* (S. Marshall & Co., 1883); Godwin, P. (ed.), *The Auto-biography of Goethe* (Wiley & Putnam, 1846-47); Gotzberg, *The Sorrows of Werter* (J. Cundee, 1808); Hayward, A., *Faust* (D. Bixby, 1840; Ticknor, Reed, & Fields, 1851; E. Moxon & Co., 1860; D. Estes & Co., 1908; Hutchinson & Co., 1927); Hedge, F. H. (ed.), *Faust, Clavigo, Egmont, The Wayward Lover* (J. D. Williams, 1882; Hurst & Co., 1888); Hedge, F. H. and Swanwick, A., *Faust* (T. Y. Crowell & Co., 1882); Hedge, F. H. and Noa, L. (eds.), *Goethe's Popular Works* (Estes & Lauriat, 1883); Heller, O., *Minna von Barnhelm* (H. Holt & Co., 1917); Howard, W. G., *Laokoon. Lessing, Herder, Goethe* (H. Holt & Co., 1910); Huth, A. H., *The Tragedy of Faustus, the First Part* (Sampson Low, 1889); Kaplan, S., *Iphigenie auf Tauris* (Barron's Educational Series, Inc., 1953); Lange, V., *Sorrows of Young Werther, New Melusina, & Novelle* (Rinehart Editions, Rinehart & Co., 1949); Latham, A. G., *Goethe's Faust* (Everyman's Library, E. P. Dutton & Co., 1928);

Lawrence, R., *Goetz of Berlingen* (H. M'Creery, 1799); Lewisohn,
L., *Goethe, the Story of a Man* (Farrar, Straus, 1949); MacIntyre,
C. F., *Goethe's Faust* (New Directions, 1941); MacNeice, L.,
Goethe's Faust (Oxford University Press, 1952); Mann, T. (ed.),
The Permanent Goethe (Dial Press, 1948); Martin, T., *Faust* (G.
Kirchner & Co., 187-?; F. Bruckmann, 1877), *The Song of the Bell,
and Other Translations from Schiller, Goethe, Uhland, and Others*
(W. Blackwood & Sons, 1889), *The Works of J. W. von Goethe*
(Bigelow, Brown & Co., Inc.,·1902); Moon, R. O., *Wilhelm Meister,
Apprenticeship and Travels* (G. T. Foulis, 1947); Morgan, B. Q.
(ed.), *Faust I*. (Crofts Classics, Appleton-Century-Crofts, Inc., 1946;
The Library of Liberal Arts, The Liberal Arts Press, Inc., 1953);
Morrison, A. J. W., *Goethe's Letters from Switzerland* (J. D. Wil-
liams, 1882), *Travels in Italy* in Morrison's *Autobiography* (London,
1864-66); Morrison, A. J. W. and Nisbet, C., *Goethe's Travels in
Italy* (G. Bell & Sons, 1892); Nisbet, C., *Annals* (Colonial Press,
1901); Noa, L., *Goethe's Roman Elegies* (Schoenhof & Moeller
(18—?); Norton, C. E. (ed.), *Correspondence between Goethe and
Carlyle* (Macmillan & Co., 1887); Oxenford, J., *The Autobiography
of Goethe* (J. D. Williams, 1882), *The Auto-biography of Goethe*
(Bohn's Standard Library, H. G. Bohn, 1848), *The Boyhood and
Youth of Goethe* (G. P. Putnam's Sons, 1890), *Goethe's Boyhood*
(G. Bell & Sons, 1888), *Conversations of Goethe with Eckermann
and Soret* (G. Bell & Sons, 1883), *Conversations with Eckermann*
(M. W. Dunne, 1901; Everyman's Library, E. P. Dutton & Co.,
1930), *Faust* (A. G. Latham, 1908); Oxenford, J. and Morrison,
A. J. W., *The Auto-biography of Goethe. Also, Letters from Switzer-
land, and, Travels in Italy* (H. G. Bohn, 1848-9; Bell & Daldy, 1872);
Page, G. A., *Wilhelm Meister's Theatrical Mission* (W. Heinemann,
1913); Priest, G. M., *Faust* (Covici, Friede, 1932; A. A. Knopf,
1941); Ramage, C. T., *Beautiful Thoughts from German and Spanish
Authors* (E. Howell, 1868); Raphael, A., *Faust* (J. Cape & H. Smith,
1930; The Heritage Club, 1939); Rawson, G. & T., *Goethe's Faust;
a New Acting Version* (J. Lane, 1936); Rose, W., *The Sorrows of
Young Werther* (The Scholastic Press, 1929); Saunders, B., *The
Maxims and Reflections of Goethe* (The Macmillan Co., 1906);
Schmitz, L. D. (ed.), *Miscellaneous Travels of J. W. Goethe* (G.
Bell & Sons, 1882); Scott, W., *Dramatic Works of Goethe* (Bohn's
Standard Library, H. G. Bohn, 1850); Scott, W., Bowring, E. A.,
and Swanwick, A., *The Dramatic Works of Goethe* (J. D. Williams,
1882); Smith, M. S., *Poetry and Truth* (Bohn's Standard Library,
G. Bell & Sons, 1908); Spingarn, J. E. (ed.), *Goethe's Literary
Essays* (Harcourt, Brace & Co., 1921); Stawell, F. M. and Purtscher-
Wydenbruck, N., *The Practical Wisdom of Goethe* (G. Allen &

Unwin, Ltd., 1933); Swanwick, A., *Egmont in Faust* (J. D. Williams, 1882), *Faust* (J. D. Williams, 1882; Hurst & Co., 1882; T. Y. Crowell & Co., 189-?; Part I., D. McKay, 1898); Taylor, B., *Faust* (Houghton, Mifflin & Co., 1870; World's Classics, Oxford University Press, 1870-1; Fields, Osgood & Co., 1871; Houghton, Osgood & Co., 1879; The Macmillan Co., 1930; Hartsdale House, 1946; The Modern Library & Modern Library College Editions, Random House, 1950; Part I, Crofts Classics, Appleton-Century-Crofts, 1947); Thomas, W. G., *The Minor Poetry of Goethe* (E. H. Butler & Co., 1859); Thompson, B., *Stella* (Vernor & Hood, 1801); Todhunter, J., *Goethe's Faust, First Part* (B. Blackwell, 1924); Vaeux, C. de, *Torquato Tasso* (London, 1827); Van der Smissen, W. H., *Goethe's Faust Done into English Verse in the Original Metres* (J. M. Dent & Sons, Ltd., 1926); Wayne, P., *Faust, Part I.* (Penguin Books, Inc., 1949); Wiegand, H. J., *Wisdom and Experience* (Pantheon, 1949); Wenckstern, O., *Goethe's Opinions on the World, Mankind, Literature, Science, and Art* (J. W. Parker & Son, 1853)

Andrews, W. P., *Goethe's Key to Faust* (Houghton Mifflin Co., 1913)

Atkins, S. P., *The Testament of Werther in Poetry and Drama* (Harvard University Press, 1949)

Austin, Mrs. S. (ed.), *Characteristics of Goethe* (E. Wilson, 1833; Lea & Blanchard, 1841)

Bancroft, G., *The Life and Genius of Goethe* (O. Everett, 1824)

Barnes, B., *Goethe's Knowledge of French Literature* (Oxford University Press, 1937)

Bergstraesser, A. (ed.), *Goethe and the Modern Age* (Regnery, 1950), *Goethe's Image of Man and Society* (Regnery, 1949)

Bielschowsky, A., *The Life of Goethe* (G. P. Putnam's Sons, 1905-8)

Boyd, J., *Notes to Goethe's Poems* (B. Blackwell, 1944)

Boyesen, H. H., *Essays on German Literature* (C. Scribner's Sons, 1892), *Goethe and Schiller* (C. Scribner's Sons, 1879)

Boynton, H. W., *The World's Leading Poets* (H. Holt & Co., 1912)

Brandes, G., *Wolfgang Goethe* (N. L. Brown, 1924; Frank-Maurice, Inc., 1925)

Brewer, W., *About Poetry and Other Matters* (Marshall Jones Co., 1943)

Brown, P. H., *Life of Goethe* (H. Holt & Co., 1920)

Browning, H. C., *Goethe: His Life and Writings* (S. Sonnenschein & Co., 1892), *The Life of Goethe* (New York, 1844)

Buxton, G. R., *Prophets of Heaven & Hell* (Cambridge University Press, 1945)

Calvert, G. H., *Coleridge, Shelley, Goethe* (Lee & Shepard, 1880), *Goethe: His Life and Works* (Lee & Shepard, 1872)

Carlyle, T., *Critical and Miscellaneous Essays* (J. Munroe & Co., 1838-9),

Essays on Goethe (Cassell & Co., Ltd., 1888), *Goethe* (J. R. Osgood & Co., 1877)

Carré, J. M., *Goethe* (Coward-McCann, Inc., 1929)

Cassirer, E., *Rousseau, Kant, Goethe* (Princeton University Press, 1945)

Croce, B., *Goethe* (A. A. Knopf, 1923)

Davidson, T., *The Philosophy of Goethe's Faust* (Ginn & Co., 1906)

De Quincey, T., *Biographical Essays* (Ticknor, Reed, & Fields, 1850)

Dudley, M. V. (ed.), *Poetry and Philosophy of Goethe* (S. C. Griggs & Co., 1887)

Emerson, R. W., *Representative Men* (Houghton, Mifflin & Co., 1888)

Enright, D. J., *Commentary on Goethe's Faust* (New Directions, 1949)

Fairley, B., *Goethe as Revealed in His Poetry* (The University of Chicago Press, 1932), *A Study of Goethe* (Clarendon Press, 1947), *Goethe's Faust* (Clarendon Press, 1953)

Fiedler, H. G., *Textual Studies of Goethe's Faust* (B. Blackwell, 1946)

Francke, K., *German Ideals of Today* (Houghton, Mifflin & Co., 1907)

Frantz, A. I., *Half a Hundred Thralls to Faust* (University of North Carolina Press, 1949)

Gray, R. D., *Goethe the Alchemist* (Cambridge University Press, 1953)

Grimm, H. F., *The Life and Times of Goethe* (Little, Brown & Co., 1880)

Hale, W. H., *Challenge to Defeat* (Harcourt, Brace & Co., 1932)

Hall, F. A., *Iphigenia in Literature* (Washington University, 1910)

Hartwig, H. A. (ed.), *The Southern Illinois Goethe Celebration* (Carbondale, 1950)

Haskell, J. C. S., *Bayard Taylor's Translation of Goethe's Faust* (Columbia University Press, 1908)

Hauhart, W. F., *The Reception of Goethe's Faust in England in the First Half of the Nineteenth Century* (Columbia University Press, 1909)

Heller, O., *Faust and Faustus; a Study of Goethe's Relation to Marlowe* (Washington University, 1931)

Herford, C. H., *Goethe* (T. C. & E. C. Jack, 1913)

Hervey, W. A., *Syllabus and Selected Bibliography of Lessing, Goethe, Schiller* (Lencke & Buechner, 1918)

Hinz, S. M., *Goethe's Lyric Poems in English Translation after 1860* (Madison, 1928)

Hitch, M., *Goethe's Faust. A Fragment of Social Criticism* (C. H. Ken & Co., 1908)

Hohfeld, A. R. (ed.), *The Goethe Centenary* (University of Wisconsin Press, 1932)

Howe, S., *Wilhelm Meister and His English Kinsmen* (Columbia University Press, 1930)

Hungerford, E. B., *Shores of Darkness* (Columbia University Press, 1941)

Jantz, H. S., *Goethe's Faust as a Renaissance Man* (Princeton University Press, 1951)

Konewka, P., *Illustrations to Goethe's Faust* (Roberts Bros., 1871)

Lewes, G. H., *The Life of Goethe* (Smith, Elder & Co., 1864), *The Life and Works of Goethe* (Ticknor & Fields, 1865), *The Story of Goethe's Life* (J. R. Osgood & Co., 1873)

Liljegren, S. B., *The English Sources of Goethe's Gretchen Tragedy* (C. W. K. Gleerup, 1937)

Ludwig, E., *Genius and Character* (Harcourt, Brace & Co., 1927), *Goethe, the History of a Man* (G. P. Putnam's Sons, 1928)

Lussky, A. E., *Tieck's Romantic Irony* (University of North Carolina Press, 1932)

Lyster, T. W., *Life of Goethe* (Macmillan & Co., 1884)

Mabie, H. W., *Backgrounds of Literature* (The Macmillan Co., 1912)

Macmurray, J. (ed.), *Some Makers of the Modern Spirit* (Methuen & Co., Ltd., 1933)

Magnus, R., *Goethe as a Scientist* (H. Schuman, 1949)

Mann, T., *The Beloved Returns, Lotte in Weimar* (A. A. Knopf, 1940), *Essays of Three Decades* (A. A. Knopf, 1947), *Freud, Goethe, Wagner* (A. A. Knopf, 1942), *Past Masters and Other Papers* (A. A. Knopf, 1933), *Three Essays* (A. A. Knopf, 1929), *Goethe and Democracy* (Library of Congress, 1950)

Marshall, M., *Studies in the Age of Goethe* (H. Milford, 1931)

Masaryk, T. G., *Modern Man and Religion* (G. Allen & Unwin, Ltd., 1938)

Maurois, A., *Mape; the World of Illusion* (D. Appleton & Co., 1926)

McCabe, J., *Goethe; the Man and His Character* (J. B. Lippincott Co., 1912)

Meesen, H. J. (ed.), *Goethe Bicentennial Studies* (University of Indiana Press, 1950)

Miller, R. D., *The Meaning of Goethe's Faust* (W. Heffer & Sons, Ltd., 1939)

Muller, S. H., *Gerhart Hauptmann and Goethe* (King's Crown Press, 1949)

Mulloy, W. J., *The German Catholic Estimate of Goethe* (University of California Press, 1944)

Murry, J. M., *Heroes of Thought* (J. Messner, Inc., 1938)

Needler, G. H., *Goethe and Scott* (Oxford University Press, 1950)

Nevinson, H. W., *Goethe: Man and Poet* (Nisbet & Co., Ltd., 1931)

Owen, J., *The Five Great Skeptical Dramas of History* (G. P. Putnam's Sons, 1896)

Pollak, G., *International Minds and the Search for the Restful* (The Nation Press, Inc., 1919), *International Perspective in Criticism* (Dodd, Mead & Co., 1914)

Raphael, A. P., *Goethe, the Challenger* (J. Cape & R. Ballow, 1932)

Reik, T., *Fragment of a Great Confession* (Farrar, Straus, 1949)

Retzsch, F. A. M., *Illustrations to Goethe's Faust* (W. W. Gibbings, 1875), *Sketches to Goethe's Faust* (J. G. Cotta, 1857)

Robertson, J. G., *Goethe* (G. Routledge & Sons, Ltd., 1927), *The Life and Work of Goethe* (G. Routledge & Sons, Ltd., 1932)

Rolland, R., *Goethe and Beethoven* (Harper & Brothers, 1931)

Rose, W., *From Goethe to Byron* (E. P. Dutton, 1924), *Men, Myths, and Movements in German Literature* (Macmillan, 1931)

Rose, W. (ed.), *Essays on Goethe* (Cassell & Co., 1949)

Roubiczek, P., *The Misinterpretation of Man; Studies in European Thought of the Nineteenth Century* (C. Scribner's Sons, 1947)

Runes, D. D. (ed.), *Goethe; a Symposium* (Roerich Museum Press, 1932)

Santayana, G., *Three Philosophical Poets* (Harvard University, 1927)

Schreiber, C. F., *A Note on Faust Translations* (J. Cape & H. Smith, 1930)

Schreiber, C. F. (ed.), *Goethe's Works, a Catalogue* (Yale University Press, 1940)

Schweitzer, A., *Goethe* (Beacon Press, 1948)

Seeley, J. R., *Goethe, Reviewed after Sixty Years* (Roberts Bros., 1893)

Sime, J., *Life of Johann Wolfgang Goethe* (W. Scott, 1888)

Snider, D. J., *Goethe's Faust . . . a Commentary* (Sigma Publishing Co., 1886), *Goethe's Life-poem as Set Forth in His Life and Works* (Sigma Publishing Co., 1915; The William Harvey Miner Co., Inc., 1922)

Spalding, J. L., *Opportunity, and Other Essays and Addresses* (A. C. McClurg & Co., 1903)

Stawell, F. M. and Dickinson, G. L., *Goethe & Faust* (G. Bell & Sons, Ltd., 1928)

Stearns, F. P., *Politics and Metaphysics* (R. G. Badger, 1915)

Steiner, R., *Goethe's Secret Revelation and the Riddle in Faust* (P. L. Humphries & Co., Ltd., 1933), *Goethe's Standard of the Soul* (Anthroposophical Publishing Co., 1925)

Strich, F., *Goethe and World Literature* (Hafner Publishing Co., 1949)

Thomas, C., *Goethe* (H. Holt & Co., 1917)

Trevelyan, H., *The Popular Background to Goethe's Hellenism* (Longmans, Green & Co., 1934), *Goethe and the Greeks* (Cambridge University Press, 1941)

United Nations Educational, Scientific and Cultural Organization, *Goethe* (UNESCO, 1949)

Viëtor, K., *Goethe, the Poet* (Harvard University Press, 1949), *Goethe, the Thinker* (Harvard University Press, 1950)

Waldman, M., *Goethe and the Jews* (G. P. Putnam's Sons, 1934)

Walsh, W. S., *Faust, the Legend and the Poem* (J. B. Lippincott Co., 1888)

Willoughby, L. A., *Unity and Continuity in Goethe* (Clarendon Press, 1947)

Wilson, H. S., *Studies in History, Legend and Literature* (E. P. Dutton & Co., 1884)

GRILLPARZER

Translations: Bramsen, J., *Sappho* (A. Black, 1820); Burkhard, A., *The Argonauts* (The Register Press, 1942), *A Faithful Servant of His Master* (The Register Press, 1941), *Family Strife in Hapsburg* (The Register Press, 1940), *The Golden Fleece* (The Register Press, 1942), *The Guest-Friend* (The Register Press, 1942), *Medea* (The Register Press, 1941); Frothingham, E., *Sappho* (Roberts Bros., 1876); Spahr, H. L., *The Ancestress* (Tyler & Co., 1938); Stevens, H. H., *Hero and Leander* (The Register Press, 1938), *Libussa* (The Register Press, 1941), *Thou Shalt Not Lie* (The Register Press, 1939)

Coenen, F. E., *Grillparzer's Portraiture of Men* (University of North Carolina Press, 1951)

De Walsh, F. C., *Grillparzer as a Poet of Nature* (Columbia University Press, 1910)

Hermann, E. A., *Histrionics in the Dramas of Franz Grillparzer* (Berkeley: University Press, 1912)

Lasher-Schlitt, D., *Grillparzer's Attitude toward the Jews* (G. E. Stechert & Co., 1936)

Pollak, G., *Franz Grillparzer and the Austrian Drama* (Dodd, Mead & Co., 1907), *International Minds and the Search for the Restful* (The Nation Press, Inc., 1919)

Pollak, G. (ed.), *International Perspective in Criticism* (Dodd, Mead & Co., 1914)

Robinson, J. G., *Essays and Addresses on Literature* (G. Routledge & Sons, Ltd., 1935)

Williamson, E. J., *Grillparzer's Attitude toward Romanticism* (University of Chicago Press, 1910)

Yates, D., *Franz Grillparzer, a Critical Biography* (B. Blackwell, 1946)

GRIMM, J. L. K.

Translation: Stallybrass, J. S., *Teutonic Mythology* (G. Bell & Sons, 1882-88)

GRIMM, J. L. K. & W. K.

Translations: *The Almond-Tree and Other Tales* (G. Routledge & Sons, 1882?); *Cherry Blossom and Other Stories from Grimm* (Blackie & Son, 192-?); *Fairy Tales, by the Brothers Grimm* (Limited Editions Club, 1931); *German Popular Stories* (H. Froude, 1904); *German Popular Tales and Household Stories* (Crosby & Nichols, 1862;

Porter & Coates, 1869); *German Stories Retold* (American Book Co., 1907); *The Golden Bird, and Other Stories* (G. W. Jacobs & Co., 1922); *Hansel and Gretel and Other Stories* (Hodder & Stoughton, 191-?); *Household Stories* (G. Routledge & Sons, Ltd., 18—?; Addey & Co., 1853); *The King of the Swans, and Other Fairy Tales* (J. Miller, 18—?); *Popular Stories, Collected by the Brothers Grimm* (H. Froude, 1905); *Popular Tales and Household Stories* (Porter & Coates, 1869); *Tales from the Brothers Grimm* (F. Etchells & H. Macdonald, 1930); Boldry, E., *Grimm's Household Fairy Tales* (McLoughlin Bros., 1890); Edwardes, M., *Grimm's Household Tales* (J. M. Dent & Co., 1901); Gág, W., *Tales from Grimm* (Coward-McCann, Inc., 1936); Hunt, M., *German Household Tales* (Houghton, Mifflin & Co., 1897), *Grimm's Fairy Tales* (Pantheon Books, 1944); Hunt, M. (ed.), *Household Tales* (G. Bell & Sons, 1884); Lewis, E., *Fairy Tales from the Brothers Grimm* (The Peter Pauper Press, 1941), *Grimm's Fairy Tales* (Bantam Books, Bantam Publications, 1940); Lucas, Mrs. E., *Fairy Tales of the Brothers Grimm* (J. B. Lippincott Co., 1902); Lucas, Mrs., Crane, Lucy and Edwardes, M., *Household and Fairy Tales* (G. W. Jacobs & Co., 1916); Paul, Mrs. H. H. B., *Grimm's Fairy Tales* (F. Earne & Co., 188-?); Taylor, E., *Fairy Tales* (Everyman's Library, E. P. Dutton & Co., 1906), *German Popular Stories* (C. Baldwyn, 1824)

GUTZKOW

Translation: Faber, Mrs., *Through Night to Light* (B. Tauschnitz, 1870)
Pasmore, D. F., *Karl Gutzkow's Short Stories; a Study in the Technique of Narration* (G. Banta Publishing Co., 1918)
Schinnerer, O. P., *Woman in the Life and Work of Gutzkow* (Columbia University Press, 1924)

HARDENBERG

See Novalis.

HEGEL

Translations: Baillie, J. B., *The Phenomenology of Mind* (The Macmillan Co., 1931); Bosanquet, B., *The Introduction to Hegel's Philosophy of Fine Art* (K. Paul, Trench & Co., 1886); Bryant, W. M., *The Philosophy of Art* (D. Appleton & Co., 1879); Haldane, E. S. (ed.), *The Wisdom and Religion of a German Philosopher* (K. Paul, 1897); Haldane, E. S. and Simson, F. H., *Lectures on the History of Philosophy* (K. Paul, Trench, Trübner & Co., 1892-96); Harris, W. T., *Hegel's First Principle* (J. Knapp & Co., 1869); Johnston, W. H. and Struthers, L. G., *Hegel's Science of Logic* (G. Allen &

Unwin, Ltd., 1929); Knox, T. M., *Early Theological Writings* (University of Chicago Press, 1948), *Hegel's Philosophy of Richt* (Clarendon Press, 1942); Loewenberg, J. (ed.), *Selections* (C. Scribner's Sons, 1929); Macran, H. S., *Hegel's Doctrine of Formal Logic* (Clarendon Press, 1912), *Hegel's Logic of World and Idea* (Clarendon Press, 1929); Osmaston, F. P. B., *The Philosophy of Fine Art* (G. Bell & Sons, Ltd., 1920); Sibree, J., *Lectures on the Philosophy of History* (G. Bell & Sons, 1881), *The Philosophy of History* (The Colonial Press, 1899; P. F. Collier & Son, 1901); Slaman, H. and Wallon, J., *The Subjective Logic of Hegel* (J. Chapman, 1855); Speirs, E. B. and Sanderson, J. B., *Lectures on the Philosophy of Religion* (K. Paul, Trench, Trübner & Co., 1895); Sterrett, J. M., *The Ethics of Hegel* (Boston, 1893); Wallace, W., *Hegel's Philosophy of Mind* (Clarendon Press, 1894), *The Logic of Hegel* (Oxford University Press, 1931); Friedrich, C. J. (ed.), *The Philosophy of Hegel* (Random House, 1953)

Adams, G. P., *The Mystical Element in Hegel's Early Theological Writings* (Berkeley: The University Press, 1910)

Bryant, W. M., *Hegel's Educational Ideas* (Werner School Book Co., 1896)

Cahill, M. C., *The Absolute and the Relative in St. Thomas and in Modern Philosophy* (The Catholic University of America Press, 1939)

Caird, E., *Hegel* (W. Blackwood & Sons, 1883; J. B. Lippincott Co., 1891)

Croce, B., *What is Living and What is Dead of the Philosophy of Hegel* (Macmillan & Co., Ltd., 1915)

Cunningham, G. W., *Thought and Reality in Hegel's System* (Longmans, Green & Co., 1910)

Flaccus, L. W., *Artists and Thinkers* (Longmans, Green & Co., 1916)

Foster, M. B., *The Political Philosophies of Plato and Hegel* (Clarendon Press, 1935)

Gray, J. G., *Hegel's Hellenic Ideal* (King's Crown Press, 1941)

Harris, W. T., *Hegel's Logic* (S. C. Griggs & Co., 1895)

Haushalter, W. M., *Mrs. Eddy Purloins from Hegel* (Watts & Co., 1936)

Hobhouse, L. T., *The Metaphysical Theory of the State* (The Macmillan Co., 1918)

Hook, S., *From Hegel to Marx* (Reynal & Hitchcock, 1936)

Kedney, J. S., *Hegel's Aesthetics* (S. C. Griggs & Co., 1892; Scott, Foresman & Co., 1897)

Mackenzie, M., *Hegel's Educational Theory and Practice* (C. W. Bardeen, 1909)

Mackintosh, R., *Hegel and Hegelianism* (C. Scribner's Sons, 1903)

Maier, J., *On Hegel's Critique of Kant* (Columbia University Press, 1939)

Marcuse, H., *Reason and Revolution* (Oxford University Press, 1941)

McTaggart, J., *A Commentary on Hegel's Logic* (Cambridge: University Press, 1910), *Studies in Hegelian Cosmology* (Cambridge: University Press, 1901)
Maier, J., *On Hegel's Critique of Kant* (Columbia University Press, 1939)
Marcuse, H., *Reason and Revolution* (Oxford University Press, 1941)
Morris, G. S., *Hegel's Philosophy of the State and of History* (S. C. Griggs & Co., 1892)
Mure, G. R. G., *An Introduction to Hegel* (Clarendon Press, 1940)
Myers, H. A., *The Spinoza-Hegel Paradox* (Cornell University Press, 1944)
Reyburn, H. A., *The Ethical Theory of Hegel* (Clarendon Press, 1921)
Stace, W. T., *The Philosophy of Hegel* (Macmillan & Co., Ltd., 1924)
Wallace, W., *Prolegomena to the Study of Hegel's Philosophy and Especially of His Logic* (Clarendon Press, 1894)

HEINE

Translations: *The Book of Songs* (The Roycrofters, 1903); *Love Songs, by Heinrich Heine* (F. A. Stokes Co., n. d.); *Prose and Poetry* (Everyman's Library, E. P. Dutton & Co., 1934); *Selections from the Poetical Works of H. Heine* (The Macmillan Co., 1878); Bowring, E. A., *Poems Complete* (London, 1859), *The Poems of Heine, Complete* (G. Bell & Sons, 1889); Carter, F., *Florentine Nights* (G. Howe, 1933); DeKay, C., *The Family Life of Heinrich Heine* (Cassell Publishing Co., 1892); Ellis, H., *The Prose Writings of Heinrich Heine* (W. Scott, 1887); Evans, T. W., *The Memoirs of Heinrich Heine* (G. Bell & Sons, 1884); Ewen, F., *The Poetry and Prose of Heinrich Heine* (Citadel Press, 1948); Fleishman, S. L., *Prose Miscellanies* (J. B. Lippincott & Co., 1876); Garron, R. R., *The Book of Songs* (E. A. Vidler, 1924); Hillman, F., *Lyrics and Ballads of Heine and Other German Poets* (G. P. Putnam's Sons, 1892); Horine, C., *Heine's Poems* (The Stratford Co., 1923); Jones, H. M., *Heine's Poem, The North Sea* (The Open Court Publishing Co., 1916); Karpeles, G. (ed.), *Heinrich Heine's Memoirs* (John Lane Co., 1910); Kesten, H. (ed.), *Works of Prose* (L. B. Fischer, 1943); Kroeker, K. F., *Poems, Selected from H. Heine* (W. Scott, Ltd., 1887); Lazarus, E., *Poems and Ballads of Heinrich Heine* (Hust & Co., 188-?; R. Worthington, 1881); Leland, C. G., *Heine's Book of Songs* (F. Leypoldt, 1864; H. Holt & Co., 1874), *Heinrich Heine's Pictures of Travel* (F. Leypoldt, 1863), *The Works of Heinrich Heine* (Crossup & Sterling Co., 190-?); Martin, T. and Bowring, E. A., *Heine's Book of Songs* (White, Stokes, & Allen, 1884); Salinger, H., *Germany, a Winter's Tale, 1844* (L. B. Fischer, 1944); Scheffauer, H., *Atta Troll* (Sidgwick & Jackson, 1913); Sharp, E. A., *Heine in Art and Letters* (W. Scott, Ltd., 1895), *Italian Travel*

Sketches (W. Scott, Ltd., 1892; Foulis, 1927; Brentano's, 1928); Snodgrass, J., *Wit, Wisdom, and Pathos* (Cupples & Hurd, 1888); Stigand, W., *Anthea, Poems and Translations* (Kegan Paul, Trench, Trübner & Co., 1907); Stirling, W., *The North Sea, and Other Poems* (A. Wingate, 1947); Storr, F., *Travel-Pictures* (G. Bell & Sons, 1901); Untermeyer, L., *Poems of Heinrich Heine* (H. Holt & Co., 1917); Wolfe, H., *Portrait of Heine* (The Cresset Press, 1930); Wood, F. T., *The Sea and the Hills* (Chapman & Grimes, Inc., 1946)

Allen, P. S., *Studies in Popular Poetry* (The University of Chicago Press, 1902)

Arnold, M., *Essays in Criticism* (Ticknor & Fields, 1865; Macmillan & Co., 1865)

Atkins, H. G., *Heine* (G. Routledge & Sons, Ltd., 1929)

Bernard, H., *Heine, the Strange Guest* (G. Bles, 1928)

Braun, W. A., *Types of Weltschmerz in German Poetry* (The Macmillan Co., 1905)

Browne, L., *That Man Heine* (The Macmillan Co., 1927)

Eliot, G., *Essays and Leaves from a Note-Book* (W. Blackwood & Sons, 1884)

Ellis, H., *The New Spirit* (The W. Scott Publishing Co., 1892; Houghton Mifflin Co., 1926)

Hess, J. A., *Heine's Views on German Traits of Character* (G. E. Stechert & Co., 1929)

Lavrin, Y., *Studies in European Literature* (Constable & Co., Ltd., 1929)

Lazaron, M. S., *Seed of Abraham; Ten Jews of the Ages* (The Century Co., 1930)

Le Gallienne, R., *Old Love Stories Retold* (The Baker & Taylor Co., 1904)

Magnus, K., *Jewish Portraits* (G. Routledge & Sons, Ltd., 1925)

Marcuse, L., *Heine, a Life between Love and Hate* (Farrar & Rinehart, Inc., 1933)

Monahan, M., *Heinrich Heine* (M. Kennerley, 1911), *Heinrich Heine; Romance and Tragedy of the Poet's Life* (M. L. Brown, 1924)

Samuel, H. B., *Modernities* (E. P. Dutton & Co., 1914)

Sharp, W., *Life of Heinrich Heine* (T. Whittaker, 1888)

Stigand, W., *The Life, Work, and Opinions of Heinrich Heine* (Longmans, Green & Co., 1875)

Takak, I., *Judaic Lore in Heine* (The Johns Hopkins Press, 1948)

Untermeyer, L., *Heinrich Heine, Paradox and Poet* (Harcourt, Brace & Co., 1937)

Vallentin, A., *Poet in Exile* (V. Gollancz, Ltd., 1934)

Walter, H., *Heinrich Heine; a Critical Examination of the Poet and His Works* (J. M. Dent & Sons, Ltd., 1930)

Wood, F. H., *Heine as a Critic of His Own Works* (Privately Printed, 1934)

Wormeley, S. L., *Heine in England* (University of North Carolina Press, 1943)

Wrenn, M. E., *A Comparative Study of the Ballads and Lyrics of Heine and Eichendorff* (Chicago, 1910)

HERDER

Translations: Burkhart, F. H., *God, Some Conversations* (Veritas Press, 1940); Churchill, T., *Outlines of a Philosophy of the History of Man* (London, 1800); Howard, W. G., *Laokoon. Lessing, Herder, Goethe* (H. Holt & Co., 1910); Marsh, J. J., *The Spirit of Hebrew Poetry* (E. Smith, 1833)

Adler, F. H., *Herder and Klopstock; a Comparative Study* (G. E. Stechert & Co., 1914)

Andress, J. M., *Johann Gottfried Herder as an Educator* (G. E. Stechert & Co., 1916)

De Quincey, T., *Essays on Philosophical Writers* (Ticknor, Reed, & Fields, 1854)

Ergang, R. R., *Herder and the Foundations of German Nationalism* (Columbia University Press, 1931)

Gillies, A., *Herder* (B. Blackwell, 1945)

Marshall, M., *Studies in the Age of Goethe* (H. Milford, 1931)

McEachran, F., *The Life and Philosophy of Johann Gottfried Herder* (The Clarendon Press, 1939)

Montgomery, M., *Studies in the Age of Goethe* (H. Milford, 1931)

Sherwood, M. P., *Undercurrents of Influence in English Romantic Poetry* (Harvard University Press, 1934)

HOFFMANN

Translations: *Beauties of German Literature* (J. Burns, 1847); *Stories by E. T. W. Hoffmann* (E. P. Dutton & Co., 1908); *Tales of Hoffmann* (G. G. Harrap & Co., Ltd., 1932); *The Tales of Hoffmann* (The Limited Editions Club, 1943); Carlyle, T. (ed.), *German Romance* (J. Munro & Co., 1841); Ewing, A., *The Serapion Brethren* (G. Bell & Sons, 1892-1908); Gillies, R. P., *German Stories* (W. Blackwood, 1826); Lazore, C. (ed.), *Tales of Hoffmann* (A. A. Wyn, 1946); Oxenford, J. and Freiling, C. A., *Tales from the German* (Harper & Brothers, 1844); Soane, G., *Specimens of German Romance* (G. B. Whittaker, 1826)

Cobb, P., *The Influence of E. T. A. Hoffmann on the Tales of Edgar Allan Poe* (Chapel Hill, The University Press, 1908)

Hewett-Thayer, H. W., *Hoffmann: Author of the Tales* (Princeton University Press, 1948)

IMMERMANN

Translations: Oxenford, J. and Freiling, C. A., *Tales from the German* (Harper & Brothers, 1844)

Porterfield, A. W., *Karl Lebrecht Immermann; a Study in German Romanticism* (Columbia University Press, 1911)

JACOBI

Crawford, A. W., *The Philosophy of F. H. Jacobi* (The Macmillan Co., 1905)

Wilde, N., *Friedrich Heinrich Jacobi; a Study in the Origin of German Realism* (Columbia College, 1894)

JEAN PAUL

Translations: *Beauties of German Literature* (F. Warne & Co., 1868); *The Campaner Thal, and Other Writings* (Ticknor & Fields, 1864); *The Death of an Angel, etc.* (J. Mowatt & Co., 1844); *Levanna; or, the Doctrine of Education* (Boston, 1863); *Reminiscences of the Best Hours of Life for the Hour of Death* (J. Dowe, 1841); Brooks, C. T., *Hesperus* (Boston, 1865), *The Invisible Lodge* (H. Holt & Co., 1883), *Titan: a Romance* (Ticknor & Fields, 1863); Carlyle, T., *German Romance* (J. Munro & Co., 1841), *Tales by Musaeus, Tieck, Richter* (Scribner, Welford & Co., 1874); De Quincey, T., *Confessions of an English Opium-Eater. And, Analects from John Paul Richter* (A. T. Crocker, 1867); Kenney, A., *The Death of an Angel and Other Pieces* (London, 1839); Lee, E. B., *Walt and Vult, or the Twins* (Wiley & Putnam, 1846; J. Miller, 1863); Noel, E. H., *Flower, Fruit, and Thorn Pieces* (Ticknor & Fields, 1863)

Brewer, E. V., *The New England Interest in Jean Paul Friedrich Richter* (University of California Press, 1943)

Carlyle, T., *Critical and Miscellaneous Essays* (J. Munro & Co., 1838-39), *Jean Paul Richter* in *The Book Worm* (J. B. Alden, 1885)

De Quincey, T., *Essays on Philosophical Writers and Other Men of Letters* (Ticknor, Reed & Fields, 1854)

Hayes, J. C., *Laurence Sterne and Jean Paul* (New York, 1942)

Lee, E. B., *Life of Jean F. Richter* (C. C. Little, 1842; J. Chapman, 1845), *Life of Jean Paul Frederic Richter* (D. Appleton & Co., 1850)

Walden, H., *Jean Paul and Swift* (New York, 1940)

KANT

Translations: *Inevitable Peace* (Harvard University Press, 1948); Abbott, T. K., *Fundamental Principles of the Metaphysics of Ethics* (Longmans, Green & Co., 1932), *Fundamental Principles of the Metaphysics of Morals* (The Library of Liberal Arts, The Liberal Arts

Press, Inc., 1949), *Kant's Critique of Practical Reason* (Longmans, Green & Co., 1883), *Kant's Introduction to Logic* (Longmans, Green & Co., 1885); Beck, L. W., *Critique of Practical Reason and Other Writings in Moral Philosophy* (University of Chicago Press, 1949); Bernard, J. G., *Kant's Critique of Judgment* (Macmillan Co., Ltd., 1914); Box, E. B., *Kant's Prologomena, and Metaphysical Foundations of Natural Science* (G. Bell & Sons, 1891); Carus, P., *Prologomena to any Future Metaphysics* (The Library of Liberal Arts, The Liberal Arts Press, Inc., 1950; The Great Books Foundation, 1951); Friedrich, C. J., *The Philosophy of Kant* (The Modern Library, Random House, 1949); Goerwitz, E. F., *Dreams of a Spirit-Seer* (S. Sonnenschein & Co., Ltd., 1900); Greene, T. M., *Religion within the Limits of Reason Alone* (The Open Court Publishing Co., 1934, *Selections* (Modern Student's Library, C. Scribner's Sons); Haywood, F., *Critick of Pure Reason* (W. Pickering, 1838); Manthey-Zorn, O., *The Fundamental Principles of the Metaphysics of Ethics* (D. Appleton-Century Co., Inc., 1938); Meiklejohn, J. M. D., *Critique of Pure Reason* (H. G. Bohn, 1855; G. Bell & Sons, 1887; The Colonial Press, 1899; Everyman's Library, E. P. Dutton & Co., 1934); Meredith, J. C., *Kant's Critique of Aesthetic Judgment* (Clarendon Press, 1911); Müller, F. M., *Critique of Pure Reason* (London, 1881; The Macmillan Co., 1922); Smith, M. C., *Perpetual Peace* (The Library of Liberal Arts, The Liberal Arts Press, Inc., 1948); Watson, J., *The Philosophy of Kant* (J. Maclehose & Sons, 1894)

Caird, E., *The Critical Philosophy of I. Kant* (J. Maclehose & Sons, 1909)

Cassirer, E., *Rousseau, Kant, Goethe* (Princeton University Press, 1945)

Cassirer, H. W., *A Commentary on Kant's Critique of Judgment* (Methuen & Co., Ltd., 1938)

De Quincey, T., *Essays on Philosophical Writers* (Ticknor, Reed & Fields, 1854)

England, F. E., *Kant's Conception of God* (G. Allen & Unwin, Ltd., 1929)

Howard, C., *Coleridge's Idealism* (R. G. Badger, 1924)

Jones, W. T., *Morality and Freedom in the Philosophy of I. Kant* (Oxford University Press, 1940)

Knox, J., *The Aesthetic Theories of Kant, Hegel, and Schopenhauer* (Columbia University Press, 1936)

Maier, J., *On Hegel's Critique of Kant* (Columbia University Press, 1939)

Paton, H. J., *The Categorical Imperative* (University of Chicago Press, 1948), *Kant's Metaphysic of Experience* (G. Allen & Unwin, 1951)

Scott, J. W., *Kant on the Moral Life* (The Macmillan Co., 1924)

Smith, A. H., *Kantian Studies* (The Clarendon Press, 1947)

Smith, N. K., *A Commentary to Kant's "Critique of Pure Reason"* (Macmillan & Co., Ltd., 1918)

Teale, A., *Kantian Ethics* (Oxford University Press, 1951)

Vaihinger, H., *The Philosophy of "As If"* (Harcourt, Brace & Co., 1925)

Wallace, W., *Kant* (W. Blackwood & Sons, 1899)

Webb, C. C. J., *Kant's Philosophy of Religion* (Oxford Press, 1926)

Weldon, T. D., *Introduction to Kant's Critique of Pure Reason* (The Clarendon Press, 1945)

Wellek, R., *I. Kant in England* (Princeton University Press, 1931)

Whitney, G. T., *The Heritage of Kant* (Princeton University Press, 1939)

Wenley, R. M., *Kant and His Philosophical Revolution* (C. Scribner's Sons, 1911)

KLEIST

Translation: Oxenford, J. and Feiling, C. A., *Tales from the German* (Harper & Brothers, 1844)

Anderson, E. N., *Nationalism and the Cultural Crisis in Prussia, 1806-1815* (Farrar & Rinehart, Inc., 1939)

Becker, H. K., *Kleist and Hebbel; a Comparative Study* (Scott, Foresman & Co., 1904)

Blankenagel, J. C., *The Attitude of Heinrich von Kleist toward the Problems of Life* (The Johns Hopkins Press, 1917)

Silz, W., *Early German Romanticism; its Founders and Heinrich von Kleist* (Harvard University Press, 1929)

Stahl, E. L., *Heinrich von Kleist's Dramas* (B. Blackwell, 1948)

Zweig, S., *Master Builders* (The Viking Press, 1939)

KLINGER

Translation: Borrow, G., *Faustus; His Life, Death, and Descent into Hell* in Borrow's *Works* (W. Simpkin & R. Marshall, 1925)

KLOPSTOCK

Translations: *Memoirs of Frederick and Margaret Klopstock* (R. Cruttwell, 1809; Farrand, Mallory & Co., 1810); Collyer, J. *The Messiah* (Shepard Kollock, 1788; Evert Duyckinck & Co., 1795); Egestorff, G. H. C., *Messiah* (Hamburgh, 1821-22); Gosse, E., Hare, J., Carlyle, T., Matheson, E. P., *Undine and Other Stories* (World's Classics, Oxford University Press, 1932); Halling, S., *The Messiah, a Poem* (Francis M. Boxter, 1910); Head, C., *The Messiah: a Poem* (Longman, Rees, Orme, Brown, & Green, 1826)

Adler, F. H., *Herder and Klopstock; a Comparative Study* (G. E. Stechert & Co., 1914)

LA MOTTE-FOUQUÉ

Translations: *Aslauga and Her Knight* (Hamilton, Adams & Co., 1843); *The Magic Ring* (Oliver & Boyd, 1825); *Minstrel Love* (E. Lumley, 1845; J. Burns, 1845); *Romantic Fiction: Shorter Tales from the German of de La Motte Fouqué* (J. Burns, 185-?); *Natalia, Aslauga's Knight and Other Tales* (Jordan & Wiley, 1845); *The Seasons: Four Romances, from the German of the Baron de La Motte Fouqué* (J. Burns, 1843); *Thiodolf the Icelander, and Aslauga's Knight* (Wiley & Putnam, 1845); *Miniature Romances from the German* (C. C. Little & J. Brown, 1841); *Undine* (E. Littell, 1824); *Undine: a Romance, and Sintram and His Companions* (G. P. Putnam's Sons, 1888); *Undine, and Other Tales* (Hurd & Houghton, 1871); *Undine, and Sintram and His Companions* (Wiley & Putnam, 1845); *Undine; or the Water Spirit. Also, Sintram and His Companions* (W. P. Hazard, 1859; J. Miller, 1863; Worthington Co., 1889); *Violina: a Miniature Romance* (H. G. Clarke & Co., 1845); *Wild Love. A Romance* (E. Ferrett & Co., 1845); *Wild Love, and Other Tales* (J. Burns, 1844); Anster, J., *Xeniola. Poems, including Translations from Schiller and De La Motte Fouque* (Milliken & Son, 1837); Bunnett, F. E., *Undine* (H. Altemus, 1895), *Undine, and Other Tales, by de La Motte Fouqué* (B. Tauchnitz, 1867); Gosse, E., *Undine* (Sidgwick & Jackson, Ltd., 1912; The Limited Editions Club, 1930); Carlyle, T., *German Romances* (J. Munro & Co., 1841); Gillies, R. P., *German Stories* (W. Blackwood, 1826); Soane, G., *Minstrel-Love* (W. Simpkins & R. Marshall, 1821); Tracy, T., *German Romance. Undine* (Wiley & Putnam, 1845), *Undine: a Miniature Romance* (W. Smith, 1839; S. Coleman, 1839)

LESSING

Translations: *Laokoon, and How the Ancients Represented Death* (G. Bell & Sons, Ltd., 1914); *Nathan the Wise* (Stevenson & Matchett, 1791); *The School for Honor* (Vernor & Hood, 1799); Beasley, E. C., *Laocoon* (Longman, Brown, Green, & Longmans, 1853); Bell, E. (ed.), *The Dramatic Works of G. E. Lessing* (G. Bell & Sons, 1891); Cohen, A., *Lessing's Masonic Dialogues* (The Baskerville Press, Ltd., 1927); Frothingham, E., *Laocoön* (Roberts Bros., 1874), *Nathan the Wise* (H. Holt & Co., 1867; Leypoldt & Holt, 1869); Haney, J. D., *Lessing's Education of the Human Race* (Columbia University, 1908); Holcroft, F., *Emilia Galotti* (Bradford & Inskeep, 1810); Howard, W. G., *Laokoon. Lessing, Herder, Goethe* (H. Holt & Co., 1910); Markun, L., *Nathan the Wise* (Haldeman-Julius Co., 1926); Maxwell, P., *Nathan the Wise* (Bloch Publishing Co., 1923); Phillimore, R., *Laocoon* (London, 1874); Robertson, J. G., *Lessing's Dramatic Theory* (Cambridge University

Press, 1939); Rönnfeldt, W. B., *The Laocoon, and Other Prose Writings of Lessing* (W. Scott, Ltd., 1895); Wrankmore, W. C., *Minna von Barnhelm* (A. Gumprecht, 1858)

Bryant, F. E., *A History of English Balladry and Other Studies* (R. G. Badger, 1913)

Coleridge, S. T., *Confessions of an Inquiring Spirit* (W. Pickering, 1849)

De Quincey, T., *Essays on Philosophical Writers and Other Men of Letters* (Ticknor, Reed, & Fields, 1854)

Garland, H. B., *Lessing, the Founder of Modern German Literature* (Bowes & Bowes, 1927)

Hervey, W. A., *Syllabus and Selected Bibliography of Lessing, Goethe, Schiller* (Lencke & Buechner, 1918)

Lowell, J. R., *The English Poets: Lessing, Rousseau* (W. J. Gage & Co., 1888)

Mann, T., *Essays of Three Decades* (A. A. Knopf, 1947), *Past Masters and Other Papers* (A. A. Knopf, 1933)

Mehring, F., *The Lessing Legend* (Critics Group Press, 1938)

Nolte, F. O., *Lessing's Laokoon* (Lancaster Press, 1940)

Perry, H. T. E., *Masters of Dramatic Comedy and Their Social Themes* (Harvard University Press, 1939)

Phelps, W. L., *Essays on Books* (Macmillan Co., 1914)

Robertson, J. G., *Essays and Addresses on Literature* (G. Routledge & Sons, Ltd., 1935), *Lessing's Dramatic Theory* (Cambridge University Press, 1939)

Rolleston, T. W. H., *Life of Gotthold Ephraim Lessing* (W. Scott, 1889)

Schmitz, F. J., *The Problem of Individualism and the Crises in the Lives of Lessing and Hamann* (University of California Press, 1944)

Sime, J., *Lessing* (Trübner & Co., 1877)

Stahr, A. W. T., *The Life and Works of Gotthold Ephraim Lessing* (W. V. Spencer, 1866)

Vail, C. C. D., *Lessing's Relation to the English Language and Literature* (Columbia University Press, 1936)

MUNDT

Translation: Radford, T. J., *Count Mirabeau* (D. Appleton & Co., 1868)

NOVALIS

Translations: *Henry of Ofterdingen: a Romance* (J. Owen, 1842; H. H. Moore, 1853); Hope, M. J., *Novalis; His Life, Thoughts, and Works* (A. C. McClurg & Co., 1891); Manheim, R., *The Novices of Sais* (C. Valentin, 1949)

Carlyle, T., *Critical and Miscellaneous Essays* (Houghton, Mifflin & Co., 1881)

Maeterlinck, M., *On Emerson and Other Essays* (Dodd, Mead & Co., 1912)

Spring, H. P., *Novalis, Pioneer of the Spirit* (Orange Press, 1946)

PAUL

See Jean Paul

RICHTER

See Jean Paul

SCHELLING

Translations: Bolman, Jr., F. de W., *The Ages of the World* (Columbia University Press, 1942); Gutmann, J., *Schelling: Of Human Freedom* (The Open Court Publishing Co., 1936)

Cahill, M. C., *The Absolute and the Relative in St. Thomas and in Modern Philosophy* (The Catholic University of America Press, 1939)

Watson, J., *Schelling's Transcendental Idealism* (S. C. Griggs & Co., 1892)

SCHILLER

Translations: *Cabal and Love. A Tragedy* (J. Bryan, 1795); *Don Carlos: a Tragedy* (W. J. & J. Richardson, 1798); *Essays, Aesthetical and Philosophical* (G. Bell & Sons, 1875); *The Ghost-Seer; or, Apparitionist* (T. & J. Swords, 1796); *History of the Revolt of the Netherlands* (Bell & Daldy, 1847); *History of the Thirty Years' War* (Hurst & Co., 1880); *The Robbers. A Tragedy* (G. G. & J. Robinson, 1800); *The Robbers. A Tragedy in Five Acts* (D. Longworth, 1808; S. French, 18—?; W. Taylor & Co., 1854); *Mary Stuart. A Tragedy* (D. & J. Allen, 1883); *William Tell; a Historical Play* (A. Gebhardt, 1873); *The Works of Frederick Schiller* (H. G. Bohn, 1853-67; Bell & Daldy, 1872-73; J. D. Williams, 188-?; G. Bell & Sons, 1881); Anster, J., *Xeniola. Poems, including Translations from Schiller and de La Motte Fouqué* (Milliken & Son, 1837); Arnold, T. J., *Das Lied von der Glocke* (D. Nutt, 1846); Blaquiere, W., *The History of the Thirty Years' War in Germany* (C. Jugel, 1842); Bohn, H. G., *The Robbers* (Stringer & Townsend, 1850); Bowring, E. A., *The Poems of Schiller* (G. Bell & Sons, 1908); Brooks, C. T., *Schiller's Homage of the Arts* (J. Miller, 1864); Bulwer-Lytton, E., *Schiller's Poems and Ballads* (G. Routledge & Sons, 1887); Calvert, G. H., *Correspondence between Schiller and Goethe, from 1794 to 1805* (Wiley & Putnam, 1845), *Don Carlos; a Dramatic Poem* (W. & J. Neal, 1834); Coleridge, D. (ed.), *The Dramatic Works of Samuel Taylor Coleridge* (E. Moxon, 1852); Coleridge, S. T., *The Piccolomini* in his *Poetical and Dramatic Works* (Boston, 1861), *The*

Tragedies of Schiller (Griffin, Bohn & Co., 1853?); Dole, N. H., *Collected Works* (D. Estes & Co., 1901-2), *The Works of Friedrich Schiller* (Bigelow, Brown & Co., Inc., 1902); Dwight, J. S., *Select Minor Poems, Translated from the German of Goethe and Schiller* (Hilliard, Gray, & Co., 1839); Fischer, J. G. (ed.), *Collected Works* (G. Barrie, 1883); Furness, W. J., *Das Lied von der Glocke* (Schäfer & Koradi, 1859); Harris, G. S., *The Nephew as Uncle* (Voigt & Günther, 1856); Hedge, F. H., *Schiller's Song of the Bell* (Hazard & Mitchell, 1850); Hempel, C. J. (ed.), *Schiller's Complete Works* (I. Kohler, 1861); Johnston, J. P., *Lyrics from the German of Schiller* (C. & H. Senior, 1839); Kaplan, S., *William Tell* (Barron's Educational Series, Inc., 1953); Lewis, M. G., *The Minister: a Tragedy* (J. Bell, 1797; Graisberry & Campbell, 1798); J. C. M., *Mary Stuart, a Tragedy* (G. Auld, 1801); Martin, T., *The Song of the Bell, and Other Translations from Schiller, Goethe, Uhland, and Others* (W. Blackwood & Sons, 1889); G. H. N. & J. S., *Fiesco; or, The Genoese Conspiracy* (J. Johnson, 1796); Moir, G., *History of the Thirty-Years' War* (Edinburgh, 1828); Morrison, A. J. W., *History of the Thirty Years' War* (Harper & Brothers, 1846), *The History of the Thirty Years' War* (A. L. Burt Co., 19—?), *History of the Revolt of the Netherlands* (Harper & Brothers, 1847), *History of the Thirty Years' War, Complete. History of the Revolt of the Netherlands to the Confederacy of the Gueux* (Bell & Daldy, 1873); Morrison, A. J. W. and Schmitz, L. D., *The Revolt of the United Netherlands* (G. Bell & Sons, 1889); Murison, A. F., *Schiller's Wallenstein* (Longmans, Green & Co., 1931); Novello, S., *Turandot; the Chinese Sphinx* (S. French, 1872); Peter, W., *Mary Stuart, a Tragedy* (H. Perkins, 1840); Ramage, C. T., *Beautiful Thoughts from German and Spanish Authors* (E. Howell, 1868); Reinhardt, G., *Maria Stuart* (Barron's Educational Series, Inc., 1950), *Nathan Der Weise* (Barron's Educational Series, Inc., 1950); Retzsch, F. A. M., *Schiller's Pegasus in the Yoke* (D. Appleton & Co. & W. Radde, 1857); Rhoades, L. A. (ed.), *Schiller's Maria Stuart* (D. C. Heath & Co., 1896); Roscoe, T. (ed.), *German Novelists* (London, 1826); Simpson, L., *Correspondence of Schiller with Körner* (R. Bentley, 1849); Steel, W. A., *Laocoön, Minna, Nathan the Wise* (Everyman's Library, E. P. Dutton & Co., 1934); Thompson, B., *The Robbers. A Tragedy, in Five Acts* (Vernor & Hood, 1800); Viereck, G. S., *The Maid of Orleans* (Haldeman-Julius Co., 1925); Weiss, J., *The Aesthetic Letters, Essays, and the Philosophical Letters* (C. C. Little & J. Brown, 1845); Weisse, J. F., *Letters of Schiller* (S. N. Dickinson, 1841); Woodhouselee, Lord, *The Robbers. A Tragedy* (Samuel Campbell, 1793)

Boyesen, H. H., *Essays on German Literature* (C. Scribner's Sons, 1892), *Goethe and Schiller* (C. Scribner's Sons, 1879)

Bryant, W. C., *Orations and Addresses* (G. P. Putnam's Sons, 1873)

Carlyle, T., *Critical and Miscellaneous Essays* (J. Munroe & Co., 1838-9), *The Life of Friedrich Schiller* (D. Appleton & Co., 1846)

Carus, P., *Friedrich Schiller* (Open Court Publishing Co., 1905)

De Quincey, T., *Biographical Essays* (Ticknor, Reed & Fields, 1850)

Duentzer, H., *The Life of Schiller* (Macmillan & Co., 1883)

Ellet, E. F., *Characters of Schiller* (Boston, 1839)

Ewen, F., *The Prestige of Schiller in England, 1788-1859* (Columbia University Press, 1932)

Florer, W. W., *German Liberty Authors* (R. G. Badger, 1918)

Francke, K., *German Ideals of Today* (Houghton, Mifflin & Co., 1907)

Garland, H. B., *Schiller* (McBride, 1950)

Hervey, W. A., *Syllabus and Selected Bibliography of Lessing, Goethe, Schiller* (Lemcke & Buechner, 1918)

Kaufmann, F. W., *Schiller, Poet of Philosophical Idealism* (Oberlin Academy Press, 1942)

Kühnemann, E., *Schiller* (Ginn & Co., 1912)

Ludwig, E., *Genius and Character* (Harcourt, Brace & Co., 1927)

Meakin, A. M. B., *Goethe and Schiller, 1785-1805* (F. Griffiths, 1932)

Moorman, L. J., *Tuberculosis and Genius* (The University of Chicago Press, 1940)

Nevinson, H. W., *Life of Friedrich Schiller* (T. Whittaker, 1889)

Palleske, E., *Schiller's Life and Works* (London, 1860)

Parry, E. C., *Friedrich Schiller in America* (Americana Germanica Press, 1905)

Phelps, W. L., *Essays on Books* (The Macmillan Co., 1914)

Steiner, R., *Schiller and Our Times* (H. Collison, 1933), *The Theory of Knowledge Implicit in Goethe's World-Conception; Fundamental Outlines with Special Reference to Schiller* (Anthroposophic Press, 1940)

Thomas, C., *The Life and Works of Friedrich Schiller* (H. Holt & Co., 1901)

Wilm, E. C., *The Philosophy of Schiller in its Historical Relations* (J. W. Luce & Co., 1912)

Witte, W., *Schiller* (B. Blackwell, 1949)

Wolf, E. and Florer, W. W., *A Guide for the Study of Schiller's Wilhelm Tell* (Sheehan & Co., 1904)

SCHLEGEL, A. W.

Translations: Black, J., *A Course of Lectures on Dramatic Art and Literature* (J. Templeman, 1840; H. G. Bohn, 1846), *Lectures on Dramatic Art and Literature* (G. Bell & Sons, 1876); Fiedler, H. G.

(ed.), *A. W. Schlegel's Lectures on German Literature from Gottsched to Goethe* (B. Blackwell, 1944); Harvey, E. L., *Ariadne* (C. Jugel's Sons, 1847); Holstein, Mme. de Staël, *An Appeal to the Nations of Europe against the Continental System* (J. M. Richardson, 1813; S. H. Parker, 1813)

Phelan, A. A., *The Indebtedness of Samuel Taylor Coleridge to August Wilhelm von Schlegel* (Madison: the University, 1907)

SCHLEGEL, K. W. F.

Translations: *Lectures on the History of Literature Ancient and Modern* (T. Dobson & Son, 1818; W. Blackwood & Sons, 1841; J. & H. G. Langley, 1841; H. G. Bohn, 1859; Moss, Brother & Co., 1860; Bell & Daldy, 1871; G. Bell & Sons, 1896); Millington, E. J., *The Aesthetic and Miscellaneous Works* (H. G. Bohn, 1849); Purcell, L. and Whitelock, R. H., *A Course of Lectures on Modern History* (H. G. Bohn, 1849); Robertson, J. B., *The Philosophy of History* (Saunders & Otley, 1835; D. Appleton & Co., 1841; H. G. Bohn, 1847; G. Bell & Sons, 1904)

STURM UND DRANG

Garland, H. B., *Storm and Stress* (Harrap, 1952)

Runge, E. A., *Primitivism and Related Ideas in Sturm und Drang Literature* (The Johns Hopkins Press, 1946)

Zeydel, E. H., *Early References to Storm and Stress in German Literature* (Indiana University Studies, Bloomington, Indiana, 1926)

TIECK

Translations: *Popular Tales and Romances of the Northern Nations* (W. Simpkin & R. Marshall, 1823); Burette, Mme., *The Rebellion in the Cevennes* (D. Nutt, 1845); Carlyle, T., *German Romance* (J. Munroe & Co., 1841), *Tales by Musaeus, Tieck, Richter* (Scribner, Welford & Co., 1874); Hare, J. C., *The Old Man of the Mountain* (E. Moxon, 1831); Hare, J. C., Froude, J. A. and Others, *Tales from the "Phantasus"* (J. Burns, 1845); Rumsey, M. C., *The Midsummer Night* (C. Whittingham, 1854); Zeydel, E. H., Matenko, P., Fife, R. H. (eds.), *Letters of Ludwig Tieck* (Modern Language Association of America, 1937); Matenko, P. (ed.), *Tieck and Solger, the Complete Correspondence* (B. Westermann Co., 1933)

Danton, G. H., *The Nature Sense in the Writings of Ludwig Tieck* (Columbia University, 1907), *Tieck's Essay on the Boydell Shakspere Gallery* (E. J. Hecker, printer, 1912)

Lang, E. A., *Ludwig Tieck's Early Concept of Catholic Clergy and Church* (The Catholic University of America, 1936)

Lussky, A. E., *Tieck's Romantic Irony* (The University of North Carolina Press, 1932)

Martin, T., *Essays on the Drama* (London, 1889)

Scheiber, M. M., *Ludwig Tieck and the Medieval Church* (The Catholic University of America Press, 1939)

Zeydel, E. H., *Ludwig Tieck and England* (Princeton University Press for the University of Cincinnati, 1931), *Ludwig Tieck, the German Romanticist* (Princeton University Press, 1935)

UHLAND

Translation: Platt, A., *Poems* (Leipzig, 1848)

WERNER

Carlyle, T., *Critical and Miscellaneous Essays* (D. Estes & Co., 1901)

WIELAND

Translations: *The Trial of Abraham* (J. Trumbull, 1777); Adams, J. Q., *Oberon, a Poetical Romance in Twelve Books* (F. S. Crofts & Co., 1940); Christmas, H., *The Republic of Fools* (W. H. Allen & Co., 1861); Cooke, T., *Oberon; or, The Charmed Horn* (J. Tabby, 1826); Sotheby, W., *Oberon, a Poem* (T. Cadell & W. Davies, 1805; J. Belcher, 1810; H. G. Clarke & Co., 1844); Wintersted, Mr., *Socrates Out of His Senses* (D. Denniston & J. Fellows, 1797)

Bach, M. G., *Wieland's Attitude toward Woman and her Cultural and Social Relations* (Columbia University Press, 1922)

Beyer, W. W., *Keats and the Daemon King* (Oxford University Press, 1947)

Elson, C., *Wieland and Shaftesbury* (Columbia University Press, 1913)

CHAPTER SEVEN

THE RISE OF REALISM

GENERAL

Alden, H. M., *Magazine Writing and the New Literature* (Harper & Brothers, 1908)

Anderson, S., *A Writer's Conception of Realism* (Olivet College Press, 1939)

Bacourt, P. D. de, *French Literature during the Last Half-Century* (Macmillan Co., 1923)

Bithell, J., *Modern German Literature (1880-1938)* (Methuen & Co., Ltd., 1939)

Brown, J. M., *The Modern Theatre in Revolt* (W. W. Norton & Co., Inc., 1929)

Courtney, W. L., *Old Laws and Modern Instances* (Chapman & Hall, Ltd., 1918)

Darrow, C. S., *Realism in Literature and Art* (C. H. Kerr & Co., 1899)

Davies, H. S., *Realism in the Drama* (Cambridge University Press, 1934)

Eloesser, A., *Modern German Literature* (A. A. Knopf, 1933)

Goodsell, W., *The Conflict of Naturalism and Humanism* (Columbia University Press, 1910)

Heller, O., *Studies in Modern German Literature* (Ginn & Co., 1905)

Hentschel, C., *The Byronic Teuton; Aspects of German Pessimism, 1800-1933* (Methuen & Co., Ltd., 1940)

Jameson, S., *Modern Drama in Europe* (Collins, 1920)

Klenze, C. von, *From Goethe to Hauptmann* (The Viking Press, 1926)

Lange, V., *Modern German Literature, 1870-1940* (Cornell University Press, 1945)

Lewisohn, L., *The Spirit of Modern German Literature* (B. W. Huebsch, 1916)

Lucas, F. L., *The Decline and Fall of the Romantic Ideal* (Cambridge University Press, 1948)

McDowall, A. S., *Realism* (Constable & Co., Ltd., 1918)

Moore, A. P., *The Genre Poissard and the French Stage of the Eighteenth Century* (Columbia University Press, 1935)

Myers, W. L., *The Later Realism* (University of Chicago Press, 1927)

Oda, W. H., *The Subject of Realism in the Revue de Paris* (University of Pennsylvania Press, 1939)

Phelps, W. L., *Essays on Books* (Macmillan Co., 1914)

Reade, A., *Main Currents in Modern Literature* (Nicholson, 1935)

Weinberg, *French Realism* (Modern Language Association, 1937)

Wells, B. W., *Modern German Literature* (Little, Brown, & Co., 1906)

AUERBACH

Translations: *Christian Gellert, and Other Sketches* (S. Low, Son, & Co., 1858); *The Foresters, A Novel* (D. Appleton & Co., 1880); *German Tales* (Roberts Bros., 1869; H. Holt & Co., 1874); Bell, C., *Brigitta. A Tale* (B. Tauchnitz, 1880); Brooks, C. T., *The Convicts and Their Children* (H. Holt & Co., 1877), *Lorley and Reinhard* (H. Holt & Co., 1877), *Poet and Merchant: a Picture of Life from the Times of Moses Mendelssohn* (H. Holt & Co., 1877); Bunnett, F. E., *On the Heights* (Roberts Bros., 1869; A. L. Burt, 191-?); Dulcken, H. W., *Little Barefoot; or, Strive and Trust* (G. Munro, 1879); Frothingham, E., *Edelweiss. A Story* (Roberts Bros., 1869); Goepp, C., *Black Forest Village Stories* (Leypoldt, Holt & Williams, 1871); Hancock, E., *Master Bieland and His Workmen* (H. Holt & Co.,

1883); Howitt, M., *The Professor's Lady* (Harper & Brothers, n. d.);
Irish, A. B., *Landolin* (H. Holt & Co., 1878); Nicholson, E., *Spinoza.
A Novel* (H. Holt & Co., 1882); Shackford, C. S., *Villa Eden: the
Country-house on the Rhine* (Roberts Bros., 1869); Stern, S. A.,
Waldfried: a Novel (John W. Lovell Co., 1874); Taylor, J. E.,
Narrative of Events in Vienna (L. D. Bogue, 1849), *The Villa on
the Rhine* (Leypoldt & Holt, 1869)

AUGIER

Translations: *The Adventuress* (F. Rullman, 1888); *Home Truths* (A.
Harris, 1860); *Paul Forrester* (N. Y. Printing Co., 1871); Clark,
B. H., *Four Plays* (A. A. Knopf, 1915), *The Green Coat* (S. French,
1915), *The House of Fourchambault* (S. French, 1915), *The Post-
Scriptum* (S. French, 1915); Lyster, F., *Faces of Brass* (F. Rullman,
1888); Matthison, A., *A False Step* (S. French, 18—?); Reynoldson,
T. H., *Good for Evil* (T. H. Lacy, 1860); Robertson, T. W., *Home*
(S. French, 1890); Rose, E., *Equals* (S. French, 18—?)

BALZAC

Translations: *Droll Stories* (The Modern Library, Random House, 1931);
Allen, F., *The School of Matrimony* (n. p., 1911); Bell, C., *About
Catherine de Medici* (E. P. Dutton & Co., 1915), *At the Sign of the
Cat and Racket* (J. M. Dent & Co., 1895), *Cat and Racket, etc.*
(Everyman's Library, E. P. Dutton & Co., 1908), *Ursule Mirouet*
(Everyman's Library, E. P. Dutton & Co., 1915); Blanchamp, H., *The
Tragedy of a Genius* (Brentano's, 191-?); Brown, E. K., Walter, D.,
and Watkins, J., *Père Goriot and Eugénie Grandet* (The Modern Li-
brary & Modern Library College Editions, Random House, 1946);
Burgan, J. A., *L'Amour Masqué* (G. Barrie's Sons, 1920); Cameron,
N., *Cousin Pons* (The Novel Library, 1950); Chambers, J. (ed.), *The
Human Comedy* (P. F. Collier, 1893); Crawford, M. A., *Old Goriot*
(Penguin Books, Inc., 1951); Dowson, E., *The Girl with the Golden
Eyes* (Illustrated Editions Co., Inc., 1931); Fowlie, W. (ed.), *Père
Goriot* (Rinehart Editions, Rinehart & Co., Inc., 1950); Griffin, S. P.
and Hill, F. T., *Miniatures from Balzac's Masterpieces* (D. Appleton
& Co., 1894); Harris, T., *The Purse* (The Dramatic Publishing Co.,
1887); Hastings, W. S. (ed.), *Balzac and Souverain; and Unpub-
lished Correspondence* (Doubleday, Page & Co., 1927); Ives, G. B.,
Albert Savarus (G. Barrie & Son, 1897), *Honoré de Balzac* [stories]
(G. P. Putnam's Sons, 1907); Iving, A. M., *Love in a Mask* (Rand,
McNally & Co., 1911); Kent, P., *The Cat and Battledore* (S. Low,
Marston, Searle, & Rivington, 1879); Loyd, Lady M., *The Two
Young Brides* (P. F. Collier & Son, 1902); MacSpadden, J. W., *The
Physiology of Marriage* (D. Estes & Co., 1901); Mapes, E., *Mon-*

triveau (n. p., 1901); Marriage, E., *Eugénie Grandet* (J. M. Dent & Co., 1901; Everyman's Library, E. P. Dutton & Co., 1907), *Old Goriot* (Everyman's Library, E. P. Dutton & Co., 1907; The Limited Editions Club, 1948); Marriage, E. and Rudd, J., *The Jealousies of a Country Town* (The Gebbie Publishing Co., 1899); May, J. L., *Unpublished Correspondence* (John Lane, 1937); Paul, C., *The Fatal Skin* (The Novel Library, 1949); Raine, K., *Cousin Betty* (The Novel Library, 1948); Rickel, H. (ed.), *The Wisdom of Balzac* (G. P. Putnam's Sons, 1923); Saintsbury, G., *The Chonans* (Cassell Publishing Co., 1890); Saintsbury, G. (ed.), *Works* (Avril Publishing Co., 1901); Sedgwick, E., *Splendour and Miseries of Courtesans* (G. Barrie & Son, 1895-6); Sims, G. R., *Droll Stories* (Privately Printed, 1874); Stenbock, E. and Wilson, W., *Don Juan* (F. M. Lipton Publishing Co., 189-?) · Tomlinson, M., *The House of the Cat and the Racket* (G. Barrie & Son, 1896); Trent, W. P. (ed.), *Works* (N. Y. Society of English and French Literature, 1900); Valcourt-Vermont, E. de, *Dramatic Works* (Laird & Lee, 1901); Verelst, M., *After-Dinner Stories* (G. J. Coombes, 1886); Walton, W., *A Double Family* (G. Barrie & Son, 1897); Waring, J. and Marriage, E., *Cousin Betty, and Other Stories* (J. D. Morris & Co., 1890); Wight, O. and Goodrich, F. B., *The Alchemist* (Rudd & Carleton, 1861), *Eugénie Grandet* (Rudd & Carleton, 1861); Walton, W., *Honorine* (G. Barrie & Son, 1897); Wormeley, K. P., *Letters to Mme Hanska* (Hardy, Pratt & Co., 1900), *Works* (Little, Brown & Co., 1903-12)

Bowen, R. P., *The Dramatic Construction of Balzac's Novels* (University of Oregon, 1940)

Brunetière, F., *Honoré de Balzac* (J. B. Lippincott Co., 1907)

Carrère, J., *Degeneration in the Great French Masters* (Brentano's, 1922)

Chapman, J. J., *Greek Genius and Other Essays* (Moffat, Yard & Co., 1915)

Dargan, E. P., *The Evolution of Balzac's Comédie Humaine* (University of Chicago Press, 1942), *Honoré de Balzac* (University of Chicago Press, 1932), *Studies in Balzac's Realism* (University of Chicago Press, 1932)

Dedinsky, B. H., *Development of the Scheme of the Comédie Humaine* (University of Chicago Press, 1943)

Faguet, E., *Balzac* (Houghton, Mifflin Co., 1914)

Floyd, J. H., *Women in the Life of Balzac* (H. Holt & Co., 1921)

Garnand, H. J., *The Influence of Walter Scott on the Works of Balzac* (Columbia University, 1926)

Gautier, T., *Famous French Authors* (R. Worthington, 1879)

Gozlan, L., *Balzac in Slippers* (R. M. McBride & Co., 1929)

Gribble, F. H., *Balzac* (E. P. Dutton & Co., 1930)

Grierson, H. J. C., *Sir Walter Scott Today* (Constable & Co., Ltd., 1932)

Hastings, W. S., *The Drama of Balzac* (Johns Hopkins, 1917)

Helm, W. H., *Aspects of Balzac* (J. Pott & Co., 1905)

James, Harry, *Notes on Novelists* (C. Scribner's Sons, 1914), *The Question of Our Speech* (Houghton, Mifflin & Co., 1905)

James, Henry, *The Art of Fiction* (Oxford University Press, 1948)

Keim, A. and Lumet, L., *Honoré de Balzac* (F. A. Stokes Co., 1914)

Lavrin, Y., *Studies in European Literature* (Constable & Co., Ltd., 1929)

Lawton, F., *Balzac* (G. Richards, Ltd., 1910)

Levin, H., *Toward Balzac* (New Directions, 1947)

Lilly, W. S., *Studies in Religion and Literature* (Chapman & Hall, 1904)

Loving, P., *M. de Balzac Entertains a Visitor* (University of Washington Book Store, 1929)

Ludwig, E., *Genius and Character* (Harcourt, Brace & Co., 1927)

Maurois, A., *Mape* (D. Appleton & Co., 1926), *Seven Faces of Love* (Didier, 1944)

McMurtrie, D. C., *Balzac, Printer and Typefounder* (Privately Printed, 1926)

Neumann, R., *Passion* (Harcourt, Brace & Co., 1932)

Royce, W. H., *Balzac As He Should Be Read* (A. Giraldi, 1946), *A Balzac Bibliography* (University of Chicago Press, 1929), *Balzac, Immortal* (Privately Printed, 1926)

Saltus, E., *Balzac* (Houghton, Mifflin & Co., 1884)

Sandars, M. F., *Balzac* (Dodd, Mead & Co., 1905)

Taine, H., *Balzac* (Funk & Wagnalls Co., 1906)

Turguet-Milnes, G. R., *From Pascal to Proust* (J. Cape, Ltd., 1926)

Wedmore, Sir F., *Life of Balzac* (W. Scott, 1890)

Wenger, J., *The Province and the Provinces in the Work of Balzac* (Princeton University, 1937)

Wormeley, K. P., *Balzac* (Little, Brown & Co., 1912)

Zweig, S., *Balzac* (The Viking Press, 1946), *Three Masters* (The Viking Press, 1930)

BEYLE (STENDHAL)

Translations: *Memoirs of Rossini* (T. Horcham, 1824); Bombet, L. A. C., *The Life of Haydn* (Miller & Hutchens, 1820); Earp, T. W., *Memoirs of an Egotist* (Turnstile Press, 1949); Le Clercq, J., *Lamiel* (Brentano's, 1929); Lloyd, Lady M., *The Charterhouse of Parma* (P. F. Collier & Son, 1901); Moncrieff, C. K. S., *The Abbess of Castro* (Boni & Liveright, 1926), *The Charterhouse of Parma* (Boni & Liveright, 1925; Chatto & Windus, 1926; Anchor Books, Doubleday & Co., Inc., 1953), *The Red and the Black* (Boni & Liveright, 1926; The Modern Library, Random House, 1929); Phillips, C. A., *The Life of Henri Brulard* (A. A. Knopf, 1925); Shaw, M. R. B.,

The Red and the Black (Penguin Books, Inc., 1954?); Woolf, P. S. and C. N. S., *On Love* (Duckworth & Co., 1915)

Brussaly, M., *The Political Ideas of Stendhal* (Columbia University, 1933)

Carrère, J., *Degeneration in the Great French Masters* (Brentano's, 1922)

Faguet, E., *Politicians and Moralists of the Nineteenth Century* (F. Benn, Ltd., 1928)

Fineshriber, W. H., *Stendhal, the Romantic Rationalist* (Princeton University Press, 1932)

Green, F. C., *Stendhal* (Cambridge University Press, 1939)

Hazard, P., *Stendhal* (Coward-McCann, Inc., 1929)

Huneker, J. G., *Egoists* (C. Scribner's Sons, 1909)

Josephson, M., *Stendhal* (Doubleday & Co., Inc., 1946)

Kayser, R., *Stendhal* (H. Holt & Co., 1930)

Krutch, J. W., *Five Masters* (J. Cape & H. Smith, 1930)

Maurois, A., *Seven Faces of Love* (Didier, 1944)

Paton, A. A., *Henry Beyle* (Trübner & Co., 1874)

Samuel, H. B., *Modernities* (K. Paul, Trench, Trübner & Co., Ltd., 1914)

Strachey, L., *Books and Characters* (Harcourt, Brace & Co., 1922)

Valéry, P., *Variety: Second Series* (Harcourt, Brace & Co., 1938)

Vinogradov, A. K., *Three Colors of Time* (Hutchinson & Co., Ltd., 1946)

Writridge, A., *Critical Ventures in Modern French Literature* (C. Scribner's Sons, 1924)

Zweig, S., *Adepts in Self-Portraiture* (The Viking Press, 1928)

BITZIUS

See Gotthelf.

DAUDET

Translations: *One of the Forty* (Continental Publishing Co., 1888), *Sapho* [sic] (Boni & Liveright, 1919); Bertault, C., *In the Midst of Paris* (Platt, Bruce & Co., 1896); Blaydes, W., *The Nabob* (P. F. Collier & Son, 1902); Champlin, V., *Kings in Exile* (Rand, McNally & Co., 1889), *Numa Roumestan* (Lee & Shepard, 1882); Cohn, A., *The Head of the Family* (G. P. Putnam's Sons, 1898); Ensor, L., *Artists' Wives* (G. Routledge & Sons, 1890), *Recollections of a Literary Man* (G. Routledge & Sons, 1889), *Robert Helmont* (G. Routledge & Sons, 1888), *Thirty Years of Paris* (G. Routledge & Sons, 1888); Frith, H., *Tartarin on the Alps* (G. Routledge & Sons, 1887); Garver, M., *Suffering* (Yale University Press, 1934); Ginty, E. B., *Sappho, a Play* (F. Rullman, 1905); Ives, G. B., *Letters from My Mill* (G. P. Putnam's Sons, 1903); Ives, G. B. and Others, *The Works* (Little, Brown & Co., 1898-1900); James, H., *Port Tarascon* (Harper & Brothers, 1891); LeClercq, J., *Tartarin of Tarascon* (The Limited Editions Club, 1930); Mansion, J. E., *Letters from My Windmill*

(G. G. Harrap & Co., Ltd., 1919); McIntyre, M., *Jack* (Little, Brown & Co., 1900); Okie, C. G., *Tartarin of Tarascon* (Folio Club, 1938); Potter, F. H., *Letters from My Mill* (Dodd, Mead & Co., 1893); Sarkar, I., *French Stories from Alphonse Daudet* (C. Chatterjee & Co., 1945); Serrano, M. J., *Rose and Ninette* (F. T. Neely, 1894); Sherwood, M. N., *The Little Good-for-Nothing* (Estes & Lauriat, 1878); Verrall, A. W. and M. de G., *One of the Forty* (Rand, McNally & Co., 189-?); Vizetelly, E. H., *Fromont Junior and Risler Senior* (J. B. Lippincott Co., 1895); Wormeley, K. P., *Kings in Exile* (Little, Brown & Co., 1900)

Daudet, L., *Alphonse Daudet* (Little, Brown & Co., 1898)

Loti, P., *On Life's By-Ways* (G. Bell & Sons, Ltd., 1914)

Matthews, B., *The Historical Novel* (C. Scribner's Sons, 1901)

Ransome, A., *Portraits and Speculations* (Macmillan & Co., Ltd., 1913)

Sherard, R. H., *Alphonse Daudet* (E. Arnold, 1894)

DUMAS, ALEXANDER (FILS)

Translations: *Camille* (The Modern Library, Random House, 1925); *La Dame aux Camilias* (F. Rullman, 1910); Bracco, A., *Francillon* (C. & T. Rosenfeld, 1893); Byrne, C. A., *The Wife of Claude* (F. Rullman, 1905); George, C., *Legend of Camille* (Dramatists Play Service, Inc., 1943); Gosse, E., *Camille* (The Limited Editions Club, 1937), *The Lady of the Camelias* (P. F. Collier & Son, 1902); Heron, M., *Camille* (S. French, 1856); Lynch, A., *The Lady with the Camelias* (L. C. Page & Co., 1906); Metcalf, H., *Camille* (S. French, 1931); Olivine, W., *Camille* (O. O. Roorbach, 1856); Reynolds, E. and Playfair, N., *The Lady of the Camellias* [sic] (E. Benn, Ltd., 1930); Slevin, L. J., *The Woman's Friend* (Privately Printed, 1928); Squier, Mrs. E. G., *The Demi-Monde* (J. B. Lippincott & Co., 1858); Vanderhoff, G., *Man-Woman* (Privately Printed, 1873); Walton, W., *The Lady of the Camelias* (G. H. Richmond & Co., 1897)

Bodington, O. E., *Quiseen* (The Richards Press, Ltd., 1927)

DeFord, M. A., *Love-Children* (The Dial Press, 1931)

Gribble, F. H., *Dumas, Father and Son* (E. P. Dutton & Co., 1930)

James, H., *Notes on Novelists* (C. Scribner's Sons, 1914)

Schwarz, H. S., *Alexander Dumas Fils* (New York University Press, 1927)

Taylor, F. A., *The Theatre of Alexander Dumas, Fils* (The Clarendon Press, 1937)

Tolstoi, L., *Stop and Think!* (Brotherhood Publishing Co., 1899)

ENGELS

See Marx.

110 BIBLIOGRAPHY OF EUROPEAN LITERATURE

FLAUBERT

Translations: *The Complete Works* (M. W. Dunne, 1904); *Madame Bovary* (The Living Library, The World Publishing Co.); Aveling, E. M., *Madame Bovary* (Boni & Liveright, Inc., 1918; The Modern Library, Random House, 1921; Everyman's Library, E. P. Dutton & Co., 1928; Rinehart Editions, Rinehart & Co., Inc., 1948; Pocket Books, Inc., 1952); Blaydes, W., *Madame Bovary* (P. F. Collier & Son, 1902); Chartres, J., *Salambô* (Everyman's Library, E. P. Dutton & Co., 1931); Francis, R., *The First Temptation of Saint Anthony* (Duckworth & Co., 1915); Goldsmith, A., *Sentimental Education* (Everyman's Library, E. P. Dutton & Co., Inc., 1941); Hearn, L., *The Temptation of St. Anthony* (The Alice Harriman Co., 1911); Honey, M. D., *The Legend of St. Julian the Hospitaller* (G. G. Harrap & Co., Ltd., 1925); Hopkins, G., *Madame Bovary* (Oxford University Press, paper 1953); Koch, T. W., *Bibliomania, a Tale* (Northwestern University Library, 1929); Mathers, E. P., *Salambo* [sic] (The Golden Cockerel Press, 1931); McDowall, A., *Three Tales* (Chatto & Windus, 1923; A. A. Knopf, Inc., 1924; New Directions Publications, 1944); Redman, B. R. (ed.), *Salammbô* (Tudor Publishing Co., 1931); Russell, A., *Madame Bovary* (Penguin Books, Inc., 1950); Sheldon, M. F., *Salammbô* (Saxon & Co., 1886); Von Schrader, G. M., *Salambo* [sic] (Sherman, French & Co., 1914); Walton, W., *Madame Bovary* (G. H. Richmond & Co., 1896)

Bradford, G., *Bare Souls* (Harper & Brothers, 1924)

Brandes, G. M. C., *Creative Spirits of the Nineteenth Century* (Thos. Y. Crowell Co., 1923)

Carrère, J., *Degeneration in the Great French Masters* (Brentano's, 1922)

Coleman, A., *Flaubert's Literary Development* (The Johns Hopkins Press, 1915)

David, H. C. E., *Flaubert and George Sand* (The Chicago Literary Club, 1924)

Faguet, E., *Flaubert* (Houghton, Mifflin Co., 1914)

Fay, P. B., *Sources and Structure of Flaubert's Salammbô* (The Johns Hopkins Press, 1914)

Ferguson, W. D., *The Influence of Flaubert on George Moore* (University of Pennsylvania Press, 1934)

Freienmuth von Helms, E. E. P., *German Criticism of Flaubert* (Columbia University Press, 1939)

Hamilton, A., *Sources of the Religious Element in Flaubert's Salambô* (The Johns Hopkins Press, 1917)

Huneker, J. G., *Egoists* (C. Scribner's Sons, 1909)

James, H., *The Art of Fiction* (Oxford University Press, 1948); *Essays in

London and Elsewhere (Harper & Brothers, 1893, *Notes on Novelists*
(C. Scribner's Sons, 1914)
Maurois, A., *Seven Faces of Love* (Didier, 1944)
Moore, T. S., *Art and Life* (Methuen & Co., 1910)
Riddell, A. R., *Flaubert and Maupassant* (University of Chicago Press,
1920)
Shanks, L. P., *Flaubert's Youth* (The Johns Hopkins Press, 1927)
Spencer, P., *Flaubert* (Grove, 1953)
Steegmüller, F., *Flaubert and Madame Bovary* (The Viking Press, 1939)
Tarver, J. C., *Gustave Flaubert as Seen in His Works and Correspondence*
(D. Appleton & Co., 1895)
Watson, P. B., *Tales of Normandie* (Marshall Jones Co., 1930)
Wilson, E., *The Triple Thinkers* (Harcourt, Brace & Co., 1938)

FREYTAG

Translations: *The Lost Manuscript* (The Open Court Publishing Co.,
1898); L. C. C., *Debit and Credit* (Harper & Brothers, 1858); Frenz,
H. and Waggoner, M., *The Weavers, Hannele, The Beaver Coat*
(Rinehart Editions, Rinehart & Co., Inc., 1951); Heinemann, H.
E. O., *Martin Luther* (The Open Court Publishing Co., 1897); Mac-
Ewan, E. J., *Technique of the Drama* (S. C. Griggs & Co., 1895;
Scott, Foresman & Co., 1904), *Freytag's Technique of the Drama*
(Scott, Foresman & Co., 1908); Malcolm, Mrs., *Ingraban* (H. Holt
& Co., 1873), *Ingo* (Holt & Williams, 1873), *The Lost Manuscript*
(D. Appleton & Co., 1887); Riemer, G. C. L., *Doctor Luther* (The
Lutheran Publication Society, 1916); Schierbrand, W. von, *Ingo*
(P. F. Collier & Son, 19—?)
Price, L. M., *The Attitude of Gustav Freytag and Julian Schmidt toward
English Literature (1848-1862)* (The Johns Hopkins Press, 1915)

GONCOURT, ED. DE and JULES DE

Translations: *Love in the 18th Century* (A. L. Humphreys, 1905);
Chestershire, J., *Germinie Lacerteux* (C. L. Page & Co., 1906);
Dowson, E., *The Confidantes of a King* (T. N. Foulis, 1907); Gal-
lentière, L., *The Concourt Journals* (Doubleday, Doran & Co., Inc.,
1937); Hallard, A., *Renée Mauperin* (P. F. Collier & Son, 1902);
Ironside, R., *French 18th Century Painters* (Phaidon Press, 1948);
Le Clercq, J. and Roeder, R., *The Woman of the 18th Century* (Min-
ton, Balch & Co., 1927)
James, H., *Essays in London and Elsewhere* (Harper & Brothers, 1903)
Lowndes, M. A. B. and Shedlock, M. L., *Edmond and Jules de Concourt*
(Dodd, Mead & Co., 1895)

GOTTHELF

Translation: *Wealth and Welfare, by Jeremiah Gotthelf (pseud.)* (A. Strahan, 1867)

HAUPTMANN

Translations: Achurch, A. and Wheeler, C. E., *The Coming of Peace* (Duckworth & Co., 1910); Archer, W., *Hannele; a Dream Poem* (W. Heinemann, 1907); Lewisohn, L. (ed.), *The Dramatic Works of Gerhart Hauptmann* (B. W. Huebsch, 1912-29); Miltzer, C. H., *Hannele. A Dream Poem* (Doubleday, Page & Co., 1908), *The Sunken Bell* (Doubleday & McClure Co., 1900; Doubleday, Page & Co., 1902); Morgan, B. F., *Phantom, a Novel* (B. W. Huebsch, Inc., 1922); Morison, M., *Lonely Lives; a Drama* (W. Heinemann, 1898), *The Weavers* (B. W. Huebsch, 1911); Muir, W. and E., *The Island of the Great Mother* (B. W. Huebsch & The Viking Press, 1925); Seltzer, A. and T., *Atlantis* (B. W. Huebsch, 1912), Seltzer, T., *The Fool in Christ, Emmanuel Quint* (B. W. Huebsch, 1911); Williams, Q., *Parsival* (Macmillan Co., 1915)

Buck, P. M., *Directions in Contemporary Literature* (Oxford University Press, 1942)

Dukes, A., *Modern Dramatists* (F. Palmer, 1911)

Francke, K., *German Ideals of Today* (Houghton, Mifflin & Co., 1907)

Hale, E. E., *Dramatists of To-day* (H. Holt & Co., 1911)

Heller, O., *Studies in Modern German Literature* (Ginn & Co., 1905)

Holl, K., *Gerhart Hauptmann; His Life and Work* (A. C. McClurg & Co., 1913)

Huneker, J. G., *Iconoclasts, a Book of Dramatists* (C. Scribner's Sons, 1905)

Klenze, C. von, *From Goethe to Hauptmann* (Viking Press, 1926)

Krause, C. A., *Gerhart Hauptmann's Treatment of Blank Verse* (Press of the New Era Printing Co., 1910)

Marble, A. R., *The Nobel Winners in Literature* (D. Appleton & Co., 1925)

Muller, S. H., *Gerhart Hauptmann and Goethe* (King's Crown Press, 1949)

Scholz, K. W. H., *The Art of Translation, with Special Reference to English Renditions of the Prose Dramas of Gerhart Hauptmann and Herman Sudermann* (Americana Germanica Press, 1918)

Weisert, J. J., *The Dream in Gerhart Hauptmann* (King's Crown Press, 1949)

HEBBEL

Translations: Ashton, W., *Herod and Mariamne* (Doubleday, Doran & Co., Inc., 1938); King, F. H., *Recollections of My Childhood* in

Francke, K. and Howard, W. G., *The German Classics* (The German Publication Society, 1913-14); Royce, K., *Siegfried's Death* in Francke, K. and Howard, W. G., *The German Classics* (The German Publication Society, 1913-14); Thomas, P. B., *Maria Magdalena* in Francke, K. and Howard, W. G., *The German Classics* (The German Publication Society, 1913-14)

Becker, H. K., *Kleist and Hebbel; a Comparative Study* (Scott, Foresman & Co., 1904)

Campbell, T. M., *The Life and Works of Friedrich Hebbel* (R. G. Badger, 1919)

Danton, A., *Hebbel's Nibelungen, its Sources, Method and Style* (The Macmillan Co., 1906)

Flygt, S. G., *F. Hebbel's Conception of Movement* (North Carolina University Press, 1952)

Graham, P. G., *The Relation of History to Drama in the Works of Friedrich Hebbel* (Smith College Studies in Modern Literature, 1934)

Gubelmann, A. E., *Studies in the Lyric Poems of Friedrich Hebbel* (Yale University Press, 1912)

Oechler, W. F., *Motivation in the Drama of Friedrich Hebbel* (Glencoe, Ill., Free Press, 1948)

Purdie, E., *Friedrich Hebbel; a Study of His Life and Work* (Oxford University Press, 1932)

Rees, G. B., *Friedrich Hebbel as a Dramatic Artist* (G. Bell & Sons, Ltd., 1930)

Schueler, H., *Hebbel and the Dream* (George Banta Publishing Co., 1941)

HEYSE

Translations: *The Children of the World* (Worthington Co., 1890); *In Paradise* (D. Appleton & Co., 1878); *Tales from the German of Paul Heyse* (D. Appleton & Co., 1879); Coleman, A. J. du P., *Mary of Magdala* (E. Lederer, 1900); Copeland, C. S., *A Divided Heart, and Other Stories* (Brentano's, 1894); John, E. M., *The Lonely Ones* (Philadelphia, 1870); Kings, E. H., *Four Phases of Love* (G. Routledge & Co., 1857); Percival, J. M., *The Romance of the Canoness* (D. Appleton & Co., 1887); Remy, A., *Nino and Maso* in Francke, K. and Howard, W. G., *The German Classics* (The German Publication Society, 1913-14); Townsend, C. L., *The Spell of Rothenburg* in Francke, K. and Howard, W. G., *The German Classics* (The German Publication Society, 1913-14); Van Santford, F. A., *The Fair Abigail* (Dodd, Mead & Co., 1894), *The Forest Laugh* (Dodd, Mead & Co., 1894), *The House of the Unbelieving Thomas* (Dodd, Mead & Co., 1894), *Mid-day Magic* (Dodd, Mead & Co., 1894); Winter, W., *Mary of Magdala* (The Macmillan Co., 1903); Witson, M.,

Blind in Francke, K. and Howard, W. G., *The German Classics* (The German Publication Society, 1913-14)

Brandes, G. M. C., *Creative Spirits of the Nineteenth Century* (Thomas Y. Crowell Co., 1923)

Marble, A., *The Nobel Prize Winners in Literature* (D. Appleton & Co., 1925), *The Nobel Prize Winners in Literature, 1901-1931* (D. Appleton & Co., 1932)

Mitchell, R. MacB., *Heyse and His Predecessors in the Theory of the Novelle* (J. Baer & Co., 1915)

Phelps, W. L., *Essays on Books* (The Macmillan Co., 1914)

KELLER

Translations: Hottinger, M. D., *The People of Seldwyla, and Seven Legends* (J. M. Dent & Son, Ltd., 1931); Schierbrand, W. von, *Seldwyla Folks* (Brentano's, 1919); Thomas, P. B., *The Governor of Greifensee* in Francke, K. and Howard, W. G., *The German Classics* (The German Publication Society, 1913-14); Wyness, M., *Seven Legends* (Gowans & Gray, Ltd., 1911)

Hauch, E. F., *Gottfried Keller as a Democratic Idealist* (Columbia University Press, 1916)

Hay, M., *The Story of a Swiss Poet* (F. Wyss, 1920)

Robertson, J. G., *Essays and Addresses on Literature* (G. Routledge & Sons, Ltd., 1935)

MARX

Translations: *The Class Struggles in France, 1848-50* (International Publishers, 1934; Laurence & Wishart, 1942); *Letters to Dr. Kugelmann* (International Publishers, 1934; Laurence & Wishart, 1941); *Wage-Labour and Capital* (International Publishers, 1933; C. H. Kerr & Co., 1935); Engels, F. (ed.), *Capital* (Humboldt Publishing Co., 1890; S. Sonnenschein & Co., Ltd., 1906; C. H. Kerr & Co., 1907; W. Glaisher, Ltd., 1918; The Modern Library, Random House, 1936; George Allen & Unwin, Ltd., 1938), *Manifesto of the Communist Party* (New York Labor News Co., 1908; C. H. Kerr & Co., 1912; Rand School of Social Science, 1919; International Publishers, 1933); Enmale, R. (ed.), *The Civil War in the United States* (International Publishers, 1937); Kuhn, H., *The Class Struggles in France, 1848-1850* (New York Labor News Co., 1924); Quelch, H., *The Poverty of Philosophy* (The Twentieth Century Press, Ltd., 1900; C. H. Kerr & Co., 1910); Torr, D., *Correspondence, 1846-1895* (M. Laurence, Ltd., 1934), *Karl Marx and Friedrich Engels Correspondence, 1846-1895* [sic] (International Publishers, 1936)

Adams, H. P., *Karl Marx in His Earlier Writings* (G. Allen & Unwin, Ltd., 1940)

Adoratskii, V. V., *Dialectical Materialism* (International Publishers, 1934)

Aveling, E. B., *The Student's Marx* (S. Sonnenschein & Co., 1892)

Balz, A. G. A., *The Value Doctrine of Karl Marx* (King's Crown Press, 1943)

Barzun, J., *Darwin, Marx, Wagner* (Little, Brown & Co., 1941)

Beer, M., *The Life and Teaching of Karl Marx* (Small, Maynard & Co., 1924)

Berlin, I., *Karl Marx; His Life and Environment* (T. Butterworth, Ltd., 1939)

Bloom, S. F., *The World of Nations; a Study of the National Implications in the Work of Karl Marx* (Columbia University Press, 1941)

Bober, M. M., *Karl Marx's Interpretation of History* (Harvard University Press, 1948)

Böhm von Bawerk, E., *Karl Marx and the Close of His System* (T. F. Unwin, 1898)

Bukharin, N. I., *Marxism and Modern Thought* (Harcourt, Brace & Co., 1935)

Carr, E. H., *Karl Marx; a Study in Fanaticism* (J. M. Dent & Son, Ltd., 1934)

Cole, G. D. H., *What Marx Really Meant* (A. A. Knopf, 1934)

Croce, B., *Historical Materialism and the Economics of Karl Marx* (The Macmillan Co., 1914)

Dobb, M. H., *Marx as an Economist* (Laurence & Wishart, Ltd., 1943)

Eastman, M., *The Last Stand of Dialectical Materialism* (Polemic Publishers, 1934)

Federn, K., *The Materialist Conception of History* (Macmillan & Co., Ltd., 1939)

Goldendach, D. B., *Karl Marx and Friedrich Engels* (International Publishers, 1927)

Haldane, J. B. S., *The Marxist Philosophy and the Sciences* (Random House, 1939)

Hook, S., *From Hegel to Marx* (Reynal & Hitchcock, 1936), *Reason, Social Myths and Democracy* (The John Day Co., 1940), *Towards the Understanding of Karl Marx* (The John Day Co., 1933)

Joseph, H. W. B., *The Labour Theory of Value in Karl Marx* (Oxford University Press, 1923)

Kautsky, K., *The Economic Doctrines of Karl Marx* (A. & C. Black, Ltd., 1925)

Korsch, K., *Karl Marx* (J. Wiley & Sons, 1938)

Lazaron, M. S., *Seed of Abraham; Ten Jews of the Ages* (The Century Co., 1930)

Liebnecht, W. P., *Karl Marx* (C. H. Kerr & Co., 1901)

Loria, A., *Karl Marx* (G. Allen & Unwin, 1920)

Macmurray, J. (ed.), *Some Makers of the Modern Spirit* (Methuen & Co., Ltd., 1933)

Mayer, G., *Friedrich Engels* (A. A. Knopf, 1936)

McFadden, C. J., *The Metaphysical Foundations of Dialectical Materialism* (The Catholic University of America, 1938)

Mehring, F., *Karl Marx; the Story of His Life* (Covici, Friede, 1935)

Neill, T. P., *Makers of the Modern Mind* (Bruce Publishing Co., 1949)

Nomad, M., *Apostles of Revolution* (Little, Brown & Co., 1939)

Osbert, R., *Freud and Marx, a Dialectical Study* (V. Gollancz, Ltd., 1937)

Parkes, H. B., *Marxism: an Autopsy* (Houghton, Mifflin Co., 1939)

Portus, G. V., *Marx and Modern Thought* (Macmillan & Co., 1921)

Rühle, O., *Karl Marx, His Life and Work* (The Viking Press, 1929; Garden City Publishing Co., Inc., 1936)

Schlesinger, R., *Marx, His Time and Ours* (Routledge & Paul, 1950)

Spargo, J., *Karl Marx; His Life and Work* (B. W. Huebsch, 1910)

Sweezy, P. M., *The Theory of Capitalist Development* (Oxford University Press, 1942)

Wilson, E., *To the Finland Station* (Harcourt, Brace & Co., 1940)

MAUPASSANT

Translations: *Best Stories* (The Modern Library, Random House, 1945); *Complete Works* (Dermotan Society, 1903); *The Life Work of Maupassant* (M. W. Dunne, 1903); Bell, C., *Pierre and Jean* (London Book Co., 1906); Boyd, E., *Bel Ami* (A. A. Knopf, 1923), *Boule de Suif* (A. A. Knopf, 1922), *The Sisters Rondoli* (A. A. Knopf, 1923); Brockway, W. (ed.), *The Great Short Stories* (Pocket Books, Inc., 1951); Craig, H., *Pierre and Jean* (G. Routledge & Co., Ltd., 1890); Dell, C., *Pierre and Jean* (P. F. Collier & Son, 1902); Ensor, L., *Afloat* (G. Routledge & Sons, 1889); Galantière, L. (ed.), *The Portable Maupassant* (The Viking Press, 1947); Hearn, L., *The Adventures of Walter Schnaffs* (The Hokuseido Press, 1931); Jameson, S., *Day and Night Stories* (A. A. Knopf, 1924), *Little Rogue* (A. A. Knopf, 1924), *The Pedlar* (A. A. Knopf, 1926), *A Woman's Heart* (A. A. Knopf, 1926); Jeffery, J. E., *Doctor Heraclius Gloss* (Brentano's, 1923); Keating, W. S., *Mlle. Fifi* (Stravon Publishers, 1949); Laurie, M., *A Woman's Life* (The Nonesuch Press, 1942), *Short Stories* (Everyman's Library, E. P. Dutton & Co., 1934); Mansion, J. E., *Mlle. Perle* (G. G. Harrap & Co., Ltd., 1926); Martindale, E., *Stories from Maupassant* (J. Cape, 1927); McMaster, A. M. C., *Monsieur Parent* (Standard Book Co., 1922); McMaster, A. M. C. and Others, *Works* (Willey Book Co., 1928); Ranous, D. K., *Selected Stories* (The Leslie-Judge Co., 1912); Smith, A., *Pierre et Jean* (J. B. Lippincott Co., 1889); Sturges, J., *The Odd Number*

(Harper & Brothers, 1889); Sutton, E., *Bel-Ami* (The Novel Library, n. d.); White, A., *A Woman's Life* (The Novel Library, 1949)

Artinian, A., *Maupassant Criticism in France* (King's Crown Press, 1941)

Boyd, E., *Guy de Maupassant* (A. A. Knopf, 1926)

Jackson, S., *Guy de Maupassant* (Duckworth, 1938)

James, H., *The Art of Fiction* (Oxford University Press, 1948)

Kirkbride, R. de L., *The Private Life of Guy de Maupassant* (Sears Publishing Co., 1932)

Lavrin, Y., *Studies in European Literature* (Constable & Co., Ltd., 1929)

Lemaître, J., *Literary Impressions* (D. O'Connor, 1921)

Riddell, A. R., *Flaubert and Maupassant* (The University of Chicago Press, 1920)

Sherard, R. H., *The Life, Work, and Evil Fate of Guy de Maupassant* (T. W. Laurie, Ltd., 1926)

Steegmuller, F., *Maupassant* (Random House, 1949)

Tassart, F., *Recollections of Guy de Maupassant* (J. Lane, 1912)

Watson, P. B., *Tales of Normandie* (Marshall Jones Co., 1930)

MÉRIMÉE

Translations: *Carmen* (Pearson's Library, 1920); *Colomba* (Phillips, Sampson & Co., 1856); *1572* (G. & C. H. Carvill, 1830); *The House of a Traitor* (F. T. Neely, 1899); *The Plays of Clara Gazul* (G. B. Whittaker, 1825); Bois, H. P. du, *Letters to an Unknown* (Brentano's, 1897); Bolton, T., *Diane de Turgis* (The Arnold Co., 1925); Fay, E., *The Slave Ship* (Northwestern University Library, 1934); Galsworthy, J. and A., *Carmen* (E. Mathews & Marrot, 1932); Garnett, E. H., *Manon Lescaut and Carmen* (Everyman's Library, E. P. Dutton & Co., 1929); Garrett, E., Lloyd, M., Waller, E., *The Loves of Carmen* (Pocket Books, Inc., 1948); Ives, G. B., *Carmen and Other Tales* (G. P. Putnam's Sons, 1903); Lloyd, Lady M., *Colomba* and *Carmen* (P. F. Collier & Son, 1901); Norton, S. and Carpenter, H., *Carmen* (University of Oklahoma Press, 1935); Saintsbury, G., *A Chronicle of the Reign of Charles IX* (J. C. Nimmo, 1890), *The Novels, Tales and Letters of Prosper Mérimée* (Himebaugh & Browne, 1915); Sherman, R., *Colomba* (Translation Publishing Co., 1920); Stoddard, R. H. (ed.), *Letters to an Incognita* (Scribner, Armstrong, & Co., 1874); Sutton, E., *Carmen and Colomba* (The Novel Library, 1949); Verelst, M., *Tales before Supper* (Brentano's, 1887)

Balch, E., *An Author's Love* (Macmillan & Co., 1889)

Derwent, G. H. J., *Prosper Mérimée* (G. Routledge & Sons, Ltd., 1926)

Irvine, L. L., *Ten Letter-Writers* (L. & V. Woolf, 1932)

Lyons, S., *The Life and Times of Prosper Mérimée* (Dial Press, 1948)

Thorold, A. L., *Six Masters in Dissillusion* (A. Constable & Co., Ltd., 1909)

NIETZSCHE

Translations: Collins, A., *The Use and Abuse of History* (The Library of Liberal Arts, The Liberal Arts Press, Inc., 1949); Common, T., *Thus Spake Zarathustra* (The Modern Library, Random House, 1921); Fademan, C., *The Birth of Tragedy* (The Modern Library, Random House, 1937), *Ecce Homo* (The Modern Library, Random House, 1937); Kerr, C. V., *The Nietzsche-Wagner Correspondence* (Boni & Liveright, 1921); Levy, O. (ed.), *The Complete Works of Friedrich Nietzsche* (Macmillan Co., 1910-27); Ludovici, A. M., *Selected Letters of Friedrich Nietzsche* (Doubleday, Page & Co., 1921); Orage, A. R., *Nietzsche in Outline & Aphorism* (A. C. Mc-Clurg & Co., 1910); Mann, H., *The Living Thoughts of Nietzsche* (Longmans, Green & Co., 1939); Mencken, H. L., *The Gist of Nietzsche* (J. W. Luce & Co., 1910); Samuel, H. B., *The Genealogy of Morals* (The Modern Library, Random House, 1937); Tille, A. and Bozman, M. M., *Thus Spake Zarathustra* (The Macmillan Co., 1896; Everyman's Library, E. P. Dutton & Co., Inc., 1933); Zimmern, H., *Beyond Good and Evil* (The Macmillan Co., 1907; The Modern Library, Random House, 1931)

Abraham, G., *Nietzsche* (Duckworth, 1933)

Bentley, E. R., *A Century of Hero-worship* (J. B. Lippincott Co., 1944), *The Cult of the Superman* (R. Hale, 1947)

Brandes, G. M. C., *Friedrich Nietzsche* (Macmillan Co., 1914)

Brinton, C., *Nietzsche* (Harvard University Press, 1941)

Carus, P., *Nietzsche and Other Exponents of Individualism* (Open Court Publishing Co., 1914)

Crookshank, F. G., *Individual Psychology and Nietzsche* (C. W. Daniel Co., 1933)

Davis, H. E., *Tolstoy and Nietzsche* (New Republic, Inc., 1929)

De Casseres, B., *The Superman in America* (University of Washington Book Store, 1929)

Dolson, G. N., *The Philosophy of Friedrich Nietzsche* (Macmillan Co., 1901)

Ellis, E. M. O. L., *Three Modern Seers: James Hinton-Nietzsche-Edward Carpenter* (M. Kennerley, 1910)

Ellis, H., *Affirmations* (Constable & Co., Ltd., 1929)

Faguet, E., *On Reading Nietzsche* (Moffat, Yard & Co., 1918)

Flaccus, L. W., *Artists and Thinkers* (Longmans, Green & Co., 1916)

Förster-Nietzsche, E., *The Life of Nietzsche* (Sturgis & Walton Co., 1912-15)

Foster, G. B., *Friedrich Nietzsche* (The Macmillan Co., 1931)

Gould, G. M., *Biographic Clinics* (P. Blakiston's Son & Co., 1903-07)

Halévy, D., *The Life of Friedrich Nietzsche* (The Macmillan Co., 1911)

Hamblen, E. S., *Friedrich Nietzsche, and His New Gospel* (R. G. Badger, 1911)

Heller, O., *Prophets of Dissent* (A. A. Knopf, 1918)

Hubber, W., *Four Prophets of Our Destiny* (Macmillan, 1952)

Huneker, J. G., *Egoists; a Book of Superman* (C Scribner's Sons, 1909)

Kaufmann, W. A., *Nietzsche* (Princeton University Press, 1950)

Kennedy, J. M., *Nietzsche* (T. W. Laurie, Ltd., 1914), *The Quintessence of Nietzsche* (T. W. Laurie, Ltd., 1909)

Knight, A. H. J., *Some Aspects of the Life and Work of Nietzsche* (Cambridge University Press, 1933)

Lavrin, J., *Nietzsche, an Approach* (Methuen, 1948), *Nietzsche and Modern Consciousness* (W. Collins Sons & Co., Ltd., 1922); *Studies in European Literature* (Constable & Co., Ltd., 1929)

Lichtenberger, H., *The Gospel of Superman* (The Macmillan Co., 1926)

Ludovici, A. M., *Who is to be Master of the World?* (T. N. Foulis, 1909), *Nietzsche and Art* (J. W. Luce & Co., 1912), *Nietzsche, His Life and Works* (Constable & Co., Ltd., 1910; Dodge Publishing Co., 1910)

Macmurray, J., *Some Makers of the Modern Spirit* (Methuen & Co., 1933)

Mann, T., *Past Masters and Other Papers* (A. A. Knopf, 1933), *Nietzsche's Philosophy in the Light of Contemporary Events* (Library of Congress, 1947)

Mencken, H. L., *The Philosophy of Friedrich Nietzsche* (Luce, 1913)

Morgan, G. A., *What Nietzsche Means* (Harvard University Press, 1943)

Muegge, M. A., *Friedrich Nietzsche; His Life and Work* (Brentano's, 1909; Dodge Publishing Co., 1912)

Nicolas, M. P., *From Nietzsche Down to Hitler* (W. Hodge & Co., Ltd., 1938)

O'Brien, E. J. H., *Son of the Morning* (Brewer, Warren & Putnam, 1932)

Orage, A. R., *Friedrich Nietzsche, the Dionysian Spirit of the Age* (T. N. Foulis, 1906)

Podach, E. F., *The Madness of Nietzsche* (Putnam, 1931)

Portalès, G. de, *The Mad King* (H. Holt & Co., 1928)

Ransome, A., *Portraits and Speculations* (Macmillan & Co., Ltd., 1913)

Reyburn, H. A., *Nietzsche; the Story of a Human Philosopher* (Macmillan, 1948)

Roubiczek, P., *The Misinterpretation of Man* (C. Scribner's Sons, 1947)

Samuel, H. B., *Modernities* (E. P. Dutton & Co., 1914)

Stewart, H. L., *Nietzsche and the Ideals of Modern Germany* (Longmans, Green & Co., 1915)

Stocker, R. D., *The Real Nietzsche* (E. MacDonald, 1915)

Wolf, A., *The Philosophy of Nietzsche* (Constable & Co., 1915)
Wright, W. H., *What Nietzsche Taught* (B. W. Huebsch, 1915)
Zweig, S., *Master Builders* (The Viking Press, 1939)

RILKE

Translations: *Thirty-one Poems by Rainer Maria Rilke* (B. Ackerman, Inc., 1946); Barrett, R. G. L., *The Life of the Virgin Mary* (C. Triltsch, 1922); Deutsch, B., *Poems from the Book of Hours "Das Stundenbuch"* (New Directions, 1941); Greene, J. B. and Norton, M. D. H., *Letters of Rainer Maria Rilke* (W. W. Norton & Co., 1945-8); Leishman, J. B., *Poems* (L. & V. Woolf, 1934), *Requiem and Other Poems* (L. & V. Woolf, 1935), *Selected Poems* (The Hogarth Press, 1941), *Sonnets to Orpheus* (L. & V. Woolf, 1936); Leishman, J. B. and Spender, S., *Duino Elegies* (The Hogarth Press, 1939); Lemont, J., *Poems* (T. A. Wright, 1918; Columbia University Press, 1943), *Sonnets to Orpheus* and *Duino Elegies* (The Fine Editions Press, 1945); Lemont, J. and Trausit, H., *Auguste Rodin* (Sunwise Turn, Inc., 1919), *Rodin* (The Fine Editions Press, 1945); Linton, J., *The Journal of My Other Self* (W. W. Norton & Co., 1930); MacIntyre, C. F., *Fifty Selected Poems* (University of California Press, 1940); Niemeyer, C., *Five Prose Pieces* (Cummington Press, 1947), *Primal Sound & Other Prose Pieces* (Cummington Press, 1943); Norton, M. D. H., *Letters to a Young Poet* (W. W. Norton & Co., Inc., 1934), *Sonnets to Orpheus* (W. W. Norton & Co., Inc., 1942), *The Tale of the Love and Death of Cornet Christopher Rilke* (W. W. Norton & Co., Inc., 1932), *Translations from the Poetry of Rainer Maria Rilke* (W. W. Norton & Co., 1938), *Wartime Letters of Rainer Maria Rilke, 1914-1921* (W. W. Norton & Co., 1940); Norton, M. D. H. and Purtscher-Wydenbruck, N., *Stories of God* (W. W. Norton & Co., Inc., 1932); Snell, R., *Letters to a Young Poet* (Sidgwick & Jackson, 1945); Nordern, H., *Letters to Benvenuta* (Hogarth Press, 1953)

Betz, M., *Rilke in Paris* (Verlag der Arche, 1948)

Butler, E. M., *Rainer Maria Rilke* (Cambridge University Press, 1941)

Fausset, H. I., *Poets and Pundits* (Yale University Press, 1947)

Kenmare, D., *The Long Pursuit* (Burrow's Press, Ltd., 1945)

Mason, E. C., *Rilke's Apotheosis* (B. Blackwell, 1938)

Mises, R. von, *Rilke in English, a Tentative Bibliography* (The Cosmos Press, 1947)

Olivero, F., *Rainer Maria Rilke; a Study in Poetry and Mysticism* (W. Heffer & Sons, Ltd., 1931)

Purtscher, N., *Rilke, Man and Poet* (J. Lehmann, 1949)

Sargeaunt, G. M., *The Classical Spirit* (The Cloanthus Press, 1936)

SAND

Translations: *The Castle in the Wilderness* (J. S. Dwight & E. L. Balch, 1856); *Fauchon the Cricket* (J. Bradburn, 1864); *The Last Aldini* (T. B. Peterson & Bros., 18—?); *Simon* (T. B. Peterson & Bros., 18—?); *The Tower of Percemont* (D. Appleton & Co., 1877); Adams, H. K., *Impressions and Reminiscences* (W. F. Gill & Co., 1877); Bauer, J., *The Uscoque* (Bunce & Bros., 18—?); Beaufort, R. L. de, *Letters* (Ward & Downey, 1886); Bloom, M., *Tales of a Grandmother* (J. B. Lippincott Co., 1930); Dewey, M. E., *The Miller of Angibault* (Roberts Bros., 1871); Hays, M. M., *Fadette* (G. P. Putnam, 1851); Howe, M. J., *The Intimate Journal of George Sand* (J. Day Co., 1929); Johnston, C. C., *The Master Mosaic-Workers* (Little, Brown, & Co., 1895); Keeler, R., *The Marquis de Villemer* (R. Worthington, 1879); Lancaster, Mrs. J. M., *Fadette* (T. Y. Crowell & Co., 1896); Leland, O. S. (ed.), *Teverino* (W. P. Fetridge & Co., 1855); Lucas, V., *Letters of George Sand* (Houghton Mifflin Co., 1930); MacKaye, M. E., *Convent Life of George Sand* (Roberts Bros., 1893); McKenzie, A. L., *The George Sand-Gustave Flaubert Letters* (Boni & Liveright, 1921); Miles, H., *The Devil's Pool* (The Scholastic Press, 1929); Owen, C., *Handsome Laurence* (R. Worthington, 1879), *A Rolling Stone* (R. Worthington, 1870); Potter, F. H., *Consuelo* (Dodd, Mead & Co., 1889), *The Haunted Pool* (Dodd, Mead & Co., 1893); Robinson, F., *Consuelo* (Stringer & Townsend, 1851), *The Countess of Rudolstadt* (Stringer & Townsend, 1851); Sedgwick, J. M. and E., *The Devil's Pool* (G. H. Richmond & Co., 1894); Sedgwick, J. M., *Fauchon the Cricket* (Duffield & Co., 1915), *François the Waif* (G. H. Richmond & Co., 1894); Shaw, F. G., *Consuelo* (W. D. Ticknor & Co., 1847), *The Countess of Rudolstadt* (W. D. Ticknor & Co., 1847), *The Journeyman Joiner* (W. H. Graham, 1847), *Monsieur Sylvestre* (Roberts Bros., 1883); Stanwood, E., *Cesarine Dietrich* (J. R. Osgood & Co., 1871); Stoddard, R. H. (ed.), *Letters to an Incognita* (Scribner, Armstrong, & Co., 1874); Vanderpolle, L., *Princess Nowmahal* (G. W. Dillingham, 1888); Vaughan, V., *Antonia* (Roberts Bros., 1870), *Mauprat* (Roberts Bros., 1870), *The Snow Man* (Roberts Bros., 1871); Waldaver, A., *Fauchon the Cricket* (S. French, 186-?); Young, S., *Mauprat* (P. F. Collier & Son, 1902)

Babbitt, I., *Spanish Character and Other Essays* (Houghton Mifflin Co., 1940)

Bradford, G., *Daughters of Eve* (Houghton Mifflin Co., 1930)

Carrère, J., *Degeneration in the Great French Masters* (Brentano's, 1922)

Coan, T. M., *Studies in Biography* (G. P. Putnam's Sons, 1883)

David, H. C. E., *Flaubert and George Sand in Their Correspondence* (The Chicago Literary Club, 1924)

Doumic, R., *George Sand* (Chapman & Hall, Ltd., 1910)
Frye, P. H., *George Sand and Her French Style* (University of Nebraska, 1903)
Gambier-Parry, M., *Studies of Childhood* (Heath Cranton, Ltd., 1925)
George, W. L., *Historic Lovers* (Hutchinson & Co., Ltd., 1926)
Gribble, F. H., *George Sand and Her Lovers* (E. Nash, 1908)
Hetzel, P. J., *Public and Private Life of Animals* (S. Low, Marston, Searle, & Rivington, 1887)
Howe, M., *George Sand* (The John Day Co., 1927)
Iwaskiewicz, J., *Summer at Nohant* (Minerva Publishing Co., 1942)
Jaeger, M., *Adventures in Living* (W. Morrow & Co., 1932)
James, H., *Notes on Novelists* (C. Scribner's Sons, 1914)
Lemaître, J., *Literary Impressions* (D. O'Connor, 1921)
Maurois, A., *Leila* (Harper & Brothers, 1953)
Mirecourt, Eugène de, *Famous French Authors* (R. Worthington, 1879)
Moeller, P., *Madame Sand* (A. A. Knopf, 1917)
Ravenel, F., *Women and the French Tradition* (Macmillan Co., 1918)
Sackett, S., *Nocturne* (S. French, 1927)
Sandars, M. F., *George Sand* (R. Holden & Co., Ltd., 1927)
Schermerhorn, E. W., *The Seven Strings of the Lyre* (Houghton Mifflin Co., 1927)
Seyd, F., *Romantic Rebel* (The Viking Press, 1940)
Thomas, B., *George Sand* (W. H. Allen & Co., 1883)
Toesca, M., *The Other George Sand* (D. Dobson, 1947)
Winwar, F., *The Life of the Heart* (Harper & Brothers, 1945)

SARDOU

Translations: *Cleopatra* (F. Rullman, 1891); *Dante* (Chiswich Press, 1903); *Divorçons* (F. Rullman, 1904); *Fedora* (F. Rullman, 1887); *Gismonda* (F. Rullman, 1918); *La Tosca* (F. Rullman, 1891); *Theodora* (F. Rullman, 1890); Albery, J., *Duty* (S. French, 18—?); Beatty-Kingston, W., *Tosca* (G. Ricordi & Co., 1900); Boucicault, D., *Seraphine* (Privately Printed, 1869); Byrne, C. A., *The Sorceress* (F. Rullman, 1905); Clark, B. H., *The Black Pearl* (S. French, 1915), *Patrie* (Doubleday, Page & Co., 1915); Daly, A., *Hazardous Ground* (S. French & Son, 1868); Galdemar, A., *Robespierre* (Dodd, Mead & Co., 1899); Ginty, E. B., *Gismonda* (F. Rullman, 1896); Howgrave, W., *La Tosca* (Drane's, Ltd., 1925); March, G., *Our Friends* (S. French, 18—?); Mayo, M., *Cyprienne* (S. French, 1941); Meltzer, C. M., *Mme Sans-Gêne* (S. French, 1901); Pritchard, J. V., *Daniel Rochat* (S. French, 18—?); Rowe, S. and B., *Diplomacy* (Privately Printed, 18—?); Schönberg, J., *Fernande* (Burnton, 1870); Simpson, J. P., *A Scrap of Paper* (S. French, 186-?); Weissert,

C. A., *The Sorceress* (R. G. Badger, 1917); Wigan, H., *Friends or Foes* (T. H. Lacy, 18—?)

Hart, J. A., *Sardou and the Sardou Plays* (J. B. Lippincott Co., 1913)

Roosevelt, B., *Victorien Sardou* (K. Paul, Trench, Trübner & Co., 1892)

SCHNITZLER

Translations: Barker, G., *Anatol* (M. Kennerley, 1911; Little, Brown & Co., 1916); Björkman, E., *The Lonely Way: Intermezzo: Countess Mizzie* (Little, Brown & Co., 1927); Colbron, G. I., *Plays by Arthur Schnitzler* (Boni & Liveright, Inc., 1917; The Modern Library, Random House, 1925); Eisemann, F., *Viennese Idylls* (J. W. Luce & Co., 1913); Gowans, A. L., *Gallant Cassian; a Puppet-Play in One Act* (Gowans & Gray, Ltd., 1914); Jacques, A., *Beatrice, a Novel* (Simon & Schuster, 1926); Loving, P., *Comedies of Words, and Other Plays* (Stewart & Kidd Co., 1923); Paul, E. and C., *Casanova's Homecoming* (Brentano's, Ltd., 1923; Simon & Schuster, 1930); Samuel, H. B., *The Green Cockatoo, and Other Plays* (Gay & Hancock, Ltd., 1913; A. C. McClurg & Co., 1914), *The Road to the Open* (H. Latimer, Ltd., 1913); Shand, P. M., *Playing with Love* (A. C. McClurg & Co., 1914); Simon, R. A., *Fräulein Else; a Novel* (Simon & Schuster, 1925)

Dukes, A., *Modern Dramatists* (F. Palmer, 1911)

Henderson, A., *European Dramatists* (D. Appleton & Co., 1926)

Liptzin, S., *Arthur Schnitzler* (Prentice-Hall, Inc., 1932)

Samuel, H. B., *Modernities* (E. P. Dutton & Co., 1914)

SCHOPENHAUER

Translations: Box, E. B. (ed.), *Selected Essays of Schopenhauer* (G. Bell & Sons, Ltd., 1926); Bullock, A. B., *The Basis of Morality* (G. Allen & Unwin, Ltd., 1915); Durant, W. (ed.), *The Works of Schopenhauer, Abridged* (Garden City Publishing Co., 1928; Simon & Schuster, 1928); Edman, I., *The Philosophy of Schopenhauer* (The Modern Library, Random House, 1928); Haldane, R. B. and Kemp, J., *The World as Will and Idea* (Trübner & Co., 1883-86; K. Paul, Trench, Trübner & Co., Ltd., 1906); Mann, T., *The Living Thoughts of Schopenhauer* (Longmans, Green & Co., 1939); Parker, *Selections* (Modern Student's Library, C. Scribner's Sons); Ramage, C. T., *Beautiful Thoughts from German and Spanish Authors* (E. Howell, 1868); Saunders, T. B., *The Art of Controversy* (G. Allen & Unwin, Ltd., 1921), *The Art of Literature* (S. Sonnenschein & Co., 1891), *Counsels and Maxims* (The Macmillan Co., 1897), *Essays of Arthur Schopenhauer* (A. L. Burt Co., 189-?), *On Human Nature* (G. Allen & Unwin, Ltd., 1926), *Religion: a Dialogue, and Other Essays* (S. Sonnenschein & Co., 1890; G. Allen & Unwin, Ltd., 1930), *A*

Series of Essays, by Arthur Schopenhauer (Willey Book Co., 1915), *Studies in Pessimism* (G. Allen & Co., Ltd., 1923; Boni & Liveright, Inc., 1925; The Modern Library, Random House, 1925), *The Wisdom of Life* (S. Sonnenschein & Co., Ltd., 1906), *The Wisdom of Schopenhauer* (G. A. S. Wieners, 1902); Saunders, T. B. and Box, E. B., *The Wisdom of Life* (M. W. Dunne, 1901)

Beer, M., *Schopenhauer* (Dodge Publishing Co., 1914)

Caldwell, W., *Schopenhauer's System in its Philosophical Significance* (W. Blackwood & Sons, 1896)

Copleston, F., *Arthur Schopenhauer, Philosopher of Pessimism* (Oates & Washbourne, 1946)

Hueffer, F., *Italian and Other Studies* (E. Stock, 1883)

Kelly, M., *Kant's Ethics and Schopenhauer's Criticism* (S. Sonnenschein & Co., 1910), *Kant's Philosophy as Rectified by Schopenhauer* (S. Sonnenschein & Co., 1909)

Knox, I., *The Aesthetic Theories of Kant, Hegel, and Schopenhauer* (Columbia University Press, 1936)

McGill, V. J., *Schopenhauer; Pessimist and Pagan* (Brentano's, 1931)

Phelps, W. L., *Essays on Books* (Macmillan Co., 1914)

Tsanoff, R. A., *Schopenhauer's Criticism of Kant's Theory of Experience* (Longmans, Green, & Co., 1911)

Wallace, W., *Life of Arthur Schopenhauer* (Walter Scott, 1890)

Zimmern, H., *Arthur Schopenhauer; His Life and His Philosophy* (Longmans, Green & Co., 1876; G. Allen & Unwin, Ltd., 1932)

SCRIBE

Translations: *Adrienne Lecouvreur* (Darcie & Corbyn, 1855); *Caesar* (T. H. Lacy, 186-?); *The Crown Diamonds* (Philadelphia Ledger Job Printing Office, 1867); *The Duc d'Olonne* (n. p., 1852); *Piquillo Alliaga* (Richards & Co., 185-?); *The Syren* (n. p., 1852); *The Woman that Was a Cat* (T. H. Lacy, 182-?); Archer, T., *Asmodeus* (T. H. Lacy, 18—?); Bernard, C. R., *The Huguenots* (Philadelphia Ledger Job Printing Office, 1870); Boucicault, D., *The Queen of Spades* (T. H. Lacy, 1856); Buckstone, J. B., *The Happiest Day of My Life* (J. Cumberland, 1829); Dent, E. J., *Fra Diavolo* (Oxford University Press, 1944); Fitzball, E., *Azael* (J. Duncombe, 185-?), *The Bronze Horse* (J. Duncombe & Co., 183-?), *The Crown Jewels* (J. H. Eastburn's Press, 1855); Grundy, S., *A Debt of Honour* (T. Scott, 1880), *Sympathetic Souls* (S. French, 1900); Harrison, Mrs. B., *A Russian Honeymoon* (The Dramatic Publishing Co., 1883); Hermann, H., *Adrienne Lecouvreur* (S. French, 18—?); Hollenius, L. J., *First Love* (R. M. DeWitt, 1873); Horncastle, H., *The Bayadere* (n. p., 1852), *Ma Part* (n. p., 1852); Lacy, M. R., *Fra Diavolo* (J. Miller, 1833), *The Jewess* (T. H. Lacy, 1835); Long, C., *The Chalet*

(C. Long, 1845), *The Crown Brilliants* (C. Long, 1852); Macfarren, G., (J. Cumberland, 183-?); Moncrieff, W. T., *The Somnambulist* (J. Cumberland, 1828); Oxenford, J., *The World of Fashion* (T. H. Lacy, 186-?); Payne, J. H., *Love in Humble Life* (Turner & Fisher, 18—?); Planché, J. R., *A Peculiar Position* (Chapman & Hall, 1837); Reade, C., *The Ladies' Battle* (T. H. Lacy, 18—?); Robertson, T. W., *The Lost Husband* (T. H. Lacy, 185-?), *The Star of the North* (T. H. Lacy, 186-?); Rodwell, J. T. G., *A Race for a Dinner* (J. Cumberland, 1828); Simpon, J. P., *Marco Spada* (T. H. Lacy, 1853); Soame, G., *Masaniello* (J. Miller, 1825); Suter, W. W., *A Glass of Water* (T. H. Lacy, 18—?); Webster, B., *The Black Domino* (National Acting Drama Office, 184-?); Welstead, H., *Giralda* (T. H. Lacy, 185-?); Wylde, Mrs. H., *The Mason* (A. S. Mallett, 1879)

Arvin, N. C., *Eugène Scribe and the French Theatre* (Harvard University Press, 1924)

Istel, E., *The Art of Writing Opera Librettos* (G. Schirmer, Inc., 1922)

SPIELHAGEN

Translations: M. S., *What the Swallow Sang* (Holt & Williams, 1873); Vere, S. de, *The Hohensteins* (Leypoldt & Holt, 1870), *Problematic Characters* (Leypoldt & Holt, 1869), *Through Night to Light* (Leypoldt & Holt, 1870)

STENDHAL

See Beyle.

STORM

Translations: Heath, J. A., *Immensee* (T. B. Mosher, 1902); Mellon, M. T., *Immensee* (Random House, 1937); Reinhardt, G., *Immensee* (Barron's Educational Series, Inc., 1950); Upton, G. P., *Immensee* (A. C. McClurg & Co., 1907)

SUDERMANN

Translations: *The Silent Mill* (Brentano's, 1919); Alexander, A., *Morituri: Three One-act Plays* (C. Scribner's Sons, 1910); Frank, G., *Roses: Four One-act Plays* (C. Scribner's Sons, 1909); Ginty, E. B., *Argument of Magda* (F. Rullman, 1896); Harding, W., *The Book of My Youth* (Harper & Brothers, 1923); Henkel, L., *The Wish, a Novel* (D. Appleton & Co., 1895); Lewisohn, L., *The Indian Lily, and Other Stories* (B. W. Huebsch, 1911); Marshall, B., *John the Baptist* (John Lane, 1909), *Regina* (J. Lane, 1898), *The Undying Past* (J. Lane, 1906); Overbeck, B., *Dame Care* (Boni & Liveright, Inc., 1891; P. Smith, 1932); Seltzer, A. S., *Iolanthe's Wedding* (Boni & Liveright, 1918), *The Song of Songs* (B. W. Huebsch, 1909);

Swickard, C., *Fires of St. John* (J. W. Luce & Co., 1904); Wharton, E., *The Joy of Living* (C. Scribner's Sons, 1902); Winslow, C. E. A., *Magda* (S. French, 1899)

Dukes, A., *Modern Dramatists* (F. Palmer, 1911)

Florer, W. W., *German Liberty Authors* (R. G. Badger, 1918)

Hale, E. E., *Dramatists of Today* (H. Holt & Co., 1911)

Heller, O., *Studies in Modern German Literature* (Ginn & Co., 1905)

Huneker, J. G., *Iconoclasts, A Book of Dramatists* (C. Scribner's Sons, 1905)

Scholz, K. W. H., *The Art of Translation, with Special Reference to English Renditions of the Prose Dramas of Gerhart Hauptmann and Herman Sudermann* (Americana Germanica Press, 1918)

TAINE

Translations: Durand, J., *The Ancient Régime* (H. Holt & Co., 1876), *Art in the Netherlands* (H. Holt & Co., 1873), *The French Revolution* (H. Holt & Co., 1878-85), *Italy: Florence and Venice* (H. Holt & Co., 1869), *Italy: Rome and Naples* (H. Holt & Co., 1877), *Lectures on Art* (H. Holt & Co., 1875), *The Modern Régime* (H. Holt & Co., 1890-4), *The Philosophy of Art* (Holt & Williams, 1873), *The Philosophy of Art: Art in Greece* (Leypoldt & Holt, 1871), *The Philosophy of Art: Art in the Netherlands* (Leypoldt & Holt, 1871); Fiske, J. S., *A Tour through the Pyrenees* (H. Holt & Co., 1874); Haye, T. D., *On Intelligence* (Privately Printed, 1871); O'Rourke, *Balzac* (Funk & Wagnalls Co., 1906); Rae, W. F., *Notes on England* (Holt & Williams, 1872); Stevens, J. H., *Notes on Paris* (H. Holt & Co., 1875); Van Laun, H., *History of English Literature* (Holt & Williams, 1871)

Babbitt, I., *The Masters of Modern French Criticism* (Houghton Mifflin Co., 1912)

Devonshire, Mrs. R. L., *Life and Letters of H. Taine* (E. P. Dutton & Co., 1902-8)

Faguet, E., *Politicians and Moralists of the Nineteenth Century* (E. Benn, Ltd., 1928)

Gummere, F. B., *Democracy and Poetry* (Houghton Mifflin Co., 1911)

Lemaître, J., *Literary Impressions* (D. O'Connor, 1921)

Morley, J., *Biographical Studies* (Macmillan & Co., Ltd., 1923), *Critical Miscellanies* (Chapman & Hall, 1871-7)

WAGNER

Translations: Translations of Wagner's Music Dramas are readily obtainable in Opera Librettos (Fred Rullman, Inc., New York City); Bozman, M. M., *Letters of Richard Wagner* (J. M. Dent & Sons, Ltd., 1927); Burlingame, E. L., *Art Life and Theories of Richard*

Wagner (H. Holt & Co., 1889); Dannreuther, E., *Beethoven* (W. Reeves, 1903); Ellis, W. A., *Family Letters of Richard Wagner* (Macmillan & Co., Ltd., 1911); Kerr, C. V., *The Story of Bayreuth as Told in the Bayreuth Letters of Richard Wagner* (Small, Maynard & Co., 1912)

Barzun, J., *Darwin, Marx, Wagner* (Little, Brown & Co., 1941)

Bekker, P., *Richard Wagner; His Life in His Work* (J. M. Dent & Sons, Ltd., 1931)

Bentley, E. R., *A Century of Hero-worship* (J. B. Lippincott Co., 1944), *The Cult of the Superman* (R. Hale, 1947), *The Modern Theatre* (R. Hale, 1948)

Berlioz, H., *Mozart, Weber, and Wagner* (W. Reeves, 1918)

Brownell, G., *The Wagnerian Romances* (A. A. Knopf, 1925)

Chamberlain, H. S., *Richard Wagner* (J. M. Dent & Co., 1900), *The Wagnerian Drama* (J. Lane, 1915)

Cleather, A. L., *The Ring of the Nibelung* (Schirmer, n. d.)

Finch, H. T., *Wagner and His Works* (C. Scribner's Sons, 1907)

Flaccus, L. W., *Artists and Thinkers* (Longmans, Green & Co., 1916)

Gilman, L., *Wagner's Operas* (Farrar & Rinehart, Inc., 1937)

Glasenapp, C. F., *Life of Richard Wagner* (K. Paul, Trench, Trübner & Co., 1900-6)

Hadow, Sir W. H., *Studies in Modern Music* (Macmillan Co., 1923)

Haweis, H. R., *My Musical Memories* (Funk & Wagnalls, 1884)

Henderson, J. W., *Richard Wagner, His Life and His Dramas* (G. P. Putnam's Sons, 1901)

Hueffer, F., *Half a Century of Music in England* (Gebbie, 1889)

Huneker, J. G., *Mezzotints* (C. Scribner's Sons, 1899)

Jacobs, R. L., *Wagner* (J. M. Dent & Sons, Ltd., 1935)

Jullien, A., *Richard Wagner* (J. B. Millet Co., 1892)

Kobbé, G., *Wagner's Life and Works* (G. Schirmer, 1890)

Lavignac, A., *The Music Drumas of Richard Wagner and His Festival Theatre in Bayreuth* (Dodd, Mead & Co., 1902)

Layton, K. A., *The Nibelungen of Wagner* (Urbana University Press, 1909)

Mann, T., *Freud, Goethe, Wagner* (A. A. Knopf, 1942)

Newman, E., *Fact and Fiction about Wagner* (Cassell & Co., Ltd., 1931), *The Life of Richard Wagner* (A. A. Knopf, 1933-46), *Wagner as Man & Artist* (J. M. Dent & Sons, Ltd., 1914; A. A. Knopf, 1924)

Shaw, G. B., *The Perfect Wagnerite* (Constable, 1929)

Steigman, B. M., *The Unconquerable Tristan; the Story of Richard Wagner* (The Macmillan Co., 1933)

Wallace, W., *Richard Wagner as He Lived* (Harper & Brothers, 1925)

Weston, J. L., *The Legends of the Wagner Drama* (D. Nutt, 1903)

Wilson, P. C., *Wagner's Dramas and Greek Tragedy* (Columbia University Press, 1919)

Zarek, O., *The Tragi-Idealist* (Harper & Brothers, 1939)

YOUNG GERMANY

See Gutzkow and Mundt.

Whyte, J., *Young Germany in its Relations to Britain* (George Banta Publishing Co., 1917)

ZOLA

Translations: *Buried Alive* (The Warren Press, 1911); *The Dreyfus Case* (J. Lane, 1898); *The Flood* (The Warren Press, 1911); *Nana* (The Modern Library, Random House, 1928; Three Sirens Press, 1933; Pocket Books, Inc., 1941; The Living Library, The World Publishing Co.); *Shell-Fish* (The Warren Press, 1911); *Travail* (Harper & Brothers, 1901); Apthorp, W. F., *Jacques Damour* (Copeland & Day, 1895); Chase, E. A., *The Dream* (Chatto & Windus, 1907); Colman, L., *The Human Beast* (Julian Press, 1932); Cox, G. D., *The Mysteries of Marseilles* (T. B. Peterson & Bros., 1882); De Lacey, C., *Drink* (Greening & Co., Ltd., 1907); Dowson, E., *La Terre* (Boni & Liveright, 1924); Ellis, H. (ed.), *L'Assomoir* (A. A. Knopf, 1938); Ellis, H., *Germinal* (A. A. Knopf, 1925; Everyman's Library, E. P. Dutton & Co., 1933); Job, T., *Thérèse* (S. French, 1947); Josephson, M., *J'Accuse* (The Macaulay Co., 1928); Lederer, A. M., *For a Night* (Brown Bros., 1911); Mattos, A. T. de, *La Curée* (Boni & Liveright, 1924); Niess, R. J. (ed.), *Letters to Kolff* (Washington University, 1940); Pinkerton, P., *Piping Hot* (Boni & Liveright, 1924), *Restless House* (Farrar, Straus & Young, 1953); Rogerson, T. F., *A Page of Love* (G. H. Richmond & Co., 1897); Serrano, M. J., *Doctor Pascal* (International Association of Newspapers and Authors, 1901); Sherman, B. M., *The Experimental Novel* (The Cassell Publishing Co., 1893); Sloane, W. M., *The Downfall* (P. F. Collier & Son, 1902); Soissons, C. S., Count de, *A Dead Woman's Work* (Greening & Co., 1902); Stirling, J., *L'Assommoir* (T. B. Peterson & Bros., 1879), *La Belle Lisa* (T. B. Peterson & Bros., 1882), *Clorinda* (T. B. Peterson & Bros., 1880), *The Joy of Life* (T. B. Peterson & Bros., 1891); Vizetelly, E. A. (ed.), *Abbé Mouret's Transgression* (Chatto & Windus, 1911), *The Conquest of Plassans* (Chatto & Windus, 1908), *The Downfall* (Chatto & Windus, 1892), *The Dram Shop* (Chatto & Windus, 1902), *Fruitfulness* (Doubleday, Page & Co., 1900), *Germinal* (Chatto & Windus, 1901), *His Excellency* (Chatto & Windus, 1897), *His Masterpiece* (Chatto & Windus, 1902), *The Honour of the Army* (Chatto & Windus, 1901), *The Joy of Life* (Chatto & Windus,

1901), *Lourdes* (Macmillan Co., 1897), *A Love Episode* (Hutchinson & Co., 1895), *Money* (Chatto & Windus, 1894), *The Mysteries of Marseilles* (Hutchinson & Co., 1895), *Paris* (G. N. Morany, 1898), *Rome* (Macmillan & Co., 1896), *Stories for Ninon* (G. H. Richmond & Son, 1898), *Thérèse Raquin* (Chatto & Windus, 1910), *Truth* (Blackwood, Scott & Co., 1903); Vizetelly, F. J., *Nana* (Limited Editions Club, 1948); Woods, K., *The Masterpiece* (Howell, Soskin, 1946)

Amicis, E. D., *Studies of Paris* (G. P. Putnam's Sons, 1897)

Barbusse, H., *Zola* (J. M. Dent & Sons, Ltd., 1932)

Carrère, J., *Degeneration in the Great French Masters* (Brentano's, 1922)

Cézanne, P., *Letters* (B. Cassirer, 1941)

Ellis, H., *Affirmations* (Constable & Co., Ltd., 1929)

Friedman, L. M., *Zola and the Dreyfus Case* (The Beacon Press, Inc., 1937)

Hemmings, F. W. J., *Emile Zola* (Oxford University Press, 1953)

Hirsch, E. G., *Émile Zola* (Bloch & Newman, 1902)

James, H., *The Art of Fiction* (Oxford University Press, 1948), *Notes on Novelists* (C. Scribner's Sons, 1914)

Josephson, M., *Zola and His Time* (The Macaulay Co., 1928)

Lemaître, J., *Literary Impressions* (D. O'Connor, 1921)

Lynch, A., *Human Documents* (B. Dobell, 1896)

MacDonald, A., *Emile Zola* (Open Court, 1898)

Murray, H., *Robert Buchanan, and Other Essays* (P. Wellby, 1901)

Patterson, J. G., *A Zola Dictionary* (G. Routledge & Sons, Ltd., 1912)

Rewald, J., *Paul Cézanne* (Simon & Schuster, 1948)

Root, W. H., *German Criticism of Zola* (Columbia University Press, 1931)

Rufener, H. B., *Biography of a War Novel* (King's Crown Press, 1946)

Sherard, R. H., *Émile Zola* (Chatto & Windus, 1893)

Sondel, B. S., *Zola's Naturalistic Theory with Particular Reference to the Drama* (University of Chicago, 1939)

Vizetelly, E. A., *Émile Zola* (J. Lane, 1904), *With Zola in England* (Chatto & Windus, 1899)

Wilson, A., *Emile Zola* (Morrow, 1952)

CHAPTER EIGHT

THE RISE OF RUSSIAN LITERATURE

GENERAL

Baring, M., *Landmarks in Russian Literature* (The Macmillan Co., 1910), *Outline of Russian Literature* (H. Holt, 1914)

Bianchi, M. G., *Russian Lyrics* (Duffield & Co., 1910)

Biddle, H. P., *Prose Miscellany* (R. Clarke & Co., 1881), *Russian Literature* (R. Clarke & Co., 1877)

Brandes, G., *Impressions of Russia* (T. Y. Crowell & Co., 1889)

Brückner, A., *A Literary History of Russia* (T. Fisher Unwin, 1908)

Cournos, J. (ed.), *A Treasury of Russian Life and Humor* (Coward-McCann, 1943)

Dupuy, E., *The Great Masters of Russian Literature* (T. Y. Crowell & Co., 1886)

Gangulee, N. (ed.), *The Russian Horizon* (G. Allen & Unwin, Ltd., 1943)

Gifford, H., *The Hero of His Time* (Arnold, 1950)

Gudzii, N. K., *History of Early Russian Literature* (Macmillan Co., 1949)

Hapgood, I. F., *A Survey of Russian Literature* (The Chautauqua Press, 1902)

Hare, R., *Russian Literature from Pushkin to the Present Day* (Methuen, 1947)

Hutton, J. A., *Guidance on Russia from Their Literature* (Hodder & Stoughton, Ltd., 1930)

Kropotkin, P., *Ideals and Realities in Russian Literature* (A. A. Knopf, 1915)

Kunitz, J., *Russian Literature and the Jew* (Columbia University Press, 1929), *Russian Literature since the Revolution* (Boni & Gaer, 1948)

Lavrin, J., *From Pushkin to Mayakovsky* (Sylvan Press, 1948), *Russian Literature* (E. Benn, Ltd., 1927)

Martyanov, N. M., *Books Available in English by Russians and on Russia* (N. M. Martyanov, 1936)

Masaryk, T. G., *The Spirit of Russia* (The Macmillan Co., 1918)

Maslenikov, O. A., *The Frenzied Poets* (University of California Press, 1953)

Mirsky, D. S., *Contemporary Russian Literature* (A. A. Knopf, 1926)

Muchnic, H., *An Introduction to Russian Literature* (Doubleday, 1947)

Olgin, M. J., *Guide to Russian Literature* (J. Cape, 1920)

Perlman, L., *Russian Literature and the Business Man* (Columbia University, 1937)

Persky, S., *Contemporary Russian Novelists* (J. W. Luce & Co., 1913)

Phelps, W. L., *Essays on Russian Novelists* (The Macmillan Co., 1916)

Rudwin, M. J., *The Gloom and Glory of Russian Literature* (Open Court, 1918)

Shaknovski, *A Short History of Russian Literature* (K. Paul, Trench, Trübner & Co., Ltd., 1921)

Simmons, E. J., *An Outline of Modern Russian Literature* (Cornell University Press, 1943)

Slonim, M., *Modern Russian Literature* (Oxford University Press, 1953)

Spector, I., *The Golden Age of Russian Literature* (The Scholastic Press, 1939), *Introduction to Russian Literary Criticism* (Seattle University Bookshop, 1945)

Trory, E., *Mainly about Books* (Acorn Press, 1945)

Turner, C. E., *Studies in Russian Literature* (S. Law, Searle & Rivington, 1882)

Volkonski, S. M., *Pictures of Russian History and Russian Literature* (Lawson, Wolffe & Co., 1897)

Waliszewski, K., *A History of Russian Literature* (D. Appleton & Co., 1900)

Williams, H. W., *Russia of the Russians* (Sir Isaac Pitman & Sons, 1914)

Wolfe, A. J., *Aspects of Recent Russian Literature* (Sewanee University Press, 1908)

Yarmolinsky, A., *Russian Literature* (American Library Association, 1931)

DERZHAVIN

Translation: Bowring, J., *Ode to Deity* (D. Lothrop Co., 1887)

DOSTOÏEVSKI

Translations: *The Brothers Karamazoff* (Everyman's Library, E. P. Dutton & Co., 1911); *Crime and Punishment* (Everyman's Library, E. P. Dutton & Co., 1911; The Living Library, The World Publishing Co.); Ackland, R., *Crime and Punishment* (H. Holt, 1948); Brasol, B., *The Diary of a Writer* (C. Scribner's Sons, 1949); Covan, J., *The Brothers Karamazoff* (Brentano's, 1923); Edwards, H. S., *Prison Life in Siberia* (Harper & Brothers, 1881); Garnett, C., *The Brothers Karamasov* (Everyman's Library, E. P. Dutton & Co., 1927; The Modern Library and Modern Library College Editions, Random House, 1929), *Crime and Punishment* (Abridged) (Signet Books, The New American Library of World Literature, Inc., 1949), *The Idiot* (The Modern Library, Random House, 1942), *The Possessed* (Everyman's Library, E. P. Dutton & Co., 1931; The Modern Library, Random House, 1936), *The Novels of Fyodor Dostoyevsky* (Macmillan Co., 1917-29); Hill, E. and Mudie, D., *The Letters of Dostoyevsky to His Wife* (Constable & Co., Ltd., 1930); Hogarth, C. J., *Letters from the Underworld, etc.* (Everyman's Library, E. P. Dutton & Co., 1913), *Poor Folk, The Gambler* (Everyman's Library, E. P. Dutton & Co., 1915); Ivan, R., *The Brothers Karamazov* (Doubleday, Page & Co., 1927); Koteliansky, S. S., *The Grand Inquisitor* (Elkin, Mathews & Marrot, 1930); Koteliansky, S. S. and Murry, J. M., *Letters and Reminiscences* (Chatto & Windus, 1923), *Pages from Dostoevsky* (J. W. Luce & Co., 1916); Magarshack, D.,

Crime and Punishment (Penguin Books, Inc., 1951); Martin, E. M., *The Idiot* (Everyman's Library, E. P. Dutton & Co., 1914); Mayne, E. C., *Letters to His Family and Friends* (Chatto & Windus, 1914); Scott, B., *Dream of a Ridiculous Man* (L. Drummond, Ltd., 1945); Thilo, M. von, *Buried Alive* (H. Holt & Co., 1881); Whishaw, F., *The Idiot* (Vizetelly & Co., 1887), *Injury and Insult* (Vizetelly & Co., 1887), *Uncle's Dream* (Vizetelly & Co., 1888)

Abraham, G. E. H., *Dostoevsky* (Duckworth, 1936)

Birdyayev, N. A., *Dostoievsky* (Sheed & Ward, 1934)

Brasol, B., *The Mighty Three* (W. F. Payson, 1934)

Carr, E. H., *Dostoevsky* (Houghton, Mifflin Co., 1931)

Clutton-Brock, A., *Essays on Books* (Methuen & Co., Ltd., 1920)

Dostoyevsky, A., *Fyodor Dostoyevsky* (W. Heinemann, 1921)

Dostoyevskaya, A. G., *The Diary of Dostoyevsky's Wife* (Macmillan Co., 1928)

Fayer, M. H., *Gide, Freedom, and Dostoevsky* (Lane Press, 1946)

Fülop-Miller, R., *Fyodor Dostoevsky* (Scribner, 1950)

Gide, A., *Dostoevsky* (A. A. Knopf, 1926)

Grant, P. S., *Essays* (Harper & Brothers, 1922)

Halperin, G., *Tolstoy, Dostoevskiy, Tourgenev* (Chicago Literary Club, 1946)

Hromadka, J. L., *Doom and Resurrection* (Madrus House, 1945)

Hubben, W., *Four Prophets of Our Destiny* (Macmillan, 1952)

Ivanov, V. I., *Freedom and the Tragic Life* (Noonday Press, 1952)

Kaun, A. and Simmons, E. J. (eds.), *Slavic Studies* (Cornell University Press, 1943)

King, H. H., *Dostoyevsky and Andreyev* (Cornell Alumni News Corporation, 1936)

Kohn, H., *Prophets and Peoples* (The Macmillan Co., 1946)

Koteliansky, S. S., *Dostoevsky Portrayed by His Wife* (G. Routledge & Sons, Ltd., 1926)

Lavrin, J., *Dostoevsky* (The Macmillan Co., 1947), *Dostoevsky and His Creation* (W. Collins Sons & Co., Ltd., 1920), *Studies in European Literature* (Constable & Co., Ltd., 1929)

Lloyd, J. A. T., *Fyodor Dostoevsky* (C. Scribner's Sons, 1947)

Mackiewicz, S., *Dostoyevsky* (Orbis, 1948)

Masaryk, T. G., *The Spirit of Russia* (The Macmillan Co., 1919)

Meier-Graefe, J., *Dostoevsky* (G. Routledge & Sons, Ltd., 1928)

Muchnic, H., *Dostoevsky's English Reputation* (Smith College Studies, 1939)

Murry, J. M., *Fyodor Dostoevsky* (M. Secker, 1916)

Neumann, R., *Passion* (Harcourt, Brace & Co., 1932)

Pfleger, K., *Wrestlers with Christ* (Sheed & Ward, 1936)

Powys, J. C., *Dostoievsky* (J. Lane, 1946)

Roe, I., *The Breath of Corruption* (Hutchinson & Co., Ltd., 1946)
Roubiczek, P., *The Misinterpretation of Man* (C. Scribner's Sons, 1947)
Shestov, L., *In Job's Balances* (J. M. Dent & Sons, Ltd., 1932)
Simmons, E. J., *Dostoevski* (Oxford University Press, 1940)
Troyat, H., *Firebrand* (Roy Publishers, 1946)
Vogüé, E. M. M., *The Russian Novelists* (D. Lothrop Co., 1887)
Warner, R., *The Cult of Power* (John Lane, 1946)
Yarmolinsky, A., *Dostoevsky* (Harcourt, Brace & Co., 1934)
Zander, L. A., *Dostoevsky* (S. C. M. Press, 1948)
Zernov, N. M., *Three Russian Prophets* (S. C. M. Press, 1944)
Zweig, S., *Master Builders* (The Viking Press, 1939)

GOGOL

Translations: *Taras Bulba and Other Tales* (Everyman's Library, E. P. Dutton & Co., 1918); Anderson, J., *The Inspector General* (S. French, 1931); Baskerville, B. C., *Taras Bulba* (The Walter Scott Publishing Co., Ltd., 1907); Berkman, A., *The Gamblers* (The Macaulay Co., 1927); Campbell, D. J., *The Government Inspector* (Sylvan Press, 1947); Field, C., *The Mantle and Other Stories* (T. W. Laurie, Ltd., 1916); Garnett, C., *Dead Souls* (Chatto & Windus, 1922; The Modern Library, Random House, 1936), *Evenings on a Farm near Dikanka* (Chatto & Windus, 1926), *The Government Inspector* (A. A. Knopf, 1927), *Mirgorod* (Chatto & Windus, 1928), *The Overcoat and Other Stories* (A. A. Knopf, 1923); Guerney, B. B., *Chichikov's Journeys* (The Readers Club, 1942); *Dead Souls* (Rinehart Editions, Rinehart & Co., Inc., 1948); Hapgood, I. F., *Taras Bulba* (T. Y. Crowell & Co., 1886); Hogarth, C. J., *Dead Souls* (Everyman's Library, E. P. Dutton & Co., 1915; J. M. Dent & Sons, Ltd., 1916); Mirsky, Prince, *The Diary of a Madman* (The Cresset Press, 1929); Reavey, G., *Dead Souls* (The Novel Library, 1948); Scott, B., *Diary of a Madman* (L. Drummond, Ltd., 1945); Seltzer, T., *The Inspector-General* (A. A. Knopf, 1916); Shoenberg, Z. and Domb, J., *The Greatcoat* (G. G. Harrap & Co., Ltd., 1944); Sykes, A. A., *The Inspector-General* (W. Scott, n. d.); Tolstoy, G., *Cossack Tales* (J. Blackwood, 1860)

Brasol, B., *The Mighty Three* (W. F. Payson, 1934)
Churchill, W., *The Marvelous Year* (B. W. Huebsch, 1909)
Lavrin, J., *Gogol* (G. Routledge & Sons, Ltd., 1925)
Nabokov, V. V., *Nikolai Gogol* (New Directions Books, 1944)
Panin, I. N., *Lectures on Russian Literature* (G. P. Putnam's Sons, 1889)
Perry, H. T. E., *Masters of Dramatic Comedy* (Harvard University Press, 1939)
Vogüé, E. M. M., *The Russian Novelists* (D. Lothrop Co., 1887)

GONCHAROV

Translations: Bryant, M., *The Precipice* (A. A. Knopf, 1916); Dudding-ton, N. A., *Oblomov* (G. Allen & Unwin, Ltd., 1929; Everyman's Library, E. P. Dutton & Co., 1932); Hogarth, C. J., *Oblomov* (Mac-millan Co., 1915)

GRIBOYEDOV

Translation: Pring, S. W., *The Misfortune of Being Too Clever* (D. Nutt, 1914)

Tynyanov, Y. N., *Death and Diplomacy in Persia* (Boriswood, 1938)

GRIGOROVICH

Translation: Rappaport, A. S., *The Fisherman* (S. Paul & Co., 1916)

KARAMZIN

Translations: *Travels from Moscow* (J. Badcock, 1803); Elrington, J. B., *Russian Tales* (G. Sidney, 1803)

KRYLOV

Translations: *Krilof and His Fables* (Strahan & Co., 1869); Coxwell, C. F., *Kriloff's Fables* (K. Paul, Trench, Trübner, & Co., Ltd., 1921); Harrison, I. H., *Kriloff's Original Fables* (Remington & Co., 1883); Pares, B., *Krylov's Fables* (J. Cape, 1926)

LERMONTOV

Translations: *Sketches of Russian Life* (Ingram, Cooke & Co., 1853); Burness, R., *The Demon* (Douglas & Foulis, 1918); Conant, S. S., *The Circassian Boy* (J. R. Osgood & Co., 1875); Cournos, J., *A Song about Tsar Ivan* (The Aquila Press, 1929); Krup, J., *Six Poems from the Russian* (The Galleon Press, 1936); Merton, R., *A Hero of Our Time* (P. Allan & Co., Ltd., 1928); Nabakov, V., *Three Russian Poets* (New Directions, 1943); Pulszky, T., *The Hero of Our Days* (D. Bogue, 1854); Richter, E., *The Demon* (D. Nutt, 1910); Robbins, J. J., *A Sheaf from Lermontov* (Lieber & Lewis, 1923); Shelley, G., *The Demon* (The Richards Press, Ltd., 1930); Voynich, E. L., *Six Lyrics from the Ruthenian* (E. Mathews, 1911); Wisdom, J. H. and Murray, M., *A Hero of Our Time* (A. A. Knopf, 1916)

Heifetz, A. S., *Lermontov in English* (The New York Public Library, 1942)

Kaun, A. and Simmons, E. J. (eds.), *Slavic Studies* (Cornell University Press, 1943)

McCarthy, D., *Lermontov* (The Five Arts Committee, 1944)

OSTROVSKI

Translations: Ackland, R., *The Diary of a Scoundrel* (S. Low, Marston & Co., 1948); Campbell, J. P. and Noyes, G. R., *At the Jolly Spot* (Poet Lore, 1925), *A Cat Has Not Always Carnivals* (Poet Lore, 1929); Colby, I. S. and Noyes, G. R., *Wolves and Sheep* (Poet Lore, 1926); Daniels, C. C. and Noyes, G. R., *Fairy Gold* (Poet Lore, 1929); Garnett, C., *The Storm* (Duckworth & Co., 1899); Holland, G. F. and Morley, M., *The Storm* (G. Allen & Unwin, Ltd., 1930); Korvin-Kronkovshy, E. and Noyes, G. R., *A Last Sacrifice* (Poet Lore, 1928); Kurlandzik, S. C. and Noyes, G. R., *Bondwomen* (Poet Lore, 1926); Magarshack, D., *Easy Money* (G. Allen & Unwin, Ltd., 1944); Martens, F. H., *Snégurotchka* (F. Rullman, Inc., 1921); Noyes, G. R. (ed.), *Plays by A. Ostrovsky* (C. Scribner's Sons, 1917); Whyte, F. and Noyes, G. R., *The Thunderstorm* (S. French, 1927); Winlow, C. V. and Noyes, G. R., *The Forest* (S. French, 1926)

Kaun, A. and Simmons, E. J. (eds.), *Slavic Studies* (Cornell University Press, 1943)

PUSHKIN

Translations: Brasol, B., *The Russian Wonderland* (Williams & Norgate, Ltd., 1936); Currall, R. T., *Three Tales* (Transatlantic Arts, Inc., 1945); Deutsch, B., *Eugene Onegin* (The Limited Editions Club, 1943); Duddington, N., *The Captain's Daughter* (J. M. Dent & Sons, 1928); Elton, O., *Eugeny Onegin* (The Pushkin Press, 1937), *Verse from Pushkin and Others* (E. Arnold & Co., 1935); Gray, M. K., *A Collection of Short Lyrics by Pushkin* (Privately Printed, 1936); Hayes, A., *Boris Godunov* (K. Paul, Trench, Trübner & Co., Ltd., 1918); Keane, T., *The Prose Tales* (G. Bell & Sons, Ltd., 1916); Krup, J., *Six Poems from the Russian* (The Galleon Press, 1936); Lewis, W. D., *The Bakchesarian Fountain* (C. Sherman, 1849); Lubimov, N., *Mozart and Salieri* (Poet Lore, 1920); Morison, W., *Pushkin's Poems* (G. Allen & Unwin, Ltd., 1945); Nabakov, V., *Three Russian Poets* (New Directions, 1944); Nachshen, D., *Tales of Bielkin* (L. Drummond, 1947); Panin, I., *Poems* (Cupples & Hurd, 1888); Radin, D. P. and Patrick, G. Z., *Eugene Onegin* (University of California Press, 1937); Spalding, Lieutenant, *Eugène Onéguine* (Macmillan & Co., 1881); Waller, H., *The Tale of the Golden Cockerel* (The Golden Cockerel Press, 1936); Yarmolinsky, A. (ed.), *Poems, Prose and Plays* (The Modern Library, Random House, 1943), *The Works of Pushkin* (Random House, 1936); Zielinska, M. H. de, *Marie* (Jansen, McClurg & Co., 1877)

Beckwith, M. W. and Others, *Pushkin* (The Paisley Press, 1937)

Brasol, B., *The Mighty Three* (W. F. Payson, 1934), *Poushkin, the Shake-
speare of Russia* (Privately Printed, 1931)
Cleugh, J., *Prelude to Parnassus* (A. Barker, Ltd., 1936)
Cross, S. H. and Simmons, E. J., *Alexander Pushkin* (American Russian
Institute, 1937)
Cross, S. H. (ed.), *Centennial Essays for Pushkin* (Harvard University
Press, 1937)
Dostoievski, F. M., *Pages from the Journal of an Author* (J. W. Luce &
Co., 1916)
Elton, O., *Essays and Addresses* (E. Arnold & Co., 1939)
Herford, C. H., *The Post-War Mind of Germany and Other European
Studies* (Clarendon Press, 1927), *A Russian Shakespearean* (Long-
mans, Green & Co., 1925)
Kaun, A. and Simmons, E. J. (eds.), *Slavic Studies* (Cornell University
Press, 1943)
Lambert, L., *Pushkin* (Doubleday & Co., Inc., 1946)
Lavrin, J., *Pushkin and Russian Literature* (Hodder & Stoughton, 1947)
Mirsky, Prince D. S., *Pushkin* (G. Routledge & Sons, Ltd., 1926)
Panin, I. N., *Lectures on Russian Literature* (G. P. Putnam's Sons, 1889)
Petrunkevitch, A. and Others, *Pushkin Centennial Meeting* (Connecticut
Academy of Arts & Sciences, 1937)
Simmons, E. J., *Pushkin* (Harvard University Press, 1937)
Talmadge, I. D. W. (ed.), *Pushkin: Homage by Marxist Critics* (Critics
Group, 1937)
Troyat, H., *Pushkin* (Pantheon, 1950)
Vogüé, E. M. M., *The Russian Novelists* (D. Lothrop Co., 1887)
Wilson, E., *The Triple Thinkers* (Harcourt, Brace & Co., 1938)
Yarmolinsky, A., *Pushkin in English* (The New York Public Library,
1937)

SUMAROKOV

Translation: Eustaphiere, *Demetrius the Imposter* (J. Nichol & Son, 1806)

TOLSTOI, ALEXIS

Translations: Covan, J., *Tsar Fyodor Ivanovitch* (Brentano's, 1922);
Galitzine, Princess, *Prince Serebrenni* (Chapman & Hall, 1874);
Hayes, A., *The Death of Ivan the Terrible* (K. Paul, Trench,
Trübner & Co., Ltd., 1926); Manning, C. A., *A Prince of Outlaws*
(A. A. Knopf, 1927)

TOLSTOI, LEO

Translations: *Anna Karenina* (The Living Library, The World Publishing
Co.); *Essays from Tula* (Sheppard Press, 1848); *Master and Man*
(Everyman's Library, E. P. Dutton & Co., 1910); *War and Peace*

(Everyman's Library, E. P. Dutton & Co., 1911); Bain, R. N., *More Tales from Tolstoi* (Brentano's, 1903); Bell, C., *War and Peace* (W. S. Gottsberger, 1886); Browne, W. R. (ed.), *Man or State* (B. W. Huebsch, 1919); Chertkov, V. (ed.), *Christian Martyrdom in Russia* (G. N. Morany, 1899); Delano, A. P., *Resurrection* (T. Y. Crowell & Co., 1911); Delano, Mrs. A., *What People Live By* (D. Lothrop & Co., 1893); Dillon, E. H., *Work While Ye Have Light* (United States Book Co., 1890); Dole, N. H., *The Dramatic Works of Tolstoi* (Harrap, 1923); Dole, N. H. (ed.), *The Novels and Other Works of Lyof N. Tolstoi* (C. Scribner's Sons, 1902); Duff, J. D. and Maude, A., *The Kreutzer Sonata, The Devil, and Other Tales* (World's Classics, Oxford University Press, 1924); England, P., *Literary Fragments* (L. MacVeagh, 1931); Evarts, Mrs. E. M., *The Living Corpse* (Brown Bros., 1912); Garnett, C., *Anna Karenina* (Random House, 1939; Pocket Books, Inc., 1951), *Christianity and Patriotism* (J. Cape, 1933), *The Death of Ivan Ilyich and Other Stories* (John Lane, 1915), *War and Peace* (W. Heinemann, 1904; The Modern Library, Random House, 1931); Hapgood, I. F., *Childhood, Boyhood, Youth* (W. Scott, 189-?), *Life* (T. Y. Crowell & Co., 1888), *What to Do?* (T. Y. Crowell & Co., 1887); Hogarth, C. J., *Childhood, Boyhood, Youth* (E. P. Dutton & Co., 1912); Hogarth, C. J. and Sirnis, A., *The Diaries of Tolstoi* (E. P. Dutton & Co., 1917); Islavin, L., *The Letters of Tolstoy and His Cousin* (E. P. Dutton & Co., Inc., 1928); Koteliansky, S. S. and Woolf, V., *Tolstoi's Love Letters* (Hogarth Press, 1923); Lewery, L., *The Cycle of Reading* (International Library Publishing Co., 1911); Loranger, A., *The Romance of Marriage* (Laird & Lee, 1890); Lyster, F., *The Kreutzer Sonata* (The Pollard Publishing Co., 1890); Maude, A., *A Confession, The Gospel in Brief and What I Believe* (World's Classics, Oxford University Press, 1921), *Kingdom of God and Peace Essays* (World's Classics, Oxford University Press, 1936), *On Life, and Essays on Religion* (World's Classics, Oxford University Press, 1934), *Recollections and Essays* (World's Classics, Oxford University Press, 1937), *Resurrection* (World's Classics, Oxford University Press, 1916), *Tolstoy on Art* (Small, Maynard & Co., 1924), *What is Art and Essays on Art* (World's Classics, Oxford University Press, 1930), *What Then Must We Do?* (World's Classics, Oxford University Press, 1925), *The Works of Leo Tolstoy* (Oxford University Press, 1928-37); Maude, L. and A., *Anna Karenina* (World's Classics, Oxford University Press, 1918), *Childhood, Boyhood and Youth* (World's Classics, Oxford University Press, 1930), *Iván Ilych and Hadji Murád* (World's Classics, Oxford University Press, 1935), *Nine Stories, 1855-63* (World's Classics, Oxford University Press, 1934), *Plays* (World's Classics,

Oxford University Press, 1923), *The Private Diary of Leo Tolstoy* (W. Heinemann, Ltd., 1927), *Tales of Army Life* (World's Classics, Oxford University Press, 1935), *Twenty-Three Tales* (World's Classics, Oxford University Press, 1906), *War and Peace* (World's Classics, Oxford University Press, 1922-3); Millet, F. D., *Sebastopol* (Harper & Brothers, 1887); Norraikow, Count, *Life is Worth Living* (C. L. Webster & Co., 1892); Perno, L., *On Insanity* (C. W. Daniel Co., Ltd., 1936); Popoff, C., *What I Believe* (Privately Printed, 1895); Rapoport, S. and Kenworthy, J. C., *Master and Man* (T. Y. Crowell & Co., 1895); Schoenberg, Z. and Domb, J., *A Captive in the Caucasus* (G. G. Harrap, 1945); Schumm, G., *The Fruits of Culture* (B. R. Tucker, 1891); Schuyler, E., *The Cossacks* (C. Scribner's Sons, 1878); Smith, H., *My Religion* (T. Y. Crowell & Co., 1885), *The Physiology of War* (T. Y. Crowell & Co., 1888); Strunsky, R., *The Journals of Tolstoi* (A. A. Knopf, 1917); Tchertkoff, V., *The Christian Teaching* (F. A. Stokes Co., 1898); Tchertkoff, V. and Fifield, A. C., *What is Religion?* (T. Y. Crowell & Co., 1902); Tchertkoff, V. and I. F. M., *Bethink Yourselves!* (T. Y. Crowell & Co., 1904), *A Great Iniquity* (The Public Publishing Co., 1905), *Tolstoy on Shakespeare* (Funk & Wagnalls Co., 1906); Tolstoy, M. K., *The Law of Love and the Law of Violence* (R. Field, 1948); Townsend, R. S., *Anna Karenina* (Everyman's Library, E. P. Dutton & Co., 1912; E. P. Dutton & Co., 1914); Traill, V., *The Cossacks* (The Novel Library, 1949), *Resurrection* (The Novel Library, 1947); Tucker, B. R., *The Kreutzer Sonata* (J. S. Ogilvie Publishing Co., 1890); Turin, Mrs. L. and Others, *Stories and Dramas* (J. M. Dent & Sons, Ltd., 1926); V. T. and A. C. F., *My Reply to the Synod's Edict* (The Free Age Press, 1901); Wiener, L., *The Complete Works of Count Tolstoy* (J. M. Dent & Co., 1905); Wolfe, A. J., *The Pathway of Life* (International Book Publishing Co., 1919), *Posthumous Works* (International Book Publishing Co., 1920), *Resurrection* (International Book Publishing Co., 1920); Yarros, V. and Schumm, G., *Church and State* (B. R. Tucker, 1891); Zweig, S. (ed.), *The Living Thoughts of Tolstoi* (Longmans, Green & Co., 1939)

Abraham, G. E. A., *Tolstoy* (Duckworth, 1935)

Acker, H., *Three Boys of Old Russia* (T. Nelson & Sons, 1944)

Arnold, M., *Essays in Criticism: Second Series* (Macmillan & Co., 1891)

Atkins, G. G., *Pilgrims of the Lonely Road* (F. H. Revell Co., 1913)

Baudouin, C., *Tolstoi* (K. Paul, Trench, Trübner, & Co., Ltd., 1923)

Behrs, C. A., *Recollections of Count Leo Tolstoy* (W. Heinemann, 1893)

Bellman, H., *Architects of the New Age* (S. Low, Marston & Co., Ltd., 1929)

Bernstein, H., *With Master Minds* (Universal Series Publishing Co., 1913)

Biryukov, P. I., *Leo Tolstoy* (C. Scribner's Sons, 1906), *The New Russia* (Independent Labour Party, 1920)

Bodde, D., *Tolstoy and China* (Princeton University Press, 1950)

Chertkov, V. G., *The Last Days of Tolstoi* (W. Heinemann, 1922)

Chesterton, G. K., *Simplicity and Tolstoy* (A. L. Humphreys, 1912)

Chesterton, G. K. and Others, *Leo Tolstoy* (J. Pott & Co., 1903)

Creelman, J., *On the Great Highway* (Lothrop Publishing Co., 1901)

Crosby, E. H., *Tolstoy and His Message* (Funk & Wagnalls Co., 1903)

Davis, H. E., *Tolstoy and Nietzsche* (New Republic, Inc., 1929)

De Selincourt, B., *Towards Peace and Other Essays* (Oxford University Press, 1932)

Dillon, E. J., *Count Leo Tolstoy* (Hutchinson & Co., Ltd., 1934)

Dixon, W. M., *An Apology for the Arts* (E. Arnold & Co., 1945)

Dole, N. H., *The Life of Count Lyof N. Tolstoi* (T. Y. Crowell Co., 1911)

Dukes, A., *Modern Dramatists* (F. Palmer, 1911)

Ellis, H., *The New Spirit* (W. Scott Publishing Co., Ltd., 1892)

Farrell, J. T., *Literature and Morality* (Vanguard Press, 1947)

Fausset, H., *Tolstoy* (J. Cape, 1927)

Flaccus, L. W., *Artists and Thinkers* (Longmans, Green & Co., 1916)

Garnett, E., *Tolstoy* (Constable & Co., Ltd., 1914)

Garrod, H. W., *Tolstoi's Theory of Art* (The Clarendon Press, 1935)

Goldenveizer, A. B., *Talks with Tolstoi* (Hogarth Press, 1923)

Gorki, M., *Reminiscences of Tolstoi* (Hogarth Press, 1921)

Griggs, E. H., *Moral Leaders* (The Abingdon Press, 1940)

Guthrie, A. M. B., *Wordsworth and Tolstoi* (T. & A. Constable, Ltd., 1922)

Hall, B., *What Tolstoy Taught* (Chatto & Windus, 1913)

Halperin, G., *Tolstoy, Dostoevskiy, Tourgenev* (Chicago Literary Club, 1946)

Harden, M., *Monarchs and Men* (The John C. Winston Co., 1913)

Heller, O., *Prophets of Dissent* (A. A. Knopf, 1918)

Holmes, J. H., *Leo Tolstoy* (Church of the Messiah, 1911)

Hunter, R., *Why We Fail As Christians* (The Macmillan Co., 1919)

Hutton, J. A., *Pilgrims in the Region of Faith* (Oliphant, Anderson & Ferrier, 1913)

Ingersoll, R. G., *Essays and Criticisms* (C. P. Farrell, 1897), *Love the Redeemer* (Progressive Publishing Co., 1890)

Jones, B. H. and Others, *Prize Essays on Tolstoy's What Shall We Do Then* (University of California Press, 1912)

Kaun, A. and Simmons, E. J. (ed.), *Slavic Studies* (Cornell University Press, 1943)

Kenworthy, J. C., *A Pilgrimage to Tolstoy* (The Brotherhood Publishing Co., 1950), *Tolstoy: His Life and Works* (The Walter Scott Publishing Co., Ltd., 1902), *Tolstoy: His Teaching* (The Brotherhood Publishing Co., n. d.)

Knowlson, T. S., *Leo Tolstoy* (F. Warne & Co., 1904)

Kuzminskaya, T. A., *Tolstoy as I Knew Him* (Macmillan Co., 1948)

Kvitko, D., *A Philosophical Study of Tolstoy* (Columbia University, 1927)

Lavrin, Y., *Studies in European Literature* (Constable & Co., Ltd., 1929), *Tolstoy* (W. Collins Sons & Co., Ltd., 1924)

Leon, D., *Tolstoy* (Routledge, 1944)

Lloyd, J. A. T., *Two Russian Reformers* (J. Lane Co., 1911)

Mann, T., *Essays of Three Decades* (A. A. Knopf, 1947), *Past Masters* (A. A. Knopf, 1933)

Maude, A. (ed.), *Family Views of Tolstoy* (G. Allen & Unwin, Ltd., 1926)

Maude, A., *Leo Tolstoy and His Works* (Oxford University Press, 1931), *The Life of Tolstoi* (Constable, 1908-10; World's Classics, Oxford University Press, 1930), *A Peculiar People* (Funk & Wagnalls Co., 1904), *Tolstoy and His Problems* (G. Richards, 1901), *Tolstoy on Art and Its Critics* (H. Milford, 1925)

Merejkowski, D. S., *Tolstoi as Man and Artist* (G. P. Putnam's Sons, 1902)

Morgan, C., *Reflections in a Mirror* (Macmillan & Co., Ltd., 1944)

Nazarov, A. I., *Tolstoy* (F. A. Stokes Co., 1929)

Newton, W. W., *A Run through Russia* (Student Publishing Co., 1894)

Noyes, G. R., *Tolstoy* (John Murray, 1919)

Panin, I. N., *Lectures on Russian Literature* (G. P. Putnam's Sons, 1889)

Polner, T. I., *Tolstoy and His Wife* (W. W. Norton & Co., Inc., 1945)

Ponsonby, A. A. W. H., *Rebels and Reformers* (G. Allen & Unwin, Ltd., 1917)

Poteat, E. M., *The Scandal of the Cross* (Harper & Brothers, 1928)

Robertson, J. M., *Explorations* (Watts & Co., 1923)

Rolland, R., *Tolstoi* (T. Fisher Unwin, 1911)

Roubiczek, P., *The Misinterpretation of Man* (C. Scribner's Sons, 1947)

Sarolea, C., *Count L. N. Tolstoi* (Thos. Nelson & Son, 1912)

Sergyeyenko, P. A., *How Count L. N. Tolstoy Lives and Works* (T. Y. Crowell & Co., 1899)

Shestov, L., *In Job's Balances* (J. M. Dent & Sons, Ltd., 1932)

Simmons, E. J., *Leo Tolstoy* (Little, Brown & Co., 1946)

Smith, J. A., *Tolstoy's Fiction in England and America* (University of Illinois, 1939)

Stadling, J. J. and Reason, W., *In the Land of Tolstoi* (J. Clarke & Co., 1897)

Stanoyevich, M. S., *Tolstoy's Interpretation of Money and Property* (Liberty Publishing Co., 1916), *Tolstoy's Theory of Social Reform* (Liberty Publishing Co., 1916)

Steiner, E. A., *Tolstoy* (F. H. Revell Co., 1914)

Stevens, H. B., *Tolstoy: a Play* (T. Y. Crowell Co., 1928)

Stockham, Mrs. A. B., *Tolstoi* (A. B. Stockham & Co., 1900)

Sukhotina, T. L., *The Tolstoy Home* (Columbia University Press, 1951)

Tolstaya, A., *The Tragedy of Tolstoy* (Oxford University Press, 1933)

Tolstaya, S., *The Autobiography of Countess Sophie Tolstoi* (L. & V. Woolf, 1922), *The Countess Tolstoy's Later Diary, 1891-1897* (V. Gollancz, Ltd., 1929), *The Diary of Tolstoy's Wife, 1860-1891* (V. Gollancz, Ltd., 1928)

Tolstoi, I. L., *Reminiscences of Tolstoi by His Son* (Chapman & Hall, 1914)

Tolstoi, L. L., *The Truth about My Father* (John Murray, 1924)

Tolstoy, A., *The Life of My Father* (E. Hapgood, tr.) (Harper & Brothers, 1953)

Tolstoy, S. A. B., *The Final Struggle* (Translated and edited by A. Maude) (G. Allen & Unwin, Ltd., 1936; Oxford University Press, 1936)

Vogüé, E. M. M., *The Russian Novelists* (D. Lothrop Co., 1887)

Wedgwood, J., *Nineteenth Century Teachers* (Hodder & Stoughton, 1909)

Wilkinson, W. C., *Some New Literary Valuations* (Funk & Wagnalls Co., 1909)

Winstanley, L., *Tolstoy* (T. C. & E. C. Jack, 1914)

Yassukovitch, A., *Tolstoi in English* (New York Public Library, 1929)

Zweig, S., *Adepts in Self-Portraiture* (The Viking Press, 1928)

TURGENIEV

Translations: *First Love and Rudin* (The Novel Library, 1950); Abbott, F., *Annouchka* (Cupples, Upham & Co., 1884); Domb, J. and Shoenberg, Z., *Mumu* (G. G. Harrap & Co., Ltd., 1945); Duddington, N., *Smoke* (Everyman's Library, E. P. Dutton & Co., 1949); Garnett, E. C., *Fathers and Sons* (The Modern Library, Random House, n. d.), *The Novels of Ivan Turgenev* (The Macmillan Co., 1906), *Three Plays* (Cassell & Co., Ltd., 1934); Gersoni, H., *Mumu* (Funk & Wagnalls, 1884), *An Unfortunate Woman* (Funk & Wagnalls Co., 1886); Hapgood, I. F., *The Novels and Stories of Ivan Turgenieff* (C. Scribner's Sons, 1903-4), *The Works of Ivan Turgenieff* (C. E. Lauriat Co., 1903-4); Hogarth, C. J., *Fathers and Sons* (Everyman's Library, E. P. Dutton & Co., 1921); Isaacs, B., *Fathers and Sons* (Foreign Languages Publishing House, 1947), *A Nest of the Gentry* (Foreign Languages Publishing House, 1947); Jerrold, S., *First Love* (W. H. Allen & Co., 1884); Mandell, M. S., *The Plays of Ivan S. Turgenev* (The Macmillan Co., 1924); Nichols, R., *Hamlet and Don Quixote* (Hendersons, 1930); Perry, T. S., *Virgin Soil* (H. Holt & Co., 1877); Ralston, W. R., *Liza* (Ward, Lock & Co., 188-?; Everyman's Library, E. P. Dutton & Co., 1914); Reavey, G., *Fathers and Sons* (The Novel Library, 1950); Schimanskaya, E., *Poems in Prose* (L.

Drummond, 1945); Schuyler, E., *Fathers and Sons* (Leypoldt & Holt, 1867); Simmons, E. J. (ed.), *Fathers and Children* (Rinehart Editions, Rinehart & Co., Inc., 1949); Townsend, R. S., *Virgin Soil* (Everyman's Library, E. P. Dutton & Co., 1911); West, W. F., *Smoke* (H. Holt & Co., 1873)

Cecil, Lord D., *Poets and Story-Tellers* (Constable, 1949)

Clutton-Brock, A., *Essays on Books* (Methuen & Co., Ltd., 1920)

Ford, F. M., *Mightier than the Sword* (G. Allen & Unwin, Ltd., 1938)

Garnett, E., *Turgenev* (W. Collins & Co., Ltd., 1917)

Gettman, R. A., *Turgenev in England and America* (University of Illinois Press, 1941)

Halperin, G., *Tolstoy, Dostoevskiy, Tourgenev* (Chicago Literary Club, 1946)

Halperine-Kaminsky, E. (ed.), *Tourgeneff and His French Circle* (T. F. Unwin, 1898)

Hershkowitz, H., *Democratic Ideas in Turgenev's Works* (Columbia University Press, 1932)

James, H., *The Art of Fiction* (Oxford University Press, 1948)

Lavrin, Y., *Studies in European Literature* (Constable & Co., Ltd., 1929)

Lloyd, J. A. T., *Ivan Turgenev* (R. Hale, Ltd., 1942), *Two Russian Reformers* (J. Lane Co., 1911)

Morgan, C., *Reflections in a Mirror* (Macmillan & Co., Ltd., 1944)

Moxom, P. S., *Two Masters* (Sherman, French & Co., 1912)

Panin, I. N., *Lectures on Russian Literature* (G. P. Putnam's Sons, 1889)

Perry, H. T. E., *Masters of Dramatic Comedy* (Harvard University Press, 1939)

Vogüé, E. M. M., *The Russian Novelists* (D. Lothrop Co., 1887)

Yarmolinsky, A., *Turgenev* (Century Co., 1926)

Zhitova, V. N. B., *The Turgenev Family* (Harvill Press, 1947)

CHAPTER NINE

OTHER NINETEENTH-CENTURY DEVELOPMENTS

GENERAL

Bertaux, F., *A Panorama of German Literature, 1871-1931* (Whittlesey House, 1935)

Bowra, C. M., *The Heritage of Symbolism* (Macmillan & Co., Ltd., 1943)

Chandler, F. W., *Modern Continental Playwrights* (Harper & Brothers, 1931)

Collison-Morley, L., *Modern Italian Literature* (Sir I. Pitman & Sons, 1911)

Jameson, S., *Modern Drama in Europe* (Collins, 1920)

Jasper, G. R., *Adventure in the Theatre* (Rutgers University Press, 1947)

Quennell, P., *Baudelaire and the Symbolists* (Chatto & Windus, 1929)
Saurat, D., *Modern French Literature, 1870-1940* (G. P. Putnam's Sons, 1946)
Schaffer, A., *The Genres of Parnassian Poetry* (Oxford University Press, 1944)
Symons, A., *The Symbolist Movement in Literature* (W. Heinemann, 1899), *Studies in Two Literatures* (Secker, 1924)
Vat, G. G. van der, *The Fabulous Opera* (J. B. Wolters', 1936)
Wilson, E., *Axel's Castle* (C. Scribner's Sons, 1931)

BAUDELAIRE

Translations: *Love Songs of France* (New Amsterdam Book Co., 1896); Bernstein, J. M. (ed.), *Baudelaire, Rimbaud, Verlaine* (The Citadel Press, 1947); Bernstein, J. M., *Eugene Delacroix* (Lear Publishers, 1947); Berthon, H. E. (ed.), *Nine French Poets* (Macmillan & Co., Ltd., 1930); Dillon, G. and Millay, E. St. V., *Flowers of Evil* (Harper & Brothers, 1936); Ford, C. H. (ed.), *The Mirror of Baudelaire* (New Directions, 1942); Hamburger, M., *Twenty Prose Poems* (Editions Poetry, 1946); Isherwood, C., *Intimate Journals* (The Blackamore Press, 1930); Laver, J. (ed.), *Flowers of Evil* (Fanfare Press, 1940); MacIntyre, C. F., *One Hundred Poems* (University of California Press, 1947); Scott, C., *The Flowers of Evil* (E. Mathews, 1909); Shanks, L. P., *Les Fleurs du Mal* (H. Holt & Co., 1925); Squire, J. C., *Poems and Baudelaire Flowers* (New Age Press, 1909); Symons, A., *Baudelaire: Prose and Poetry* (A. & C. Boni, 1926), *The Letters of Baudelaire* (A. & C. Boni, 1927); Varèse, L., *Paris Spleen* (New Directions, 1947); Wagner, G., *Flowers of Evil* (New Directions Publications, 1946); Campbell, R., *Poems of Baudelaire* (Harvill Press, 1953)
Bandy, W. T., *Baudelaire Judged by His Contemporaries* (Columbia University Press, 1933)
Bennett, J. D., *Baudelaire* (Princeton University Press, 1944)
Buchanan, R. W., *The Fleshly School of Poetry* (Strahan & Co., 1872)
Carrère, J., *Degeneration in the Great French Masters* (Brentano's, 1922)
Clapton, G. T., *Baudelaire* (Oliver & Boyd, 1934)
Eliot, T. S., *For Lancelot Andrewes* (Doubleday, Doran & Co., 1929)
Fowlie, W., *Clowns and Angels* (Sheed & Ward, 1943), *The Spirit of France* (Sheed & Ward, 1944)
Gautier, T., *Charles Baudelaire* (Greening & Co., 1915), *Famous French Authors* (R. Worthington, 1879)
Gilman, M., *Baudelaire the Critic* (Columbia University Press, 1943)
Huneker, J. G., *Egoists* (C. Scribner's Sons, 1925)
Jones, P. M., *Baudelaire* (Yale University Press, 1952)
Laforgue, R., *The Defeat of Baudelaire* (L. & V. Woolf, 1932)

Lavrin, Y., *Studies in European Literature* (Constable & Co., Ltd., 1929)

Loving, P., *Gardener of Evil* (Brewer & Warren, Inc., 1931), *Monsieur de Balzac Entertains a Visitor* (University of Washington Book Store, 1929)

Mary, Mother A., *The Influence of Joseph de Maistre on Baudelaire* (Bryn Mawr, 1943)

Morgan, E., *Flower of Evil, a Life of Chas. Baudelaire* (Sheed & Ward, 1943)

Porché, F., *Chas. Baudelaire* (H. Liveright, 1928)

Quennell, P., *Baudelaire and the Symbolists* (Chatto & Windus, 1929)

Raymond, M., *From Baudelaire to Surrealism* (Schultz, 1950)

Rhodes, S. A., *The Cult of Beauty in Baudelaire* (Columbia University, 1929)

Shanks, L. P., *Baudelaire* (Little, Brown, & Co., 1930)

Starkie, E., *Baudelaire* (G. P. Putnam's Sons, 1933)

Symons, A., *Chas. Baudelaire* (E. Mathews, 1920)

Turguet-Milnes, G., *The Influence of Baudelaire in France and England* (Constable & Co., Ltd., 1913)

Valéry, P., *Variety: Second Series* (Harcourt, Brace & Co., 1938)

White, C. M., *The Midnight Gardner* (Harper & Brothers, 1948)

Wright, M. G., *The Rôle of the Auditive Sense in Baudelaire* (University of Pennsylvania, 1929)

CHEKOV

Translations: *The Cherry Orchard and Other Plays* (Grosset & Dunlap, 1936); Baukhage, H., *The Boor* (S. French, 1915); Calderon, G., *Two Plays* (G. Richards, Ltd., 1912); Chamot, A. E., *The Grasshopper and Other Stories* (S. Paul & Co., Ltd., 1926), *The Shooting Party* (S. Paul & Co., Ltd., 1926), *Short Stories* (Simpkin Marshall, Ltd., 1946); Cournos, J., *That Worthless Fellow Platanov* (E. P. Dutton & Co., Inc., 1930); Covan, J., *The Cherry Orchard* (Brentano's, 1922), *Uncle Vanya* (Brentano's, 1922); Fell, M., *Five Famous Plays by Anton Tchekoff* (Duckworth, 1939), *Plays* (C. Scribner's Sons, 1912-16), *Russian Silhouettes* (Duckworth & Co., 1915), *Stories of Russian Life* (C. Scribner's Sons, 1915); Fen, E., *Three Plays* (Penguin Books, Inc., 1951); Friedland, L. S. (ed.), *Letters on the Short Story, the Drama and Other Literary Topics* (G. Bles, 1924); Garnett, C., *The Letters of A. P. Tchekov to Olga L. Knipper* (G. H. Doran Co., 1925), *Letters to His Family and Friends* (The Macmillan Co., 1920), *Plays* (The Modern Library, Random House, 1930), *The Plays of Chekov* (The Macmillan Co., 1923-4), *The Tales of Chekov* (The Macmillan Co., 1916-22); Goldberg, I. and Schnittkind, H. T., *Nine Humorous Tales* (The Stratford Co., 1918); Kaye, A. L., *The Steppe and Other Stories* (F. A. Stokes, 1916);

Koteliansky, S. S. (ed.), *Anton Tchekhov: Literary and Theatrical Reminiscences* (G. Routledge & Sons, Ltd., 1927); Koteliansky, S. S., *Plays and Stories* (Everyman's Library, E. P. Dutton & Co., 1937), *Three Plays* (Penguin Books, 1940), *The Wood Demon* (The Macmillan Co., 1926); Koteliansky, S. S. and Canaan, G., *The House with the Mezzanine* (C. Scribner's Sons, 1917); Koteliansky, S. S. and Woolf, L., *The Notebooks of Anton Tchekhov* (L. & V. Woolf, 1921); Linscott, R. N. (ed.), *Short Stories* (The Modern Library, Random House, 1932); Long, R. E. C., *The Black Monk and Other Stories* (F. A. Stokes Co., 1916), *The Kiss and Other Stories* (F. A. Stokes Co., 1915); Mandell, M. S., *The Cherry Garden* (Yale Courant, 1908); West, J., *Plays* (Duckworth & Co., 1916); Yarmolinsky, A. (ed.), *The Portable Chekov* (The Viking Press, 1947); Young, S., *The Sea Gull* (C. Scribner's Sons, Ltd., 1939)

Avilova, L. A., *Chekov in My Life* (J. Lehrmann, 1950)

Bruford, W. H., *Chekov and His Russia* (K. Paul, Trench, Trübner, 1947)

Chukovskii, K. I., *Chekov the Man* (Hutchinson & Co., Ltd., 1945)

Dukes, A., *Modern Dramatists* (F. Palmer, 1911)

Elton, O., *Chekov* (The Clarendon Press, 1929), *Essays and Addresses* (E. Arnold & Co., 1939)

Gerhardi, W. A., *Chekov: A Critical Study* (Richard Cobden-Sanderson, 1923)

Gorki, M., *Reminscences* (B. W. Huebsch, Inc., 1921)

Heifetz, A. S., *Chekov in English* (New York Public Library, 1949)

Hingley, R., *Chekhov* (Allen & Unwin, 1950)

Koteliansky, S. S., *Anton Tchekhov: Literary and Theatrical Reminiscences* (G. Routledge & Sons, Ltd., 1927)

Koteliansky, S. S. and Tomlinson, P., *The Life and Letters of A. Chekov* (Cassell, 1925)

Lavrin, Y., *Studies in European Literature* (Constable & Co., Ltd., 1929)

Magarshack, D., *Chekhov, the Dramatist* (J. Lehmann, 1952)

Nemirovich-Danchenko, V. I., *My Life in the Russian Theatre* (Little, Brown & Co., 1936)

Perry, H. T. E., *Masters of Dramatic Comedy* (Harvard University Press, 1939)

Persky, S., *Contemporary Russian Novelists* (J. W. Luce & Co., 1913)

Toumanova, N. N., *Anton Chekhov* (Columbia University Press, 1937)

HERÉDIA

Translations: Kennedy, J., *Modern Poets and Poetry of Spain* (Longman, Brown, Green & Longmans, 1852); O'Hara, J. M. and Hervey, J., *The Trophies* (The John Day Co., 1929); Wright, M. St. C., *Translations from Heredia* (H. Vinal, Ltd., 1927)

Bailey, J. C., *The Claims of French Poetry* (M. Kennerley, 1909)

IBSEN

Translations: Archer, W. and Others, *The Collected Works* (C. Scribner's Sons, 1907-14); Aveling, E. M., *The Wild Duck* (W. H. Baker & Co., 1890); Bell, C., *The Lady from the Sea* (W. H. Baker & Co., 1900); Carmichael, M., *Rosmersholm* (W. H. Baker & Co., 1900); Carstarphen, H., *The Young Men's League* (W. H. Baker & Co., 1900); Dawson, M. M., *Brand* (The Four Seas Co., 1916); Dehly, A. G., *Eagle Wings* (Maydell Publications, 1943); Ellis-Fermor, U., *Three Plays* (Penguin Books, Inc., 1950); Farquarson, *A Doll's House, An Enemy of the People and The Master Builder* (The Modern Library, Random House, 1921), *Eleven Plays* (The Modern Library, Random House, 1935); Garrett, F. E., *Brand* (Everyman's Library, E. P. Dutton & Co., 1915), *Lyrics and Poems from Ibsen* (J. M. Dent & Sons, Ltd., 1912); Gosse, E., *Hedda Gabler* (W. H. Baker & Co., 1891); Herford, C. H., *Brand* (C. Scribner's Sons, 1894), *Love's Comedy* (C. H. Sergel Co., 1900); Hult, G., *Peer Gynt* (G. P. Putnam's Sons, 1933); Kildal, A., *Speeches and New Letters* (N. G. Badger, 1916); Laurvik, J. N. and Morison, M., *Letters of Henrik Ibsen* (Fox, Duffield & Co., 1905); Lord, H. F., *The Doll's House* (D. Appleton & Co., 1889); Orbeck, A., *Early Plays* (The American-Scandinavian Foundation, 1921); Parker, L. N., *Rosmersholm* (Griffith, Farran, Okeden & Welsh, 1889); Pressey, B. (ed.), *Ghosts, The Wild Duck, An Enemy of the People* (Rinehart Editions, Rinehart & Co., Inc., 1952); Ray, C., *The Emperor and the Galilean* (S. Tinsley, 1876); Roberts, R. E., *Peer Gynt* (World's Classics, Oxford University Press, 1936); Sharp, R. F., *A Doll's House, The Wild Duck, The Lady from the Sea* (Everyman's Library, E. P. Dutton & Co., 1910), *Ghosts, An Enemy of the People, Warriors of Helgeland* (Everyman's Library, E. P. Dutton & Co., 1911), *Peer Gynt* (Everyman's Library, E. P. Dutton & Co., 1921; G. G. Harrap & Co., Ltd., 1936), *The Pretenders, Pillars of Society* (Everyman's Library, E. P. Dutton & Co., 1913); Sharp, R. F. and Aveling, E. M., *A Doll's House* (E. P. Dutton & Co., 1920); Wilson, W., *Brand* (Methuen & Co., 1899)

Acker, H., *Four Sons of Norway* (T. Nelson, 1948)

Anstensen, A., *The Proverb in Ibsen* (Columbia University Press, 1936)

Bell, C., *Pot-Boilers* (Chatto & Windus, 1918)

Boyesen, H. H., *A Commentary on the Works of Ibsen* (W. Heinemann,, 1894)

Bradbrook, M. C., *Ibsen the Norwegian* (Chatto & Windus, 1946)

Brandes, G., *Creative Spirits of the Nineteenth Century* (T. Y. Crowell Co., 1923)

Burchardt, C. J. B., *Norwegian Life and Literature* (H. Milford, 1920)

Davies, T. H., *Spiritual Voices in Modern Literature* (George H. Doran Co., 1919)

Dobrée, B., *The Lamp and the Lute* (The Clarendon Press, 1929)

Downs, B. W., *Ibsen* (Cambridge University Press, 1948), *A Study of Six Plays of Ibsen* (Cambridge University Press, 1950)

Eikeland, P. J., *Ibsen Studies* (St. Olaf College Press, 1934)

Ellis, H., *The New Spirit* (W. Scott Publishing Co., Ltd., 1892)

Firkins, I. T. E., *Henrik Ibsen: a Bibliography* (H. W. Wilson Co., 1921)

Flores, A. (ed.), *Ibsen* (Critics Group, 1937)

Franc, M. A., *Ibsen in England* (The Four Seas Co., 1919)

Gosse, E. W., *Henrik Ibsen* (C. Scribner's Sons, 1911), *Northern Studies* (W. Scott, 1890)

Gregersen, H., *Ibsen and Spain* (Harvard University Press, 1936)

Heller, O., *Henrik Ibsen* (Houghton Mifflin Co., 1912)

Henderson, A., *European Dramatists* (Stewart & Kidd Co., 1913), *Interpreters of Life* (M. Kennerley, 1911)

Herrmann, O., *Living Dramatists* (Brentano's, 1905)

Huneker, J. G., *Egoists* (C. Scribner's Sons, 1909), *Iconoclasts* (C. Scribner's Sons, 1905)

Jaeger, H. B., *Henrik Ibsen* (A. C. McClurg & Co., 1901)

James, H., *Essays in London and Elsewhere* (Harper & Brothers, 1893), *A Most Unholy Trade* (The Scarab Press, 1923)

Jorgenson, T., *Henrik Ibsen* (St. Olaf College Press, 1945)

Joyce, J., *Ibsen's New Drama* (Ulysses Bookshop, 1930)

Koht, H., *The Life of Ibsen* (W. W. Norton & Co., 1931)

Lavrin, Y., *Ibsen and His Creation* (W. Collins Sons & Co., Ltd., 1921), *Studies in European Literature* (Constable & Co., Ltd., 1929), *Ibsen, an Approach* (Methuen, 1950)

Lee, J. B. P., *The Ibsen Secret* (G. P. Putnam's Sons, 1907)

Macfall, H., *Ibsen* (M. Shepard Co., 1907)

Merezkovski, D. S., *The Lifework of Henrik Ibsen* (A. Morning, Ltd., 1915)

Moses, M. J., *Henrik Ibsen* (Little, Brown & Co., 1920)

Roberts, R. E., *Henrik Ibsen* (M. Secker, 1912)

Robertson, J. G., *Essays and Addresses on Literature* (G. Routledge & Sons, Ltd., 1935)

Robins, E., *Ibsen and the Actress* (L. & V. Woolf, 1928)

Rose, H., *Henrik Ibsen* (A. C. Fifield, 1913)

Shaw, B., *The Quintessence of Ibsenism* (B. R. Tucker, 1891)

Wergeland, A. M., *Leaders in Norway* (Geo. Banta Publishing Co., 1916)

Wiegand, H. J., *The Modern Ibsen* (H. Holt & Co., 1925)

Wicksteed, P. H., *Four Lectures on Henrik Ibsen* (S. Sonnenschein & Co., 1892)

Zucker, A. E., *Ibsen* (H. Holt & Co., 1929)

JAMMES

Translations: Edgerton, G., *Romance of the Rabbit* (N. L. Brown, 1920);
    Smith, L. H., *My Daughter Birnadette* (B. Humphries, Inc., 1933)
Lowell, A., *Six French Poets* (Houghton, Mifflin Co., 1921)

KAHN

Translation: Jackson, W., *Fantin-Latour* (J. Lane, 1927)

LECONTE

Translations: Berthon, H. E. (ed.), *Nine French Poets* (Macmillan & Co.,
    Ltd., 1930)
Bailey, J. C., *The Claims of French Poetry* (M. Kennerley, 1909)
Brown, I. H., *Leconte de Lisle* (Columbia University Press, 1924)
Fairlie, A., *Leconte de Lisle's Poems on The Barbarian Races* (Cam-
    bridge University Press, 1947)
Grierson, F., *Parisian Portraits* (J. Lane, 1913)
Henry, S. O., *French Essays and Profiles* (E. P. Dutton & Co., 1921)

MAETERLINCK

Translations: Allinson, A., *The Massacre of the Innocents* (G. Allen &
    Unwin, Ltd., 1914); Archer, W. and Sutro, A., *Alladine and Pa-
    lomides* (Duckworth & Co., 1899); Atkinson, F. M., *The Cloud That
    Lifted* (The Century Co., 1923); Coleman, A. I. du P., *Monna Vanna*
    (Harper & Brothers, 1903); Hovey, R., *The Intruder* (Dodd, Mead
    & Co., 1916), *The Plays of Maurice Maeterlinck* (Stone & Kimball,
    1894-6); Mattos, A. T. de, *The Betrothal* (Dodd, Mead & Co., 1918),
    The Blue-Bird (Dodd, Mead & Co., 1909), *The Burgomaster of
    Stilemonde* (Methuen & Co., Ltd., 1918), *Chrysanthemums* (Dodd,
    Mead & Co., 1907), *Death* (Dodd, Mead & Co., 1912), *The Double
    Garden* (Dodd, Mead & Co., 1904), *Hours of Gladness* (Dodd,
    Mead & Co., 1912), *The Intelligence of Thomas* (Dodd, Mead &
    Co., 1907), *Joyzelle* (G. Allen, 1907), *Life and Flowers* (G. Allen,
    1907), *The Light Beyond* (Dodd, Mead & Co., 1917), *Mary Magda-
    lene* (Dodd, Mead & Co., 1910), *The Measure of the Hours* (Dodd,
    Mead & Co., 1907), *The Miracle of St. Anthony* (Dodd, Mead & Co.,
    1918); *Mountain Paths* (Methuen & Co., Ltd., 1919), *News of
    Spring* (Dodd, Mead & Co., 1913), *Our Eternity* (Dodd, Mead & Co.,
    1913), *The Unknown Guest* (Dodd, Mead & Co., 1914), *The Wrack
    of the Storm* (Dodd, Mead & Co., 1916); Miall, B., *Before the Great
    Silence* (G. Allen & Unwin, Ltd., 1935), *The Great Secret* (The Cen-
    tury Co., 1922), *The Hour-Glass* (G. Allen & Unwin, Ltd., 1936),
    The Life of Space (Dodd, Mead & Co., 1928), *The Life of the Ant*
    (The John Day Co., 1930), *Pigeons and Spiders* (G. Allen & Unwin,
    Ltd., 1935), *Poems* (Dodd, Mead & Co., 1915), *Sister Beatrice*

(Dodd, Mead & Co., 1902); Moses, M. J., *On Emerson* (Dodd, Mead & Co., 1912); Neufeld, M. K. and Spodheur, R., *The Great Beyond* (Philosophical Library, 1947); Schütze, M., *Twelve Songs* (R. F. Seymour, 1902); Shelvankar, K. S., *The Supreme Law* (Rider & Co., 1934); Sutro, A., *Aglavaine and Selysette* (G. Allen, 1904), *Ancient Egypt* (G. Allen & Unwin, Ltd., 1925), *The Buried Temple* (Dodd, Mead & Co., 1912), *The Death of Tintagiles* (Gowane & Gray, 1911), *The Life of the Bee* (Dodd, Mead & Co., 1901), *The Life of the White Ant* (G. Allen & Unwin, Ltd., 1927), *The Magic of the Stars* (Dodd, Mead & Co., 1930), *Monna Vanna* (Dodd, Mead & Co., 1907), *The Treasure of the Humble* (Dodd, Mead & Co., 1903), *Wisdom and Destiny* (Dodd, Mead & Co., 1898); Tadema, L. A., *Pelléas and Mélisanda* (W. Scott Publishing Co., 1913); Winslow, E., *Pelléas and Mélisande*

Bailly, A., *Maeterlinck* (Rider & Co., 1931)

Bithell, J., *Life and Writings of Maurice Maeterlinck* (Walter Scott Publishing Co., Ltd., 1913)

Björkman, E., *Voices of Tomorrow* (M. Kennerley, 1913)

Bridges, H. J., *Criticisms of Life* (Houghton Mifflin & Co., 1915)

Clark, M., *Maurice Maeterlinck* (G. Allen & Unwin, Ltd., 1915)

Dewey, J., *Characters and Events* (H. Holt & Co., 1929)

Dukes, A., *Modern Dramatists* (F. Palmer, 1911)

Ellehange, M., *Striking Figures* (Levin & Munksgoard, 1931)

Fidler, F. G., *The Bird That Is Blue* (Selwyn & Blount, 1928)

Flaccus, L. W., *Artists and Thinkers* (Longmans, Green & Co., 1916)

Freeman, J., *The Moderns* (R. Scott, 1916)

Frothingham, P. R., *All These* (Harvard University Press, 1927)

Griggs, E. H., *Maeterlinck* (B. W. Huebsch, 1916)

Hale, E. E., *Dramatists of Today* (H. Holt & Co., 1911)

Harry, G., *Maurice Maeterlinck* (G. Allen & Sons, 1910)

Heller, O., *Prophets of Dissent* (A. A. Knopf, 1918)

Henderson, A., *European Dramatists* (Stewart & Kidd Co., 1913), *Interpreters of Life* (M. Kennerley, 1911)

Huneker, J. G., *Iconoclasts* (C. Scribner's Sons, 1905)

Leblanc, G., *Maeterlinck and I* (Methuen & Co., Ltd., 1932)

Marble, A. R., *The Nobel Prize Winners in Literature* (D. Appleton & Co., 1925)

Moses, M. J., *Maurice Maeterlinck* (Duffield & Co., 1911)

Newman, E., *Musical Studies* (J. Lane, 1914)

Phelps, W. L., *Essays on Modern Dramatists* (The Macmillan Co., 1921)

Rose, H., *Maeterlinck's Symbolism* (Dodd, Mead & Co., 1911)

Slosson, E. E., *Major Prophets of Today* (Little, Brown & Co., 1914)

Staples, L. M., *An Interpretation of Maeterlinck's Blue Bird* (J. J. Newbegin, 1914)

Sturgis, G. F., *The Psychology of Maeterlinck* (R. G. Badger, 1914)
Taylor, W., *Maurice Maeterlinck* (W. Secker, 1914)
Thomas, E., *Maurice Maeterlinck* (Dodd, Mead & Co., 1911)
Thorold, A. L., *Six Masters in Disillusion* (A. Constable & Co., Ltd., 1909)

MALLARMÉ

Translations: Fry, R., *Poems* (Chatto & Windus, 1936); Mills, C., *Herodias* (J. A. Decker, 1940); Shipley, J. T., *Herodiade* (Poet Lore, 1921)
Cooperman, C., *The Aesthetics of Stéphane Mallarmé* (The Hoffern Press, 1933)
Fowlie, M., *Mallarmé* (Dennis Dobson, 1953)
Grierson, F., *Parisian Portraits* (J. Lane, 1913)
Quennell, P., *Baudelaire and the Symbolists* (Chatto & Windus, 1929)
Trombly, A. E., *A Translator of Poe* (Privately Printed, 1942)
Woolley, B., *Stéphane Mallarmé* (Drew University, 1942)

MERRILL

Translations: AEon, *Walt Whitman* (H. S. Saunders, 1922); Merrill, S., *Pastels in Prose* (Harper & Brothers, 1890)

RÉGNIER

Translations: Brown, S., *The Libertines* (The Macaulay Co., 1929); Mengers, C., *The Guardian* (Poet Lore, 1940)
Lowell, A., *Six French Poets* (Houghton Mifflin Co., 1921)

RIMBAUD

Translations: Abel, L., *Some Poems of Rimbaud* (Exiles' Press, 1939); Belitt, B., *Four Poems* (A. Swallow, 1947); Bernstein, J. M. (ed.), *Baudelaire, Rimbaud, Verlaine* (The Citadel Press, 1947); Cameron, N., *Selected Verse Poems* (Hogarth Press, 1942); Lees, G. F., *A Season in Hell* (The Fortune Press, 1932); Rootham, H., *Prose Poems* (Faber & Faber, Ltd., 1932); Schwartz, D., *A Season in Hell* (New Directions, 1939); Varèse, L., *The Illuminations* (New Directions Publications, 1946), *A Season in Hell* (New Directions Publications, 1945, 1952); Hill, B., *The Drunken Boat* (Hart-Davis, 1953)
Bacon, L., *Dream and Action* (Harper & Brothers, 1934)
Bercovici, K., *Savage Prodigal* (Beechhurst Press, 1948)
Boston, H., *The Book of Gallant Vagabonds* (Geo. H. Doran Co., 1925)
Carré, J. M., *A Season in Hell: the Life of Arthur Rimbaud* (The Citadel Press, 1931)
Chisholm, A. R., *The Art of Arthur Rimbaud* (Macmillan & Co., Ltd., 1930)

Fowlie, W., *Rimbaud* (New Directions, 1946), *Rimbaud's Illuminations* (Grove Press, 1953)

Hare, H., *Sketch for a Portrait of Rimbaud* (Brendin Publishing Co., 1937)

Quennell, P., *Baudelaire and the Symbolists* (Chatto & Windus, 1929)

Rickword, E., *Rimbaud* (W. Heinemann, Ltd., 1924)

Sackville-West, E., *The Apology of Arthur Rimbaud* (L. & V. Woolf, 1927)

Starkie, E. M., *Arthur Rimbaud* (Faber & Faber, 1938)

Wilson, E., *Axel's Castle* (C. Scribner's Sons, 1931)

SAMAIN

Lowell, A., *Six French Poets* (Houghton Mifflin Co., 1921)

STRINDBERG

Translations: *Lucky Peter's Travels, and Other Plays* (J. Cape, 1930); Baukhage, H. R., *Honor* (S. French, 1915); Björkman, E., *Master Olof* (Amer-Scandinavian Foundation, 1915), *Plays by August Strindberg* (C. Scribner's Sons, 1912-26), *There Are Crimes and Crimes* (C. Scribner's Sons, 1912); Classen, E., Locock, C. D., Palmstreina, E. and Fagan, J. B., *Easter and Other Plays* (J. Cape & H. Smith, 1929); Field, C., *Advent* (R. G. Badger, 1914), *The German Lieutenant, and Other Stories* (T. W. Laurie, Ltd., 1915), *The Growth of a Soul* (W. Rider & Son, Ltd., 1913), *Historical Miniatures* (G. Allen & Co., Ltd., 1913), *The Inferno* (G. P. Putnam's Sons, 1913), *Legends, Autobiographical Sketches* (A. Melrose, 1912), *The Son of a Servant* (G. P. Putnam's Sons, 1913), *Zones of the Spirit* (G. Allen & Co., 1912); Howard, V. S., *Easter* (Stewart & Kidd Co., 1912), *Lucky Pehr* (Stewart & Kidd Co., 1912); Locock, C. D. and Bulman, J., *Master Olof and Other Plays* (J. Cape & Harrison Smith, 1931); Oland, E. and W., *Plays* (Luce & Co., 1912-14); Recht, C., *Countess Julia* (Brown Bros., 1912); Samuel, H. B., *Comrades* (Hendersons, 1914), *Paria, Simoon* (Hendersons, 1914); Schleussner, E., *The Confessions of a Fool* (The Viking Press, 1925), *The German Lieutenant and Other Stories* (A. C. McClurg & Co., 1915), *In Midsummer Days and Other Tales* (H. Latimer, 1913), *The Red Room* (G. P. Putnam's Sons, 1913); Seltzer, T., *Married* (Boni & Liveright, Inc., 1917; The Modern Library, Random House, 1925); Westergren, E. C., *On the Seaboard* (Stewart & Kidd Co., 1913); Ziegler, F. J., *Motherlove* (Brown Bros., 1910), *Swanwhite* (Brown Bros., 1909)

Björkman, E. A., *Voices of Tomorrow* (M. Kennerley, 1913)

Bulman, J., *Strindberg and Shakespeare* (J. Cape, 1933)

Campbell, G. A., *Strindberg* (Duckworth, 1933)

Dahlstrom, C. E. W. L., *Strindberg's Dramatic Expressionism* (University of Michigan, 1930)

De Ford, M. A., *Love Children* (The Dial Press, 1931)

Dukes, A., *Modern Dramatists* (F. Palmer, 1911)

Heller, O., *Prophets of Dissent* (A. A. Knopf, 1918)

Henderson, A., *European Dramatists* (Stewart & Kidd Co., 1913)

Huneker, J. G., *Iconoclasts, a Book of Dramatists* (C. Scribner's Sons, 1905)

Lavrin, J., *Studies in European Literature* (Constable & Co., Ltd., 1929)

Lind-af-Hageby, L., *August Strindberg; the Spirit of Revolt* (S. Paul & Co., 1913)

McGill, V. J., *August Strindberg, the Bedeviled Viking* (Brentano's, 1930)

Mortensen, B. M., *Strindberg* (Cambridge University Press, 1949)

Neumann, R., *Passion; Six Literary Marriages* (Harcourt, Brace & Co., 1932)

Nicholson, H., *A Voyage to Wonderland, and Other Essays* (W. Heinemann, 1947)

Palmblad, H. V. E., *Strindberg's Conception of History* (Columbia University Press, 1927)

Robertson, J. G., *Essays and Addresses on Literature* (G. Routledge & Sons, Ltd., 1935)

Samuel, H. B., *Modernities* (E. P. Dutton & Co., 1914)

Sprigge, E., *The Strange Life of A. Strindberg* (Macmillan Co., 1949)

Strindberg, F., *Marriage with Genius* (J. Cape, 1937)

Uddgren, C. G., *Strindberg, the Man* (The Four Seas Co., 1920)

Uppvail, A. J., *August Strindberg: a Psychoanalytic Study with Special Reference to the Oedipus Complex* (R. G. Badger, 1920)

SULLY-PRUDHOMME

Grierson, F., *Parisian Portraits* (J. Lane, 1913)

Marble, Mrs. A., *The Nobel Prize Winners in Literature* (D. Appleton & Co., 1925)

VERHAEREN

Translations: Edwards, O., *The Cloister* (Constable & Co., Ltd., 1915); Edwards, O. and Others, *The Plays* (Constable & Co., Ltd., 1916); Flint, F. S., *The Love Poems of Émile Verhaeren* (Constable & Co., Ltd., 1916); Murphy, C. R., *Afternoon* (John Lane Co., 1917), *The Evening Hours* (John Lane Co., 1918), *The Sunlit Hours* (J. Lane Co., 1916); Sadler, M. T. H., *Belgium's Agony* (Houghton Mifflin Co., 1915); Strettell, A., *Poems* (J. Lane, 1915); Symons, A., *The Dawn* (Duckworth & Co., 1898); Wallis, K., *Five Tales* (A. & C. Boni, 1924)

Baudonin, C., *Psychoanalysis and Aesthetics* (G. Allen & Unwin, Ltd., 1924)

Corell, A. F., *The Contribution of Verhaeren to Modern French Poetry* (Buffalo University, 1927)

Jones, P. M., *Emile Verhaeren* (The University of Wales Press Board, 1926)

Lowell, A., *Six French Poets* (Houghton, Mifflin Co., 1921)

Samuel, H. B., *Modernities* (K. Paul, Trench, Trübner & Co., Ltd., 1914)

Zweig, S., *Emile Verhaeren* (Houghton Mifflin Co., 1914)

VERLAINE

Translations: Bernstein, C. P. (ed.), *Baudelaire, Rimbaud, Verlaine* (The Citadel Press, 1947); Berthon, H. E. (ed.), *Nine French Poets* (Macmillan & Co., Ltd., 1930); Gant, R. and Apcher, C., *Forty Poems* (The Falcon Press, 1948); Hall, G., *Poems* (Stone & Kimball, 1895); Wingate, A., *Poems* (The Walter Scott Publishing Co., 190-?)

Applegate, B., *Paul Verlaine* (Alderbrink Press, 1916)

Blunt, H. F., *Great Penitents* (The Macmillan Co., 1921)

Carrère, J., *Degeneration in the Great French Masters* (Brentano's, 1922)

Coulon, M., *Poet under Saturn* (H. Toulmin, 1932)

Grierson, F., *Parisian Portraits* (J. Lane, 1913)

Hare, H., *Sketch for a Portrait of Rimbaud* (Brendin Publishing Co., 1937)

Huneker, J. G., *The Pathos of Distance* (C. Scribner's Sons, 1913)

Lepelletier, E., *Paul Verlaine* (T. W. Laurie, 1909)

Lowell, A., *Six French Poets* (Houghton Mifflin Co., 1921)

Morgan, C., *Reflections in a Mirror: Second Series* (Macmillan & Co., Ltd., 1946)

Nicolson, H., *Paul Verlaine* (Constable & Co., Ltd., 1921)

Roberts, C. E. B., *Paul Verlaine* (Jarrolds, 1937)

Rothenstein, W., *Paul Verlaine* (Hacon & Ricketts, 1898)

Symons, A., *Colour Studies in Paris* (E. P. Dutton & Co., 1918)

Valéry, P. A., *Variety: Second Series* (Harcourt, Brace & Co., 1938)

Zweig, S., *Paul Verlaine* (Luce & Co., 1913)

VILLIERS DE L'ISLE-ADAM

Translations: Barclay, T., *The Revolt* (Duckworth & Co., 1910); Finberg, H. P. R., *Axel* (Jarrolds, Ltd., 1925); Symons, A., *Claire Lenoir* (A. & C. Boni, 1925), *Queen Ysabeau* (The Pembroke Press, 1925)

Huneker, J. G., *Iconoclasts* (C. Scribner's Sons, 1905), *The Pathos of Distance* (C. Scribner's Sons, 1913)

Whitridge, A., *Critical Ventures* (C. Scribner's Sons, 1924)

Wilson, E., *Axel's Castle* (C. Scribner's Sons, 1931)

INDEX

155

156   INDEX

Dancourt, 43
Dante, 13-17
Dares and Dictys, 8
Daudet, 108-109
Delavigne, 63
Delille, 63
De Lisle. See Leconte
Derzhavin, 131
Diderot, 43-44
Dostoievski, 131-133
Du Bartas, 25
Du Bellay, 25
Dumas Fils, 109
Dumas Père, 64
D'Urfé, 25
Dutch Literature (General), 2, 56

Early Middle Ages (General), 5-6
Eddas and *Sagas,* The, 8-9
Eichendorff, 81
Encyclopedists, The, 44
Engels. See Marx
Erasmus, 26
European Literature (General), 1-2,
   55-56

Fénelon, 45
Flaubert, 110-111
Fontenelle, 45
Fouqué. See La Motte-Fouqué
French Eighteenth-Century Literature
   (General), 40-41
French Literature (General), 2-3, 56-
   57
French Renaissance Literature (Gen-
   eral), 19
French Romantic Literature
   (General), 60-61
French Seventeenth-Century Literature
   (General), 40
Fréron, 45
Freytag, 111
Froissart, 27

Gautier, 64-65
Gellert, 81
Gérard de Nerval, 65
German Eighteenth-Century Literature
   (General), 78-79

German Literature (General), 3-4, 58
Goethe, 81-88
Gogol, 133
Goldoni, 45-46
Goncharov, 134
Goncourt, 111
Gotthelf, 112
Grazzini, 27
Gresset, 46
Griboyedov, 134
Grigorovich, 134
Grillparzer, 88
Grimm, 88-89
Guarini, 27
Gutzkow, 89

Hardenberg. See Novalis
Hauptmann, 112
Hebbel, 112-113
Hegel, 89-91
Heine, 91-93
Helvétius, 65
Herder, 93
Herédia, 145
Heyse, 113-114
Hoffman, 93
Holbach, 66
Hugo, 66-69
Humanists, The (General), 27-28

Ibsen, 146-147
Immermann, 94
Isidore of Seville, 9
Italian Eighteenth-Century Literature
   (General), 41
Italian Literature (General), 3, 57-58
Italian Renaissance Literature (Gen-
   eral), 19-20
Italian Romantic Literature (General),
   60-61

Jacobi, 94
Jacopo da Voragine, 9
Jammes, 148
Jean Paul, 94
Jodelle, 28

Kahn, 148
Kant, 94-96